T0330595

# Espionage and Subversion in an Industrial Society

First Published in 1967, *Espionage and Subversion in an Industrial Society* presents a comprehensive overview of the true significance of industrial espionage and its relationship with the struggle for economic supremacy of a nation. Industrial espionage is a growth industry and the new battlefield where nations and ideologies struggle for economic supremacy. This and subversive activity may seem relatively harmless in comparison with a 'hot war'. It is however precisely because the temperature of an all-out war would destroy the civilization, we know that industrial espionage and subversion assume importance. In this book Mr Hamilton has combined his own extensive security knowledge with thorough research in his subjects. This is an interesting read for scholars of diplomacy, international economics, and international politics.

# Espionage and Subversion in an Industrial Society

## An Examination and Philosophy of Defence for Management

Peter Hamilton

First published in 1967
by Hutchinson & Co Ltd.

This edition first published in 2023 by Routledge
4 Park Square, Milton Park, Abingdon, Oxon, OX14 4RN

and by Routledge
605 Third Avenue, New York, NY 10017

*Routledge is an imprint of the Taylor & Francis Group, an informa business*

© 1967 Peter Hamilton

**Publisher's Note**
The publisher has gone to great lengths to ensure the quality of this reprint but points out that some imperfections in the original copies may be apparent.

**Disclaimer**
The publisher has made every effort to trace copyright holders and welcomes correspondence from those they have been unable to contact.

A Library of Congress record exists under LCCN: 67105965

ISBN: 978-1-032-45900-4 (hbk)
ISBN: 978-1-003-37919-5 (ebk)
ISBN: 978-1-032-45902-8 (pbk)

Book DOI 10.4324/9781003379195

# Espionage and Subversion in an Industrial Society

*An examination and philosophy of defence for management*

## Peter Hamilton

*Foreword by Sir Richard Jackson,*
*Formerly Assistant Commissioner CID New Scotland Yard and*
*President of Interpol*

HUTCHINSON OF LONDON

HUTCHINSON & CO (*Publishers*) LTD

*178-202 Great Portland Street London W1*

London Melbourne Sydney
Auckland Bombay Toronto
Johannesburg New York

*First published 1967*
*Reprinted 1969*

*This book has been set in Times, printed in Great Britain
on Antique Wove paper by Balding & Mansell Ltd, of London and Wisbech
and bound by Wm. Brendon & Son Ltd, of Tiptree, Essex.*

SBN
09 084170 0

To Patricia Douglas Hamilton

# Contents

Appendices

# Foreword

*by Sir Richard Jackson, Formerly Assistant Commissioner CID New Scotland Yard and President of Interpol*

Industrial espionage, like professional crime, has grown steadily in recent years and the press, radio and television have rightly drawn public attention to many instances of it which have occurred in this country and abroad. I can say of my own knowledge that it is an international threat which is worrying the authorities in many countries particularly France, Germany and America.

It may be thought that obtaining commercial secrets is a matter of private rather than public concern however valuable the secrets may be; and that industrial espionage must be relatively harmless by comparison with the widespread political and military espionage carried out by practically every country in the world today.

Mr. Hamilton, however, believes that since it has been generally recognised that an all-out 'hot' war would destroy the civilisation we know, industrial espionage must assume a new importance and that the new battlefield is the industrial arena where nations and ideologies will struggle for economic supremacy.

If he is right industrial espionage may really become as vital as, and may alternatively become indistinguishable from, its political and military counterparts. It can be employed not only to obtain such things as research secrets but to determine at what points subversion can be most effectively employed to bring about moral degeneration and industrial anarchy in a country in order to weaken its economy; to show for example where industrial relations are bad and how they can be made still worse.

Some of the author's opinions and conclusions are controversial; for example, his ideas about the future functions of the police in the field of security.

Mr. Hamilton could have written an interesting if somewhat superficial book based on case histories. Instead he has combined his own extensive security knowledge with a great deal of research, to produce a book which makes clear to his readers the true significance and the dangers of industrial espionage and gives an expert and thorough description of the methods and techniques by which it can be fought.

ix

# Introduction

It has been argued that sooner or later there will be no military secrets on the earth's surface: by the mid-seventies observation satellites will be feeding the computers of the Kremlin and Pentagon with virtually all the military information they need.

Although this is probably true, it is also important to realise that the outcome of the struggle between East and West is more likely to be decided in the industrial field than on the battlefield. The ability to make nuclear war depends on industrial capacity and skill; in terms of nuclear balance it is economic wealth that is the most decisive influence in international affairs, as several British Foreign Secretaries have lamented and the prestige of France testifies.

Today the importance of the military man has been largely deflated and the art has metamorphosed. The Scientific Adviser to the Minister of Defence is the most important general in Britain. If war between the great powers does take place it is inconceivable that it will be anything but nuclear, in which the soldiers would play little part. It would probably be one short sharp game of computerised chess between the previously stored brainpower of opposing scientists. Russian supremacy on the checker is a disquieting omen of the result.

It is to be expected that in this situation there would be a shift of emphasis in espionage. Although espionage against industry is as old as industry itself, political and military espionage have hitherto been regarded as of paramount importance. International political espionage was and is mainly concerned with the discovery of the intentions of hostile or potentially hostile foreign powers, and military espionage with their power to implement their hostile policies in terms of armed strength. Since today the success of foreign policy rests increasingly on industrial power, industrial espionage, as it is loosely termed, begins to overshadow its military sister.

The terminology is comparatively new but not the process. The advent of the term 'industrial espionage' has, however, served a useful purpose in that, largely because of the romantic association of the word 'espionage' with brave men and glamorous women, with murder and lechery, public attention is now being drawn to trends which may add sinister and corrupting influences to what has been hitherto a common business practice, that is to say, the obtaining of information about competitors. It is doubtful whether industrial espionage has in fact much glamour or romance since finer motives, such as patriotism, are usually absent.

It is in the tough and virile competition of the American economy that industrial espionage has become an important factor. The massive cost of technological research—the United States spends something like £7,000 million a year on it, about ten times that of the United Kingdom—has created conditions in which the rewards of industrial espionage by savings in research costs could be very great indeed.

It is of interest that in two recent cases of industrial espionage in the United Kingdom the firms to which the stolen information was offered would have none of it. Traps were arranged and the spies were caught. It is probable that the majority of boardrooms in this country would regard industrial espionage as completely unethical and refuse to be party to it. This is the finest defence, but it would be naïve to think that there are not a number of circumstances in which industrial espionage could flourish amongst such firms; for example, it could be carried out at lower level. A managing director, one of whose subordinates may say, 'By the way, sir, have you heard that X & Co. are buying Y & Co. shortly?' would not necessarily demand the source. If he did, it would be easy enough to convey the impression that the information had arisen from normal business contacts. An ambitious subordinate might be willing to pay out of his own pocket or to channel some of the firm's expenses for the purpose of establishing a reputation for far-sightedness. In any case, there are other firms whose approach to the subject would be less ethical, especially in conditions of tough competition and increasing research costs.

The necessity for obtaining political and military information by espionage has always been accepted, although it was the convention not to acknowledge that one went in for it oneself. It was only other countries which engaged in this dirty game. This convention was broken by President Eisenhower in the Gary Powers case[1], but it re-

1. It will be remembered that Gary Powers was the pilot of a U-2 American reconnaissance aircraft shot down over the Soviet Union in 1960. President Eisenhower subsequently admitted that Powers had been taking aerial photographs for espionage purposes.

mains the general practice of the major powers. The basis for this acceptance was undoubtedly the belief that where the national safety is concerned the government not only has the right, but the duty, to protect the country by any means within its power.

It is a truism that a prerequisite of most successful operations, whether business, political or military, is knowledge of the opposition; its state and its intentions. As Wellington said, 'All the business of life is to endeavour to find out what you don't know by what you do. That is what I called guessing what was at the other side of the hill.' In the face of the intense economic struggle for survival in which this country is engaged there is a sound case for studying industrial espionage in relation to the world in general and this country in particular. Britain is in some way peculiarly vulnerable to it. As John Buchan said, 'We are the leakiest society on earth, and we safeguard ourselves by keeping dangerous people out of it.' This may no longer be a sound defence in our increasingly mixed society.

If ever there is another British Empire it will be as the others; commercially based. Napoleon called us a nation of shop-keepers, and he was probably right. British military power was not developed so much for reasons of glamour or lust for conquest, as for the acquisition and safeguarding of wealth. The main basis of the defence of the homeland has not been, as so many people believe, the navy, which was designed primarily to protect our commerce from pirates, but our ability to form alliances, the strength of which has almost always been decisive.

The British are not only politically clever; they are also one of the most original and inventive people in the world, which incidentally makes them a natural target for industrial espionage. Many had expected in the immediate post-war world that Britain would lead a resurgent Europe—a third force which might provide a guarantee that Russia and America would keep the peace—a *pax Europa*! This meant, of course, a continuation on a wider scale of that traditional pillar of British strategy, maintenance of the balance of power in Europe. Certainly Britain's stock in Europe when the war ended in 1945 was of the highest. She was admired even by the conquered. Through her underground links and the BBC her spirit had sustained for four terrible years the hopes of occupied Europe. But when the time came it was not victorious Britain who took over the leadership of Europe—it was defeated France supported by conquered Germany, whose ruined industry had been reconstructed on modern lines by the victors, principally America.

Germany, Holland, Italy and, to some extent, France lost their empires by surgery. This has enabled them to clear their minds, see their objectives and work towards them. Britain, preoccupied with changing the empire into a multiracial commonwealth failed to see what they saw—the managerial revolution.

Furthermore, Britain, proceeding as usual in her leisurely, empirical fashion, is taking longer to solve her class and industrial relations problems. In other countries, these had been solved by extreme inflation, defeat in war, the guillotine or other forms of levelling upheaval, or through the prosperity of prolonged neutrality.

Nowadays it is *economic* power that matters. Whether Britain will regain her former prominence in the world or survive as a major power depends less on her famous regiments or 'the few' of the RAF or the Silent Service than on the managers and technicians of industry. Britain has always been a family business and this has been reflected in her services, both civil and military. It seems likely that in future the families of Britain will be more concerned with the industrial regiment. Their best cadets will not be at Sandhurst or Cranwell, but at the Manchester and London Business Schools.

These trends are not only essential if Britain is to maintain an affluent society, but they also indicate the beginning of a return to her original rôle—that of a trading nation. This is perhaps what Mr. Dean Acheson meant when he said in 1964 that Britain had not yet found her new rôle. There will be new forces abroad—undercurrents, perhaps the result of no war and a changing morality—forces which Britain must understand and come to terms with if she is to succeed. These will include the impact on our society of an increasing amount of highly organised crime, and more nebulous, but even more dangerous, what may be termed subversive activity. This will be defined in detail later in the book, but for present purposes its nature is well summed up in the aim of 'Plan D' in Peter Fleming's book *The Sixth Column*[1]—'To accelerate the current deterioration of the national character with a view to undermining and eventually eliminating British influence in the affairs of the world.'

It is argued then that international relations of the future will be almost wholly concerned with economics. There will be few armament races, except perhaps temporarily in emergent countries. Disarmament races are much more likely. At first the economic struggle will be to a large extent on a company or group or consortium basis, but later, by reason of mergers and takeovers—a natural economic force—many industries may assume a national character to enable

1. (Rupert Hart-Davis, 1951.)

them to attain effective competitiveness. Therefore the scene is set for the principal industrial economies of the world to compete with all the fervour of war. Because of the improbability of major wars, many of those with natural military gifts and tendencies, for whom service life was an outlet, will through force of circumstances be in the sales forces and in the boardrooms.

In the world-wide jungle of competition there will be other denizens, bent and perverted people whose help may be invoked in subversive activity to further the interests of one firm or one economy. There may be industrial guerilla warfare. Although it seems far-fetched to suggest that bombs may be exploded in rival aeroplanes to discredit the make or the airline, or that key personnel in rival firms will be liquidated, goods and services may be discredited by subliminal salesmanship and employees may be bought.

Intermingled with and perhaps indistinguishable from such activities will be the corruptive influence of totalitarian ideologies whose agents, often unconscious of the real purpose for which they are being used, will proselytise by intimidation and punish by secret and illegal courts those who will not conform. The destructive energies which hitherto had used force to achieve their aim, or as an outlet, may be concentrated consciously and unconsciously on destruction of the order of love and peace by 'peaceful' means.

Two things are clear: firstly, it will not be possible for any firm or perhaps any economy to survive the battle without good industrial intelligence. Organised industrial espionage would be a logical outcome of this need. It has been part of the industrial scene in America for some time. It is here and it will probably grow. To what extent it will grow, what shape it will take, how significant it will be, and how it can be defeated are some of the questions this book will try to answer.

Secondly, management on whom our future power and prosperity primarily depend cannot be effective without a loyal and contented staff and labour force. The disaffection manifested in British industry today is at once a fertile soil for industrial espionage and a cause of competitive inefficiency. That it may be due to external causes such as political and moral subversion does not diminish management's responsibility. Apart from self-interest, the welfare of an urban and industrial people a major portion of whose life is spent in the office or on the factory floor is as much the responsibility of management as that of a rural and agricultural community was the concern of the good squire. The blankets of Lady Bountiful may no more be needed by an affluent and centrally heated society, but the advice and loving care still are. (It is to be hoped that the Inland Revenue will not drive the good manager out of existence as it has done the good squire.)

Thus this book is also designed to contribute to the manager's understanding of subversion, which is likely to prove an even more disturbing factor in the sphere of his responsibility than industrial espionage, and which is, as will be shown, more difficult to counter. It can and must be countered. Failure to do so could result in the destruction of our way of life as completely as could nuclear war.

# Acknowledgements

Like many other authors I owe an immense debt to the press for its intelligence process. The ability of editors and journalists to uncover secrets, to select news of public interest and importance, to evaluate it, interpret it and summarise it, is unsurpassed by any intelligence agency. Democracy might survive without intelligence services, but it could never do so without the press.

My principal personal debt of gratitude for this book intended for management is to Leonard W. Dunham, Managing Director of Chubb &Son Limited. I thank him for much good advice and example, and considerable tolerance during the writing of this book, which, though a private task has inevitably impinged on my work as a member of his staff.

I would like particularly to thank Sir Richard Jackson, that most distinguished police officer, for many words of wisdom and for being so kind as to write the Foreword. Among the many other people to whom I am indebted for help and encouragement during the preparation of this work I am especially grateful to the following colleagues and friends: Donald Baber, Bill Bannochie, Noel Currer-Briggs, M.A., David Dring, Philip Henslow, Marjorie Jeacock, M.A., Ph.D., Charles Kemble, A.C.I.S., Alfred Markham, Garry Owen, Lt.-Col. Colin Paddock, M.C., Denis Read, Murray Sinclair, and David Uglow. Ronald Seth, well-known writer on espionage and one-time spy, kindly made available to me the fruits of his own research. Also, throughout the preparation of this book the support and professional advice of Tom Dalby of Hutchinson has been invaluable.

The interest and support of my mother, Joan Hamilton, was of great value to me, as was that of my uncle, Dr. Hubert Trumper, himself an established writer, who gave me several useful introductions. Mention must be made of my mother-in-law, Kathleen Hirst, who brought her immense commonsense to bear on my more fanciful ideas and, not least, provided a commissariat while my wife and I were struggling with the book at a very critical period. Through her, I was put in touch with Noel Osborne who kindly provided me with information on frithborh and frankpledge.

I am indebted to the following for permission to reproduce copyright material: the executors of the Garrett Mattingly Estate and Jonathan Cape Ltd., *The Defeat of the Spanish Armada*; Arthur M. Schlesinger, Jr., and Andre Deutsch Ltd., *A Thousand Days*; Sanche de Gramont and Andre Deutsch Ltd., *The Secret War*; Vance Packard and Longmans, Green & Co. Ltd., *The Naked Society*; G. M. Trevelyan and Longmans, Green & Co. Ltd., *English Social History*; Peter Fleming and Rupert Hart-Davis Ltd., *The Sixth Column*; Aubrey Wilson and Hutchinson & Co. (Publishers) Ltd., *The Marketing of Industrial Products*; Leon Radzinowicz and Heinemann Educational Books Ltd., *Ideology and Crime*; James Sutherland, *Defoe*, published by Longmans Green in the *Writers and Their Work* series for the British Council; Curtis Brown Ltd., *The Fourth Seal* by Sir Samuel Hoare (later Viscount Templewood); Ronald Seth and Arthur Barker Ltd., *Anatomy of Spying*; Granada Television, extracts from their programme *The Mind Race*; McGraw-Hill Publishing Co. Inc., extracts from *Chemical Engineering*; *TV Times*; *The Spectator*; The Controller, Her Majesty's Stationery Office, extracts from *Royal Commission on Local Government in Greater London*, 1957–60 (Cmnd. 1164), *Attitudes to Efficiency*, *First Report of the Court of Inquiry into certain matters concerning the Shipping Industry* (Cmnd. 3025), *Hansard*, 11th August 1966 (Vol. 733, No. 74), *Security Procedures in the Public Service* (Cmnd. 1681), *Lord Denning's Report* (Cmnd. 2152), and *Report by Mr. A. J. Scamp, J.P. on the activities of the Council; The Times; Financial Times; The Guardian; Sunday Times; Sunday Express; The People; Daily Telegraph; Daily Express; Daily Sketch; Daily Mirror; Evening Standard.*

Miss Diana Reader Harris, B.A., F.R.S.A., the distinguished Head Mistress of Sherborne School for Girls, has kindly allowed me to reproduce a letter she sent to parents in 1965.

My thanks are due to William E. Randall, D.F.C., A.F.C., Managing Director of Chubb & Son's Lock and Safe Company Limited, for permission to draw on material previously written in the course of my duties and for giving me my first literary opportunity.

Two superlative secretaries have shared the burden of reducing scribbling and babbling to coherence and legibility: Sheila Mann has also given up much time to research and copying of passages from documents; my wife, full-time secretary to a managing director, as well as in her 'spare' time running a large house and organising myself and the children, has been the main prop of my morale and strength, and my inspiration.

*The Attack*

# CHAPTER 1

## A General Survey of Industrial Espionage

Industrial espionage is a part of the family tree of what may be termed the dark forces of our civilisation. To counter it, it is necessary to know it, and to know it, it is necessary to look at the whole family, which includes virtually the gamut of all that is furtive and corruptive in human nature, the antithesis of love, honesty and openness. It operates outside morality and is, or probably soon will be, outlawed in most civilised countries. Yet like its political and military counterparts, it may be necessary and justifiable in certain circumstances.

### THE OBJECTS

For the purposes of this book industrial espionage is espionage undertaken with the object of obtaining industrial information which will be of economic or political advantage. It may be set up

for personal or corporate profit (this includes espionage for criminal purposes);
to strengthen national foreign policy;
to increase national war or defence potential;
for subversive political purposes.

The second and third may be the deliberate motives of the industrial espionage, or by-products of the first. Increased profit, the result of successful espionage against a foreign competitor carried out from a purely profit motive, may in addition strengthen a country's war potential. If the increased profit is in an overseas market, the country's balance of payments will be improved. As some of the profit will in any case be taken away from the company concerned by taxation, additional financial resources are available to the government to support its foreign policy, for example, by enabling it to make loans to an important emergent country and thereby increase its influence there, or reduce that of another power. Or it

3

may be in a better position to apply economic sanctions, which may be an important international weapon of the future.

The fourth type is more sinister than the others because its motive is political. A vital national industry is selected. By mingling with the labour force, the industrial spy can detect shop-floor grievances for use by the subversive political party to increase its influence in the trades unions concerned. Through rapid communications it airs the complaint long before the cumbrous consultative machinery or the union has had time to act, making it look as if the latter were being dilatory or were in league with management. Espionage methods may also be used to discover management plans which could affect the labour force. By premature release and misrepresentation the party can cause insecurity in the work force and again increase its influence. By passive sabotage, that is, strikes, go-slows, and so on, the firm and the national economy are weakened, and thus the foreign policy of a hostile power is aided, sometimes incidentally, sometimes deliberately and in concert.

It will be seen that there are close links between the four main types of industrial espionage, and there may often be difficulty in distinguishing its purpose.

THE LEGAL POSITION

There has been correspondence in *The Times* drawing attention to the ridiculous legislative situation which exists *vis-à-vis* industrial espionage. A letter published on 18th November 1965 from a Mr. D. V. B. Unwin cited a case (the Downey case, p. 60) in which, because there was no 'Official Trade Secrets Act', a person who had stolen secret papers which would have been of value to a competitor had had to be charged with and was convicted of stealing three pounds worth of paper. In the writer's own words, 'All the integers of an offence against the public as such seem . . . to be present and to justify the creation of a new criminal offence of "industrial espionage".' A further letter published on 24th November 1965 from Mr. Alan Campbell, Q.C., doubted whether the revision of our own law would be apt or effective to deal with industrial espionage and suggested the problem was essentially international; it recommended that it should be taken within the framework of an international convention dealing with the protection, retention, sharing and theft of 'know-how'.

An official of Mercedes Benz, Dr. Riester, advocated prison sentences for industrial espionage in a memorandum he prepared for the Federation of German Industries. According to *The Times* of 17th June 1966,

'*West German law, he (Dr. Riester) says, takes no account of the fact that foreign espionage organisations damage the interests not just of individual firms and the economy but also of the state. The eastern block, Yugoslavia and China are trying to make themselves less dependent on imports and more competitive in their export markets. East Germany, he adds, has earned millions as a result of industrial espionage and West Germany has suffered accordingly.*'

Mercedes Benz have themselves been victims of industrial espionage.[1]

The Council of Europe's legal committee agreed with Mr. Campbell in a report presented to its parent body in early 1966. After pointing out the difficulty of effective defence on a national basis, they recommended that member countries should introduce legislation creating the offence of industrial espionage based on identical principles.

The British government's position in this matter of amending the law was stated by the Attorney-General in reply to a question in the House of Commons on 3rd August 1966. He said that, although he had no information that it was extensive, industrial espionage was going on in Britain. It was not a criminal offence and consequently there had been no such prosecutions, but there were provisions in criminal law which could be applied and in appropriate cases this had been done. The President of the Board of Trade was inviting evidence of cases of inadequacy of the present legal position. *It was a very important matter for British industry* (author's italics).

The Attorney-General did not point out that:

because industrial espionage was not a criminal offence it was unlikely that the already overburdened police forces would be giving deep thought to the subject;

it is often against a firm's interests to report industrial espionage—the publicity may widen the breach or adversely affect the company's image (and because it is not a crime there is no obligation to report it unless of course crimes have been committed as part of the espionage);

a primary characteristic of industrial espionage is that unlike cash the loss often goes unnoticed for a considerable time. A document can be photographed without trace being left and it may be some time before the firm which steals the information can develop it to its own ends. Even then the victim firm may assume that the other firm had carried out the same research with the same results.

1. See p. 61

For all these reasons it could certainly be argued that the government's information might not be complete.


THE ETHICAL ARGUMENTS

Before going into the question of whether industrial espionage can be justified it is logical to ask whether industrial secrecy can be justified. Professor S. A. Tobias, head of the Department of Mechanical Engineering of Birmingham University, was rebuked by the Institute of Directors when he dared to suggest recently that he would like to see a great deal more industrial espionage. A warning that economic advance will be curtailed if British industry persists in being over-secretive about new manufacturing and marketing techniques was given by Mr. John Davies, the Director-General of the Confederation of British Industry. Speaking at the annual luncheon of the London Branch of the Purchasing Officers' Association and reported in the press of 27th November 1965, he said, 'Industrial security has been a great impediment and will continue to be . . . an impediment in the coming years unless associations like yours can find out what its members do to improve their activities and make these techniques known.'

The right to publish discoveries is a treasured one amongst scientists. Much fruitful scientific work is the result of free exchange of information, the continual exposure of ideas to criticism. Creative minds, always rare and thus in heavy demand, are often reluctant to do work which must be shrouded in secrecy. Secrecy may inhibit proper advertising to attract such men.

In theory men and companies can legitimately protect their discoveries, inventions and effort by patent, but in practice this offers only temporary protection, since the filing of a patent implies eventual publication, and the delay between filing and public availability may be as little as three months. Nowadays technology is advancing so rapidly that a formidable competitor, once he had seen the idea sent him by an astute patent agent, might be able to be first on the market, with perhaps an improved version which did not infringe the original patent. If there were no security, the early stages and direction of research might become known long before a patentable invention resulted and yield a considerable advantage to such a competitor. Not every idea is patentable. Only a device or machine which serves a practical purpose can be patented and this leaves out, for example, scientific concepts resulting from basic research. (And patenting will not protect government secrets, industrial or otherwise.)

Security, which is a logical consequence of the international political situation, has certainly eroded the right to publish, but stands are made from time to time. For example, Dr. Gaylord Hanwell, president of the University of Pennsylvania, has announced that the university will no longer accept contracts for classified or secret research. Their future policy will be that the results of research shall be published. Moreover, it seems wasteful in the extreme to have a large number of firms in the same field of business engaged in similar research without exchange of information.

It can be argued, too, that industrial espionage is a natural balancing force, as has indeed been argued about political and military espionage. Certainly the nuclear balance of today is in no small measure due to acts of espionage. If peace is a balance of opposing forces, then war may result from lack of balance.

For national purposes, therefore, industrial espionage is no less ethical than political or military espionage, whose inevitability in an imperfect and disunited world is generally accepted. This is not to say that it should be openly permitted any more than are the political and military varieties.

Political subversion, especially in its more obnoxious forms, is only slightly less detestable than war itself—bent minds instead of bent bodies—but it must be reckoned a major industrial factor.

The argument is often advanced that industrial espionage for profit between competitors is a logical and natural consequence of the increasing need for information which is perhaps the most influential of all the factors bearing on profitability in a highly complex industrial world. There are two answers to this: in the first place espionage of whatever kind, whether unlawful or not, is socially speaking corruptive and therefore justifiable, if at all, only where the highest national interest is concerned—that is, the safety of the nation. All spies in industry are two-way agents and therefore as dangerous to the firm which employs them as to the firms against which they operate. Secondly, industrial espionage between competitors is not really necessary.

Those who wish to know more about what is and what is not ethical and legal are invited to study Appendix L.

### COMMERCIAL DIPLOMACY AND MARKET RESEARCH

Industry and commerce's problem is not paucity of information but that they are drowning under it. Unlike military and political intelligence services, which often do require to gain small but vital pieces of closely guarded information, business usually needs a reasoned digest of the overall situation. A skilled commercial diplomatic service (which is what public relations ought to have been) to sieve, select and interpret, and a good patent agent coupled with orthodox market research for specialist problems, will produce most of the answers. In the few cases where these fail, the required information or product may have to be bought from the owners—a perfectly normal business operation. Any of these means will in the end be cheaper than industrial espionage, whose influence on its practitioners is morbid. The idea of a management diplomatic service is expanded in Chapter 11.

### THE INTERNATIONAL SCENE

When in the middle of the nineteenth century, as a result of American initiative, the Japanese recognised the tremendous possibilities of western industrial development, they quickly seized their opportunity. Large numbers of able young men were sent to many of the industrial countries of the world, including the United States and Great Britain. Ostensibly these young men were sent with the object of making contact with the western world. In fact, they took jobs in key industries and soon learned the industrial secrets of their employers. They then returned to Japan and in a short space of time, largely because of their ability to copy and improve the original and partly because of abundant cheap labour, a low cost of living and their energy and skill, they were able to compete on favourable terms with the western industrial economies, some of whose industries—the Lancashire cotton industry being a major case in point—never recovered from the Japanese competitive onslaught. Today the Japanese are equally ubiquitous and their young businessmen are to be seen in all the important parts of the western business world, and, in spite of rising costs of labour and a much higher standard of living, their advanced techniques and industrial attitudes enable them to remain highly competitive.

It is perhaps no coincidence, therefore, that the more important of the two suspected schools for industrial spies is reported to be in Japan; the other is said to be in Switzerland.

If the Japanese owe much of their industrial power today to information from, if not espionage against, the West, the tables may soon be turned. No less a person than the managing director of the Steel Company of Wales, Mr. W. F. Cartwright[1], has advised British

1. Now Chairman.

industry to copy the Japanese. Speaking to the Economics Section of the British Association for the Advancement of Science on 1st September 1966 at Nottingham, he confessed that his company continually had people in Japan trying to get information as to how the Japanese got the 'extraordinary performance' they did out of their industrial plant. Mr. Cartwright said he was extremely impressed with their philosophy, which amounted to 'Find out the best practice in the world and improve on that.' He added that there was no point in being proud and slowly catching up from behind. He thought British industry would be wise to adopt the Japanese policy.

In 1964 the *Harvard Business Review*, the official organ of the Graduate School of Business Administration, Harvard University, published an article entitled 'The U.S. Businessman Faces the Soviet Spy'. It was written by no less a person that Mr. J. Edgar Hoover, director of the Federal Bureau of Investigation. Mr. Hoover revealed that the FBI, whose task is to protect the internal security of the United States, was heavily involved in industrial counter-espionage. He said that there was 'a current massive systematic and purposive attempt by the intelligence services of the Soviet-block nations, headed by Moscow, to obtain information legally and illegally about American industry.' He related stories of actual attempts to gain industrial information and made it clear that all the methods used by the Russians in the defence intelligence fields were also used for industrial purposes. He said that overall management was probably the biggest Russian intelligence target and that about ninety-five per cent of the material needed for its intelligence objectives was obtained by agents of the Russian Embassy openly and legally. He stressed the variety of information in which they were interested—'not only highly secret technical and military data, but such things as road maps, population statistics, *per capita* income, 'phone directories, agricultural production, transit systems and penicillin production', and also 'data regarding the personal lives of key national leaders'. 'In other words,' said Mr. Hoover, 'their intelligence attack is total. It involves every facet of our national life.'

In the meantime, espionage for inter-company competitive purposes is assuming considerable importance in the United States. To many people there industrial security connotes measures against industrial espionage whereas in Britain it is thought of mainly in relation to theft. A measure of the interest which the subject arouses there is provided by a recent series of articles in the American journal *Chemical Engineering*. It should be borne in mind that much if not most of recorded industrial espionage today has been against research targets in the chemical industry. One of the series is entitled 'Gathering Competitive Intelligence' which is described in the blurb in the following way:

*Here, uncensored, is the report a prominent consultant prepared for a client on legal—if not always nice—ways of gathering competitive information.*

It is only fair to add an extract from the Editor's Note.

*Chemical Engineering does not endorse all the techniques described in this consultant's report. However, we feel that the reader would be left with an incomplete picture of the intelligence arena—and might be lulled into a false sense of security—if we were to describe only those methods that are ethically beyond reproach.*

Extracts from the advice given are reproduced in Appendices to this book as follows:

Appendix A:   The Nature of Competitive Information
          B:   Hiring a Competitor's Employee
          C:   How to Hire and Use a 'Special' Investigator
          D:   Cost of Competitive Information

The French intelligence service claims to have irrefutable evidence of widespread industrial espionage in France and it recently issued a booklet called, *L'Espionnage—une Réalité*, which has been distributed to more than nine thousand heads of industry.

In Belgium there is mounting concern about industrial espionage and particularly in the military and political contexts. A certain Belgian security expert was invited recently to prepare a 'doctoral dissertation' on the subject; a body representative of government, industry and other interested parties has been set up to give detailed consideration to security matters, including industrial espionage. A Belgian resident has been identified as a professional industrial spy, who had worked for an East German state-owned firm.

Several cases have been reported from West Germany and one of the most recent concerns East German attempts to suborn a West German scientist working at an important laboratory.

One of the most astonishing cases yet reported is of Italian-sponsored attempts to learn important drug manufacturing secrets from an American drug manufacturer.

In Britain there is now convincing evidence that industrial espionage is replacing more traditional and open methods of gaining information.

An examination of the more interesting cases is made in Chapter 6.

PROFIT TARGETS

Most recorded industrial espionage for profit concerns operation against research targets, but it can also be used—

to learn secret future economic intentions of governments;

to discover other firms' marketing plans;

to identify key persons in other firms whose services might be bought and to appraise the inducements which should be offered;

to determine the strength and weakness of rival firms, or of firms which are being considered for takeover;

for the establishment and maintenance of personal power;

for criminal, i.e., robbery, purposes;

to discover in advance information which when published will affect Stock Exchange share prices;

to discover quotations of rival companies in competitive tender.

To know the future economic intentions of a government gives the opportunity to make money, often in considerable quantity; for example, the knowledge of forthcoming loans to emergent countries will enable firms to set up in advance appropriate organisations, such as agents and servicing, so as to be in a better position to get whatever business is going. Likewise, the knowledge of another firm's plans to enter a particular field may enable a competitor to be there first, perhaps at a better price. The new firm with money behind it, with only a small share of a particular market, may be able to topple its major competitor if it can identify and suborn its key employees. The usual method of obtaining their services, having identified them and discovered how much they earn, is first to create disaffection. The new firm makes it generally known that its rates of pay and prospects are better; or it may try to make inroads into the market by selling at a loss; by identifying and approaching key customers whose loss will be a prestige blow to its formidable competitor, again by undercutting the price if necessary, or by more concentration of effort. In essence, the new firm wages a sort of psychological war to undermine morale in the big company. Many large firms in semi-monopoly conditions tend to become complacent; they may adopt an attitude of 'we know best' or 'you are lucky to be able to get our products', thus tending to become product-oriented rather than customer-oriented. Service and delivery dates may get slack. Careful industrial espionage will show the up-and-coming firm the weaknesses which can be exploited. It is a combination of these factors which will create the climate in which attractive offers to key employees are more likely to bear fruit, whereas such offers made outright without preparation might well be scorned by a contented employee.

A novel way of identifying key employees in a particular industry was used in London recently. Some foreign competitors held an exhibition of their own products which they knew would attract technical experts from the industry in the United Kingdom. By discussion with them on the stands the foreign businessmen were able to select their potential victims. Follow-ups were arranged on the basis of giving agencies and eventually suitably attractive offers were made. One astute British technical director was able to unload a rather tiresome second-in-command in this way.

Industrial mergers or takeovers are governed by Stock Exchange regulations, and by the law, which require as much openness as possible, but before they declare their intentions firms naturally wish to know as much as possible about their potential victims. If they make enquiries openly rival bids may be provoked, or the board of the firm which is to be taken over will be given time to create obstacles. Very little of the information required for a takeover can be discerned from published accounts and therefore secret enquiries are often made. When these are completed, a surprise bid can be made, and for this reason alone will often be successful.

Knowledge is power and, other things being equal, the man who knows most will be the most powerful. Some of the most powerful men in business and politics have maintained their power by ensuring that they and they only had all the knowledge. Their colleagues were given or they acquired pieces of the picture, but only the top man had the whole picture. This enabled him to hold sway. It is well known that in most branches of life only a proportion of the knowledge which a man at the top needs comes to him through the 'usual channels'. This knowledge is apt to be 'filtered' so that only emaciated or tendentious information reaches him in a form which it is thought he will like. In complex modern structures such as corporations and armies this is particularly true. Much of Field Marshal Montgomery's success with the Eighth Army may have been due to his so-called 'J' service, which was a team of young men placed at strategic points throughout the army and able to communicate direct with him. They could supply him immediately with what he really wanted to know. It would not be unfair to describe this as an internal espionage service and, of course, it caused considerable discontent in the 'usual channels'. Such procedures are far from unknown in industry.

Market research is not the prerogative of legitimate industry, but is carried out by organised crime whose onslaught is largely directed at industrial and commercial wealth and which, contrary to the methods employed by orthodox market research, relies to a large extent on the weapon of espionage. Crime, with a known annual turnover in excess of £34 million in England and Wales, is now a capitalised industry of its own. This figure represents money stolen only through known indictable offences, and the grand total may be over £100 million. Gone are the days when a simple 'casing of the joint' was sufficient reconnaissance for a plan to be made. The planning of major financial operations such as the great train robbery or the rescue of important prisoners may involve months of espionage and intelligence work. Penetration of the target organisation by criminal agents or the suborning of its employees must be regarded as norms of criminal operations today.

Early warning of the fortunes or misfortunes or takeover intentions of industrial firms enables a stock exchange operation to be carried out with the virtual certainty of profit. The City of London has one of the finest organisations in the world for this purpose. This is not espionage—which has not so far been necessary due to the 'old boy' net and detailed knowledge of the market and individual firms built up over a long period. The big stockbrokers have come to be regarded as the City intelligence service, whose latest development is a central computer for storing the records and information of individual brokers. In addition to the obvious dangers of misuse of the power which the combined knowledge of the various brokers would bring, there is no reason why the information appetite of such a central computer should be satisfied by what is fed into it by brokers. Industrial information from many sources would be attracted, and thus industrial espionage for financial speculation might be promoted. This type of espionage is in any case likely to grow as the efficiency of the 'old boy net' dwindles in an increasingly mixed society, and industrial security becomes more effective and widespread which it rapidly is doing.

When a very large firm or a government department has business to offer, it almost always does so by competitive tender. Considerable sums of money are often involved. Clearly, it is of immense advantage for a firm to know what its rival may be contemplating by way of tender. In a number of countries it is possible for an energetic sales representative to purchase (on the black market) a copy of a rival tender which may enable him to alter that of his own firm, or even to re-quote if necessary.

*       *       *       *

Many people think of industrial espionage purely as a weapon of competition between rival firms, but as has been shown the term embraces a wide variety of recondite activity. Before it can be fully understood and countered, it is necessary to consider the genus.

# CHAPTER 2

## *The Parent Art—Intelligence*

Any serious espionage encountered by industrial firms, whether inspired by a competitor, a hostile foreign power or a subversive political party will be part of an intelligence process.

Intelligence is more than espionage and a great deal is produced without recourse to the latter at all. Amongst many non-espionage (usually called overt as opposed to secret or covert) sources are newspapers, weekly journals, especially technical, house magazines of important companies, catalogues, telephone directories, commercial directories, commercial agents, diplomatic representatives, radio and television programmes, gossip, patent registers, stockbrokers, market research reports. Of all these overt sources, the daily press is far and away the most important.

Journalism and espionage perform much the same information task by different, not always very different, means, and most intelligence officers would agree that ninety per cent of the information they require can be obtained by thorough study of the world's press (see also Chapter 12, p. 117).

The ability of journalists to obtain the most closely guarded secrets is a constant source of amazement to intelligence officers and of worry to security authorities; it is also a considerable safeguard for democracy. Exposure to the light of day is one of the finest antidotes to subversive activity, or indeed any nefarious plans or plots.

An apt demonstration of this journalistic ability is provided by the disclosure in *The Guardian* of 4th January 1967 of the contents of a hitherto 'top secret' report prepared by the Economist Intelligence Unit on the efficiency of the newspaper industry. Because the findings of the report were unpalatable to the industry and the trades unions concerned, strong pressures against publication were expected.

It is perhaps no coincidence therefore that modern journalism and modern intelligence were founded at about the same time. Not only did they arise to serve roughly the same need, but both may be attributed to the same man.

Daniel Defoe is perhaps best known for his novels *Robinson Crusoe* and *Moll Flanders*—even these, as Trevelyan[1] says, 'are imaginary "reports" of daily life, whether on a desert island or in a thieves' den'—but his main contributions to civilisation are new concepts of journalism and espionage. Further details of both are given in Chapter 12; here it is sufficient to note that in 1704 Defoe was commissioned by Robert Harley, Speaker of the House of Commons, to design and take charge of an espionage service. Defoe submitted to Harley a document entitled *A Scheme for General Intelligence* (see Appendix I) whose concept is the basis of modern intelligence systems. It also marks an important phase in the development of espionage, defined in Colliers Encyclopaedia as 'The seeking, obtaining and transmitting, through secret means, of information about one country by agents of another', and which Encyclopaedia Britannica extends by including the obtaining of information 'by false pretences'.

Hitherto espionage had been regarded as an art on its own. When a need arose, men were selected as spies or informers and sent off to find the answer to a particular problem.

Defoe saw that such casual arrangements were not suited to the rapidly developing Great Britain and Europe of Queen Anne's and Louis XIV's day. To be able to rule effectively, to ensure the safety and prosperity of the state, the central government must be well informed as to thought, plans and events, military, political and economic, at home and abroad. He envisaged the use of secret and open agents in both spheres, the maintenance of reliability records, and he stressed the importance of security. (He asked in his Scheme, 'How many miscarriages have happened in England for want of silence and secrecy'.)

From Defoe's time onwards, therefore, espionage is seen as but one of the arms of the new art of intelligence.

Information is the stuff of intelligence, and throughout history the ability to obtain quick and reliable information about events, trends and plans has been highly valued. This information can be of three kinds: that which relates to events which have happened, to events which are happening, or which predicts future events. All three types are of significance in many fields of human activity, but whereas the first two can be (they often are not) exact sciences, the third, while it may be correct, is in the end guesswork, because nothing is certain until it happens.

1. G. M. Trevelyan, *English Social History* (Longmans Green, 1944).

Most decisions are based, consciously or unconsciously, on a combination of these three kinds of information, that is, what has happened, what is happening, and what will probably happen. The first two are usually important guides to the third, or, to quote Galsworthy (in another context): 'The present is linked with the past and the future with both'. The complete process of discovering all facts and probabilities for the purpose of enabling a correct decision to be made is therefore at once historical, contemporary and conjectural and when honestly performed is correctly described as the art of intelligence. This is intelligence in its highest form, but, unfortunately, it is often the product of amateurish conjecture, misreporting and tendentious reasoning according to the belief or motive of the source, rather than the result of an objective survey of the relevant evidence. Bacon described the very real difficulty of avoiding tendentiousness in the following terms: 'The human understanding when any proposition has been once laid down (either from general admission and belief or from the pleasure it affords) forces everything else to add fresh support and confirmation; and although most cogent and abundant instances may exist to the contrary, yet either does not observe or despises them or gets rid of and rejects them by some distinction with violent and injurious prejudice, rather than sacrifice the authority of its first conclusions'. Intelligence of this kind is not intelligence at all and can be dangerous and wasteful in the highest degree.

More will be said about the practice of intelligence in a later chapter. Here we must take note that it is an art whose purpose is to provide processed information from which a sound decision and course of action may be conceived.

Much can be done by remote deduction from the events of the past and the present, and from such indications of the future as there may be. However, missing indications or confirmations of those which exist must ultimately be actively sought in the field. If the information required is readily available there, the process remains as it began— overt. It is when information pertaining to the past, present or future is not readily accessible and the legitimate possessor of it is unwilling to reveal it that it has to be obtained covertly, and this is the main rôle of espionage. Intelligence (including espionage) may also be called upon to predict the reactions of people in given situations.

The treatment of information whether about the past, the present or the future is known as the Intelligence Process and is carried out in four stages; in theory these are consecutive, but in practice there is considerable overlapping especially as the process is, of course, continuous.

*Collection.* This is the obtaining of information from all sources including informers and spies. Information is not, of course, collected for its own sake but in accordance with a target system. One of the most skilled aspects of this stage is the collecting of the information without revealing that this is being done.

*Collation.* This is the comparing and relating of various pieces of information so that a composite picture emerges.

*Assessment.* Usually there will be alternatives, contradictions and missing links. It is the job of the assessor to determine from the evidence and his own knowledge the most likely answer to the problem, carefully separating fact from deduction and probability.

*Dissemination* is the communicating of the processed information—i.e. the intelligence—to whoever is responsible for decision and action.

\*      \*      \*      \*

No discourse on intelligence would be complete without actual examples. The two chosen are of a politico-military kind for the simple reason that comparable examples in industry are hard to come by and, so far, ill-documented: partly because there is less public interest, and partly because boardroom activities are well protected by law from the public gaze.

Both examples are American and concerned with Cuba and the late President Kennedy.

In 1960 United States' sensitivity to the development of Cuba as a Russian sphere of influence reached a climax. At the same time the Central Intelligence Agency (CIA) attained a new height of power and influence, a height, let it be said, that no specialist intelligence agency should ever be permitted to attain. But then the CIA was not merely an intelligence agency. Encouraged perhaps by President Eisenhower—certainly by Mr. Foster Dulles whose brother Allen headed it—the CIA had acquired a power rôle that was at once political, military and intelligence. It saw itself as a vital cold war agency; a major operator of the US policy of the containment of communism; capable not only of collecting and processing information, but of taking action on it—a logical successor perhaps to Mc-Carthyism, and in any case by no means out of tune with a major and influential body of American opinion. In the particular case, apart from *amour propre* and the Monroe doctrine, there was little doubt in many American minds that Castro posed a real threat.

During the administration of President Eisenhower the CIA had made a political and operational plan for the re-establishment of American influence in Cuba. Before it was mounted the Eisenhower administration was replaced by that of President Kennedy and it seems clear from Arthur M. Schlesinger's book[1] that Kennedy was a reluctant partner in CIA's ill-starred venture against Cuba.

In essence, the plan consisted of the military training and subsequent lodgment in Cuba of a force composed of some fourteen hundred supposedly right-wing Cuban exiles, with an appropriate follow-up. The CIA's intelligence assessment was that after some initial skirmishing the bulk of the Cuban people, guided of course by CIA agents, would gladly reject Castro and Moscow and joyously acclaim the return to a good old American type way of life. The Central Intelligence Agency, according to Schlesinger, also advised that the Cuban air force was 'entirely disorganised, its planes for the most part obsolete and inoperative, its combat efficiency almost non-existent'.

In the event, as all the world knows, the whole enterprise, usually referred to as the Bay of Pigs, ended in failure. The reasons are summed up by Schlesinger as follows: 'For the reality was that Fidel Castro turned out to be a far more formidable foe and in command of a far better organised régime than anyone had supposed. His patrols spotted the invasion at almost the first possible moment. His planes reacted with speed and vigour. His police eliminated any chance of sabotage or rebellion behind the lines. His soldiers stayed loyal and fought hard. He himself never panicked; and, if faults were chargeable to him, they were his over-estimate of the strength of the invasion and undue caution in pressing the ground attack against the beachhead. His performance was impressive'.

Schlesinger goes on to say: 'One reason Washington miscalculated Castro, of course, was a series of failures in our own intelligence'. Almost every major intelligence principle was flouted. The most important of these is the principle that those whose responsibility it is to collect, collate and disseminate information must not be also responsible for acting upon it. Quite apart from the fact that to do otherwise offends democratic checks and balances, it is a truism to say that those who are clever at providing intelligence are seldom men of sound political or military judgment; moreover, those who have the responsibility to act will almost certainly be tendentious in their intelligence approach, *vide* Bacon, p. 16. Apart from all this, the

1. *A Thousand Days* (Andre Deutsch, 1965).

information on which the intelligence assessment was based was clearly wrong, probably because the sources themselves wished for what they reported to be true.

There could have been no more inauspicious beginning to a President's term of office, and it is a measure of the greatness of Mr. Kennedy that he learned the lessons of this disaster, initiated the necessary reforms, and was able when the time came, as a result of sound intelligence, to take the decision and the action which history may show to have saved the world from nuclear war. Before passing on from how not to do it to how to do it, it may be of interest to quote again from Schlesinger about the Bay of Pigs: 'David Ormsby-Gore (British Ambassador to the United States) told me that British intelligence estimates, which had been made available to CIA, showed that the Cuban people were still predominantly behind Castro and that there was no likelihood at this point of mass defections or insurrections'.

There is no better illustration of American resilience and power to recover from disaster and learn lessons than the Administration's handling of the next Cuban crisis. We are concerned here with the intelligence angle, and the first step of this kind taken by President Kennedy was, as a direct result of the Bay of Pigs fiasco, to reduce the CIA from *imperium in imperio* status to that of a technical department. Dulles was replaced by Mr. John McCone and under his guidance CIA reverted to the proper role of an intelligence agency.

The test of Kennedy's concept and McCone's diligence came in the summer of 1962, when the Russian and Cuban governments took a decision to install Soviet nuclear missiles in Cuba in the autumn. There was no precedent for this Russian action—they had not previously installed nuclear missiles in any other country. The reason for the choice of Cuba for such a venture (an area in which the Americans had immense local military superiority and must also regard the action as a direct threat) is not entirely clear. It was probably due in part to an internal power struggle in the Kremlin and in part to the fascination of challenging the United States in her own back garden.

The first indication that something was afoot came from CIA agents who reported the arrival in Cuba of some 5,000 Russian technicians and unidentified equipment on a considerable scale. The White House assessment of this having regard to the past was that these measures were defensive in character. It is of particular interest, however, that, according to Schlesinger, McCone considered the possibility that the equipment might conceivably go beyond defensive weapons. There is no evidence to suggest that this was more than a 'hunch'; but even so, stemming perhaps from some form of mental process like a woman's intuition, beyond the comprehension of more ordinary minds, flair, in the very highest form of intelligence, is a recognised and highly valued attribute.

Up to this point, apart from McCone's presentiment, the available evidence of *current* happenings and precedent suggested in effect nothing more than increased Russian and Cuban activity of a defensive kind, probably concerned with the establishment of a modern Cuban air defence based on the Russian surface-to-air anti-aircraft missiles, which had shot down the U-2 reconnaissance aircraft flown by Gary Powers some two years earlier. This belief was correct as far as it went, but, as we now know, their immediate purpose was to deter and defeat US reconnaissance so that the more nefarious part of the plan might be put into effect—the establishment of surface-to-surface nuclear missiles which could directly threaten the heart of the United States.

Although reports began to come in which suggested that these missiles might in fact be arriving, or being prepared for, in Cuba, there was considerable scepticism in CIA and the White House. Nevertheless the intelligence momentum was maintained and on 14th October a U-2 (a modern form of espionage) was sent on reconnaissance over the critical area. Photographic interpretation revealed preparations for the launching of surface-to-surface missiles (and one actual missile) capable of carrying nuclear warheads to the USA.

The rôle of intelligence did not finish there. Apart from maintaining continual watch on Russo-Cuban manoeuvres in the Caribbean, its next or concurrent task was to predict the likely political and military reactions of the Russian government to various courses open to the United States. It is possible, although there is no confirmation of this, that Penkovsky, the Russian intelligence colonel who was working for US intelligence at about this time, played a significant part in these predictions.[1] At any rate, we now know that President

1. As an erstwhile intelligence officer himself, the author was very pleased to see the following passage in an excellent espionage book *Spies of the Twentieth Century* by Charles Franklin, published by Odhams since this book went to press: 'President Kennedy has always taken the sole credit for calling Kruschev's bluff over Cuba, a decision which required iron judgment and steely nerves. But his decision was to a large extent based upon Penkovsky's reports which enabled the American experts to judge precisely the extent and nature of the Soviet missile threat in Cuba. Kennedy was only able to deal with the Cuban crisis with confidence because of the knowledge he possessed about Soviet strategic capabilities. If Penkovsky had not given the West this knowledge, there is no telling what the end of the Cuban crisis might have been.'

Kennedy was able to take the best course; perhaps the only course which could prevent all-out nuclear war.

It is of course of paramount importance to realise that intelligence alone, however good, is not enough. In the end it is the skill of the man who must judge its value and take the final responsibility for action that is the deciding factor. In President Kennedy the western world, indeed the whole world, had that man, and posterity may decide that his was the most significant decision and action of all time. What is quite clear is that he was thus enabled by good intelligence: without it his decision could have been wrong, and fatal to civilisation.

It should be noticed that this United States intelligence triumph was apparently matched by Russian intelligence and security failure. In the intelligence sense, the Russians seem to have failed to appreciate American reaction to discovery of their Cuban venture, and in the security sense they failed to prevent the Americans' discovery of their actions and intentions. Both triumph and failure bring out the tremendous importance of intelligence, and for that matter, security, in the world in which we live.

One of the most difficult decisions that can face a government arises when the action which the intelligence indicates may uncover the sources which provide the intelligence. This may mean that espionage or counter-espionage networks painstakingly built up over the course of years are 'blown', to use a technical term. Apart from the personal danger to individual men and women, clearly the flow of information will cease and there will be a gap until the system can be rebuilt; it can be fatal to have lack of intelligence coverage at critical moments. No doubt this was one of the considerations that made the British Prime Minister delay so long before revealing the political influence and pressures being used to prolong the seamen's strike in 1966.

# CHAPTER 3

## *Espionage*

While intelligence is a backroom job, espionage is practical, front line work. The word espionage probably derives from an old French verb *espier*, meaning to see at a distance, or to see or discover something intended to be hid. The art is not therefore confined to the visual, but extends to discovery by any means.

Although 'seeing is believing' in espionage, as elsewhere, the spy may use any other of the human senses to get the information his masters require. Through his ears he may eavesdrop conversations, or hear movements which reveal the enemy's purpose. He may feel the shape of some equipment, or smell a particular scent, or taste a particular taste which will yield the relevant knowledge.

All technical aids to espionage are extensions of one or other of the senses—usually the eyes and ears. The long-range camera, the recon-naissance 'plane (e.g., the American U-2), binoculars, are visual aids to the spy increasing the range of the eye and the memory connected with it; the concealed microphone and its transmitting device in-creases the sensitivity and range of the ear.

In addition to having nowadays the advantage of modern techno-logy, the spy almost always operates as part of an organisation and in accordance with techniques which have been developed over the years. Technical aids and techniques are explained in more detail in Chapter 7.

Espionage should never be used when the required information may be obtained by open means. Good spies are rare and continually in danger while spying; their actions may be compromising to their employers and their launching and maintenance are usually ex-ceedingly expensive; a caught spy may give propaganda points to an enemy, or, since he is almost bound to know something of his em-ployers' own secrets and some of his fellow spies and networks, may be of considerable use to the enemy, especially today when new psychological methods of breaking men are available.

Counter-espionage is very similar to espionage in regard to the techniques and technical aids. Both are concerned with and justified by the same consideration—the safety of the state. But in very broad terms, the espionage services operate overseas and the counter-espionage in the home country; the latter are also concerned with possessions and dependencies overseas. Both these and other terms have been used rather loosely in this book so far, and it is now necessary to be more precise.

The two opposing arts are intelligence and counter-intelligence, usually today called security, but security connotes far more than counter-intelligence. Intelligence, as we have seen, is concerned with the provision of processed information upon which sound decisions and courses of action can be based. Security in this sense is the art of preventing the enemy discovering information which it is wished to conceal from him. It is also an essential part of intelligence and intelligence may, and often does, assist security. Intelligence includes espionage which, as already shown, is one of its arms or tools. Espionage is usually set up for the purpose of discovering the answer not otherwise available to a particular problem. Security is also concerned with the prevention and detection of sabotage, subversive activity and crime.

Security divides into protective security and detective security. Protective security describes the physical and administrative measures which can be taken to protect secrets and property and also the art of preventing the employment of unreliable persons in key positions and the revelation of secrets by careless talk. It should be noted that property may need to be protected against both espionage and sabotage. For example, a spy may wish to steal an instrument or piece of equipment of technical interest for use by his masters; a saboteur may wish to destroy it to prevent its use by its owners. Protective security is normally an advisory function, the responsibility for, and therefore the cost of, protection lying with the owner or user of the information or property. Detective security is the art of detecting the efforts of an enemy to perform an espionage or sabotage operation or to overthrow the state; it includes the employment of counter-spies for this purpose, and this function is usually called counter-espionage.

As has been shown already, there are many overlaps. It is axiomatic that security is of fundamental importance to the gamut of intelligence. For example, a major counter-espionage purpose is to penetrate the opposing intelligence services or subversive organisations, whose security is their defence against such penetration. But because of opportunity, this penetration may be carried out by the espionage services.

A prime example of the penetration for security purposes of a subversive organisation is the story of ' "Miss X" in the Enemy Camp' related by John Bulloch.[1] 'Miss X' was a young MI5 agent who, as part of her job, became a full member of the Communist Party of Great Britain and lived under cover for six years, and throughout was able to pass valuable information about Russian espionage activities in this country to MI5. She was responsible for the arrest of three Russian agents and at the conclusion of their trial the judge said of 'Miss X': 'I think that young woman must be possessed of extraordinary courage and I think she has done a great service for her country'. Intelligence may aid and impinge upon counter-intelligence and security. We now know that the 'lead' which led to the arrest and subsequent conviction of the Russian spy in the British Foreign Office, George Blake, came from an intelligence agent in Berlin. Even pure intelligence may be protective in that the information it yields may enable a country to increase its own security. There is, therefore, every excuse for lay misunderstanding.

Postal censorship is both protective and detective security. In the latter sense it helps to detect espionage, and in the former it prevents secrets being given away inadvertently. Press censorship is primarily intended for protective security, but of course it can always be and is often used for political purposes, e.g., the suppression of news hostile to the interest of a particular regime, or to bolster national morale by preventing publication of defeats or disasters.

If the reader was not previously aware of it, the labyrinthine nature of the intelligence and security worlds will by now be apparent to him, and what we have discussed is but the half of it.

ESPIONAGE SECURITY

A spy's security can be breached in many ways; by indiscreet talk, wrong clothes, wrong habits, and so on, but his communications are his point of maximum vulnerability. A spy must get the fruits of his espionage back to those who can use them. He may do this by going personally to his next in line, which is dangerous, since at least two links can then be compromised. He may send letters either through the post in code to accommodation addresses, or arrange to leave them to be picked up; postal censorship may counter the first, but the second is generally less easy to detect.

Radio and telephone communications suffer from the snag that conversations can be overheard and messages intercepted and it is

1. *MI5* (Arthur Barker, 1963).

a very serious difficulty that the spy does not know whether he has been overheard or intercepted. It is also possible by the use of direction-finding apparatus to pinpoint radio installations with consequent danger to the spy.

Other important security devices to protect an espionage network include what may be termed 'compartmentalisation' or 'the need to know' and 'cover'. A spy should never be told more about the plans, tasks and organisation of his own side than he needs to know for the performance of his task. If he doesn't know he can't tell the enemy if he is caught, or if he defects. If possible he should not learn the surname of his colleagues but should simply know them as John or James or Elizabeth as the case may be. He should be told as little as possible about other espionage operations—only enough to avoid confusion with any adjacent activity.

Cover is the false identity which a spy assumes to conceal his real identity and the story he tells to mask his true purpose. It is the spy's primary protection against discovery and thus of first importance to him, calling for the highest skill and attention to detail. There have been remarkable cases where a spy has so perfectly impersonated another man that even close relations, including in at least one case a wife, have been deceived by the impersonation.

The purposes of all security devices in espionage are to prevent discovery and limit the damage that discovery may cause.

### ESPIONAGE AS A BUSINESS

Espionage is not only a function of states performed for their own security. There have been and still are international peddlers of information whose interest is solely money. Where other men trade in goods, these gentlemen trade in secrets. They are used by the national networks to find out particular information and their operators may be hired out for particular jobs. They also collect 'routine' information which they think may have a sale value and sell it, perhaps by a form of secret auction, to the highest bidder. There have certainly been cases in which they have dealt in industrial secrets and this form of diversification may well become more popular and perhaps more profitable. National networks are notoriously bad payers, mainly because of the weak bargaining power of those trying to sell national secrets which is always contrary to law.

One of the best known international spies was a certain R. H. Peterssen who operated from various continental countries including Norway, Belgium and Switzerland. On behalf of the German Secret

Service he employed a number of spies in England just prior to the Great War. These included a certain Heinrich Grosse, whose task was to discover British naval secrets, and a couple known in England as Mr. and Mrs. Gould (although Mr. Gould's real name was Schroeder) who were also interested in naval secrets. All three were caught; Schroeder got six years and Grosse three. The age of chivalry was not yet dead, and although she was deeply involved no evidence was offered against Mrs. Gould.

ESPIONAGE AND SUBVERSION

In his book *The Secret War*,[1] Sanche de Gramont makes reference to what he terms total espionage. By this he means nearly all aspects of clandestine activity. It is obvious that an espionage machine together with its intelligence bureau, its highly trained spies and agents and their communications, can be used for more purposes than espionage; for personal ends such as power and money, for example.

In Imperial Russia there are said to have been at one time no less than eleven organised espionage services, some at least of which were more concerned with maintaining or augmenting the power of an individual than with the safety of the state. Rasputin, the Csar and the Csarina certainly appear to have had their own networks. Some departments had their own services over and above the official state secret service. Much intelligence and espionage effort which should have been devoted to the prosecution of the war against Germany was, in fact, spent on interdepartmental and personal spying. However misdirected it may have been, espionage is an art in which the Russians excel and especially in the communications branch in which they have for long been renowned for their codes and ciphers. In his account of his intelligence mission to Russia during the Great War, the late Sir Samuel Hoare (afterwards Viscount Templewood) comments as follows:

*'I learnt many interesting details about secret codes and ciphers. In this branch of Intelligence the Russians excelled. Their experts could unravel almost any cipher in an incredibly short period of time. One o them (an officer of the Naval General Staff) implored me as a friend and ally to ask the British Foreign Office to change a cipher that he would read almost as easily as his daily paper.'*

It is perhaps no coincidence that Russia leads the world in chess ability; which came first is not clear.

1. (Andre Deutsch, 1962).

Coupled with the Russian gifts for espionage, chess and cryptography is a love of intrigue, perhaps the result of centuries of autocracy, all of which has made them the natural recipients and exponents of communism, whose principal method of reproduction is clandestine, by cellular division and infiltration. An espionage network is an excellent vehicle for the spread of communism and the qualities required of communist agents are often similar to those required of spies. Espionage and counter-espionage are in any case necessary parts of communism; for example, espionage identifies potential recruits in vital and vulnerable places, and counter-espionage maintains a security surveillance of its probationers and members.

The espionage system is the basis of sabotage and subversive organisations wherever they are found. This is not to say that a particular espionage network will necessarily have the triple roles of seeking information, blowing up key points and attempting to overthrow or undermine some foreign state, although this may be so. It is more likely that separate branches of the same organisation will carry out the different functions and be co-ordinated at high level.

An important example of the use of an espionage-type network for subversive activity is the attempt a few years ago by communists to maintain and increase their control of the Electrical Trades Union by ballot-rigging. The reason for their selection of the ETU as a victim is not without interest. The electrician, perhaps more than any other tradesman, is a lone wolf and has to visit almost every part of every factory to carry out maintenance and installations; he must also visit many homes and government offices, including those where secrets are held or discussed. No one is in a better position for widespread subversive activity, including espionage, sabotage and proselytisation, and to defeat security, for he also maintains intruder alarm systems. Electricians, more than any other branch of organised labour, are in a position to bring any civilised country to a standstill and overthrow its government by passive or active sabotage (see Chapter 4, pp. 33-38).

Sabotage and subversion are, of course, not the only functions which can be based on an espionage type of organisation. There are, for example, intimidation and planned crime generally, kidnapping and murder for political and military purposes. Deception, which is the passing of false information to disorganise and deceive the enemy, is a highly specialised type of espionage. The usual method is to begin by passing a certain amount of true information of little value, so

that confidence in the source is established, and later to pass some
seriously false information which really matters.

## TOTAL ESPIONAGE IN EAST AND WEST

The Russian espionage service long since became the basis of most if
not all of these functions. In addition to the excellent information it
provides, it is omnipresent wherever there are weak non-communist
regimes, or it may try to create weakness were there is strength; it
foments and supports local wars to weaken the west with considerable success in such places as Korea and Indo-China, where enormous
western effort has been expended with hardly the loss of a Russian
soldier.

However, through hot and cold war experience, the principal
espionage agency of the West, the United States Central Intelligence
Agency, has become a good match for its Russian equivalent so far as
totality is concerned. Thus, according to de Gramont, in

'*1950: The CIA established a cover organisation on Formosa called
Western Enterprises Inc., which armed, trained and equipped Nationalist Chinese Guerillas that raided the Red Chinese mainland from the
offshore islands.*

'*1951: The CIA supported a guerilla force of Chinese Nationalists
that had fled to Northern Burma after the Communist take-over of China.*

'*1952: The CIA supported the coup that ousted King Farouk from
Egypt and brought Gamal Abdel Nasser to power.*[1]

'*1953: The CIA plotted the coup that ousted Premier Mohammed
Mossadegh from Iran and brought back the Shah Mohammed Reza
Pahlevi.*

'*1953: The CIA set up an independent intelligence organisation in
West Germany under Reinhard Gehlen, an intelligence chief under
Hitler. Gehlen sent agents into East Germany during the 1953 riots.*

'*1954: The CIA supported Colonel Carlos Castillo Armas in his
successful overthrow of the pro-Communist regime of Jacobo Arbenz
Guzman (in Guatemala).*

'*1955: The CIA built an underground tunnel into East Berlin and
tapped the Soviet East sector's telephone lines.*

'*1956: During the Hungarian uprising, arms were supplied by the CIA
and by Gehlen agents to the Hungarian patriots.*

'*1958: The CIA urged military intervention in Lebanon and was in-
strumental in the decision to order the Sixth Fleet there and land
Marines.*

1. This makes curious reading today (May 1967).

'*1960: The CIA backed General Phoumi Nosavan in Laos. Phoumi turned out to be little more than an unpopular and ineffective war lord and the United States was burdened with another losing proposition.*'

De Gramont says that the above examples are based on published reports. To these must be added CIA's rôle in Cuba which has already been related. It would appear that the operations of the CIA in so-called peacetime are on an even wider scale than those of its predecessor, the Office of Strategic Services, and its British counterpart, SOE, during the Second World War.[1]

This, then, is what is meant by total espionage; its scale and importance in the world today are due to the conditions of nuclear balance in which we live, and they are likely to increase, especially the psychological aspect.

Finally, it is obvious that any competent espionage organisation constituted for the primary purpose of obtaining military and political information could easily turn its attention to purely industrial information, which is in any case a frequent by-product of the pursuit of the other two. There is no evidence available to the writer that industrial information thus gleaned is put to direct commercial use, by the CIA for instance. But since a country's power to wage war, including cold war, and the impact of its foreign policy are commensurate with the strength of its economy, the temptation to do so would be very great; some would say irresistible.

---

1. Since this book was written there have been further revelations and indications of the 'total' nature of CIA's operation. For example, the downfall of the Left-wing Jagan government in the colony of British Guiana (now independent Guyana) in 1964 was apparently engineered largely by the CIA. The Anglo-American magazine *Encounter*, according to Mr. Melvin Lasky, American co-editor, had been 'the unwitting recipient of indirectly derived CIA funds'. As a result of this, Stephen Spender, the well-known poet, resigned as co-editor in May 1967. On 19th February 1967, twenty-six foundations and organisations were listed by the *New York Times* as recipients of CIA 'donations' during the past fifteen years. They included the National Student Association; the American Newspaper Guild, a journalists' union, which denied knowledge of receiving almost a million dollars; the American Fund for Free Jurists; the Foreign Policy Research Institute of Pennsylvania; the National Education Association, and the International Confederation of Free Trade Unions of Brussels.

# CHAPTER 4

## Subversion and Sabotage

It has been argued that if an enemy wanted to capture and subjugate Britain or any other western democracy today he would not use military force but a *sixth column*. World War II saw the emergence of a fifth column or Quisling type of operation—an organised body sympathising with and working for the enemy within a country at war. The idea of a sixth column was first put forward by Peter Fleming in his book of that name published in 1951, some parts of which seem prophetic in the light of many subsequent trends and events. Instead of an army, an enemy would infiltrate sixth columnists who would quietly and subtly attack the morale and character of the people. They would try to undermine established values and institutions without replacement. They would be ideological saboteurs.

It is not a coincidence that industrial espionage has become news is this country at a time when a number of equally disturbing new forces are manifesting themselves. In the present uneasy no-man's land between total peace and nuclear war there are social and moral developments which are not yet fully comprehended. Many of them arise from and cause rapidly changing beliefs and values.

Men and nations alter their beliefs either by reason of experience and changing environment or through persuasion. The latter has played a considerable part in human affairs: the pages of history are full of the doings of great persuaders—politicians, preachers and generals—using a variety of means ranging from exhortation to physical force. Although the end of persuasion, the changing of beliefs, that is, remains the same, the means change. There are indications that the next supreme means of persuasion will be of an advanced psychological nature—a mass brainwashing based upon development of Pavlovian research and taking advantage of modern mass communication techniques, whose 'fall-out' area is even greater than that of nuclear weapons. Some experiments carried out in

Moscow show that it is possible to learn a language while asleep.[1] The sleeping pupils hear thirty-six tape-recorded English lessons and, so it is believed, end their 'course' with a mastery of basic English grammar and a vocabulary of about 1,000 words and phrases. On this basis the will or the political views of a nation could be changed or modified whilst its people slept. A slight case of mental rape! But as gunpowder is still used and remains a potent weapon, so the next take-over will be gradual and there can be no guaranteed deadline after which physical force will not be used. The object of physical force, in conjunction with other means, is to destroy the enemy's will to resist and to impose another will upon him. Physical force is the court of last resort and, unless there are special factors such as internal pressures or emotions like cruelty or sadism, it is only used when peaceful persuasion, including the threat of force, has failed. Even then, physical force is used as an aid to persuasion and seldom as an end in itself.

Persuasion by word, written or spoken, can be very powerful—St. Paul, John Wesley, and, at the other end of the scale, Hitler, Goebbels and Mussolini are examples of great persuaders. The latter three used persuasion sooner rather than later in a threat or physical fear context, and in the end were compelled to resort to force to try to achieve their evil ends. But nearly all persuasion contains or implies some degree of intimidation. To be successful it has to show to the subject of the persuasion some advantage of following or disadvantage of not following the course advocated: hell-fire and damnation if one does not, commercial gain if one does, are examples. The similarity between persuasion, intimidation, threat and force is that all are aimed at the will of the victim; the differences are of degree and whether the means are mental or physical in character.

Roughly the same period of time which has seen the development of weapons of mass destruction has also seen the arrival of mass communication which enables more people to be influenced more quickly, and perhaps more certainly, because rehearsal leading to perfection of presentation (and skilled slanting) is now practicable through the use of edited film or tape. What would have been the effect of someone like Wesley had these modern means of communication been available to him? Certainly Hitler and Goebbels owed much of their success to the radio, and recent history might have been altogether different had these forms of communication not been

---

1. There is a Sleep-Learning Association with headquarters in London which has published a booklet called *Learn While You Sleep.*

developed. To give but one example, the 1944 plot against Hitler might well have succeeded had the radio not been available to Hitler or, conversely, had the plotters secured radio and telephone communication to themselves.

The power of modern communications is enormous. Far-reaching themes suitable only for highly sophisticated and educated people can now reach tens or hundreds of millions of people too immature or simple to comprehend them. Subversive messages may be conveyed subliminally with incalculable consequences.

One of the features of contemporary scientific and medical development has been a notable advance in psychology and psychiatry. Pavlov's experiments on animals and the human application of the knowledge thereby gained have taught us that by psychological means a man can be made to hate what he previously loved and love what he previously hated. The techniques of brainwashing and of public relations are extreme and mild examples. In other words, scientific development of persuasion has brought about a situation in which it is possible to impose another will on a man with virtual certainty of success and without the use or threat of physical force. This means has two major advantages over physical force: first it is well known that physical force used against certain people may have the opposite result to that intended; secondly 'voluntary' conversion does away with any desire for revenge. It is cheaper, less risky to its perpetrators and more certain of success.

This idea of 'voluntary' conversion was well illustrated in a programme called '*The World Tomorrow*' put out by the Independent Television network on 23rd August 1966. This programme, entitled 'The Mind Race,' featured in particular psychopharmacology—the science which studies the effect of drugs on the human mind. Commenting on this programme in the *TV Times*, John Cohen, professor of psychology at Manchester University and adviser to the programme, said: 'Many a tyrant has been moved by greed for power or religious fanaticism. But only in our time has mind control become an applied science, open to many abuses as well as to beneficent uses in medicine'.

One of the leading psychologists interviewed in the programme, Professor James McConnell of Michigan University, said:

'*If I wanted to control the world, I would find ten bright people and, one by one, gain control of their behaviour. Then I'd send each one out to grab ten more. It would take a matter of a year or two to take over, say, the 50 million people of Britain.*

'*The atom bomb is a child's toy compared to the way we can, theoretic-*

*ally, control people and things. I say this theoretically, because they won't let me do the experiments to prove it.*

*'If they would let us take a thousand children from Asia who are going to die of starvation, we would guarantee them a full and happy life— and simply use them as subjects.*

*'Man is going to become a different animal, and I'm worried the wrong people are going to take charge.*

*'We're getting close to the point where, if you want to go to Oxford University, you will be able to get a brain injection of instant knowledge.'*

To sum up so far, it is suggested that in the following conditions the argument that attacks on the hearts and minds of men as a means of imposing personal or national wills will rapidly supplant physical force is at least tenable—

nuclear balance;

mass communications which enable almost every home to be reached;

rapidly increasing understanding of the workings of the human brain.

With this argument and the sixth column in mind, let us now take a look at some examples of new forces of persuasion from the current industrial and accompanying social scene.

SUBVERSION

The term subversion is increasingly used today. The Pope referred to it in his 1965 Christmas message as one of the great dangers confronting the world. Lord Denning in his 1963 report on the Profumo affair said of the rôle of the Security Service:

*'They are not to be used so as to pry into any man's private conduct, or business affairs, or even into his political opinions, except in so far as they are subversive, that is, they would contemplate the overthrow of the Government by unlawful means.'*

The layman might well consider the Guy Fawkes plot a good example of subversion, as indeed it is, but it is important to realise that there is a variety of ways of overthrowing a government unlawfully. To blow its members up with gunpowder is but one.

What would happen if the following conditions occurred simultaneously in the United Kingdom?

Significant numbers of the judiciary or the magistracy became intimidated and many criminals went unpunished.

The police refused to carry out their duties.

Key trades unions, such as those concerned with transport, electricity and post office communications, were taken over by the communists and went on prolonged strike.

There was serious disaffection in the armed services and for this and other reasons they could not provide essential services.

The Government might well be reduced to impotence in such circumstances, although not overthrown in the Guy Fawkes sense. A most serious situation analagous to that in Russia in 1917 might arise. Those who believe that 'it could not happen here' should consider and investigate these statements:

It is common knowledge that jurors and witnesses are being intimidated on an increasing scale. Why should intimidation stop there? Officials of the Police Federation have, according to press reports, been making 'blunt pay demands' and other pronouncements which are not unlike strike threats (see p. 93).

To maintain and increase their hold on the Electrical Trades Union, communist officials resorted to ballot-rigging (see Appendix E and also p. 27). Although this was exposed and the communists lost control after a legal process, there are recent indications that they have not given up the struggle. An overall electrical stoppage more surely and quickly than any other could bring disaster to this country. The National Union of Seamen did go on strike; it was prolonged by the influence of communists, who according to the Prime Minister made a take-over bid for control of that union, with the aim of destroying a Government policy—the prices and incomes policy (see Appendix F).

To use the armed forces for prolonged strike breaking would throw a great strain on their loyalties, and seriously hamper national defence. It is in any case doubtful if in the conditions postulated they could provide all the services essential to life and government.

But even if the government were not immediately overthrown, there can be no doubt that many of their policies would be. The tune would be called by bodies not answerable to the electorate, who would thus be held to ransom. It is not difficult to imagine the ultimate ransom, the forfeiture of democratic government and its replacement by a totalitarian form.

The true nature of subversion is beginning to emerge. It is a hidden persuader, acting through the mind. To subvert is defined in a dictionary as 'to overthrow from the foundation' and 'to pervert the mind'. It overthrows by attacking the fabric, the foundation or the mind of its target. Its attack is insidious and at first not perceptible; like certain types of cancer, its presence may not be detected until the body is completely corrupted. It is highly flexible, adapting itself to the nature of its target; if one method fails, it will try another—if the timbers are too sound to be battered down by brute force, it will use white ants. It also fosters and uses natural disintegrative forces such as moral and physical perversion for breaking down whatever order or institution it is attacking.

Subversive activity may take many forms, but its two most important manifestations in Britain are in industry and its social environment. Communism is the main subversive threat in this country today, and its ultimate purpose is of course political. Since it is very unlikely that communists will ever be voted into power they must choose other means, the most important of which is to gain control of the trades unions. From this position they might well be able to achieve their object, especially if the moral strength of likely opposition has been rotted.

Before we look in more detail at 'peaceful' industrial subversion, let us briefly survey subversion in its violent forms.

GUERILLA WARFARE

Guerilla warfare, like criminal warfare, is an area operation. It is not fought on a linear front; it in fact has no front, which is why it is so hard to defeat. For much of the time the guerillas are legitimate tillers of fields, in perfect camouflage, and then briefly they become Saturday-night soldiers. Their success in defeating or containing immensely more powerful military forces in such places as Yugoslavia, Cyprus and Indo-China was due in a large part to their ability psychologically to identify themselves with the will of the indigenous peoples. That the true aim of guerilla warfare may be the establishment of another form of tyranny merely increases the subversiveness.

Guerilla warfare has the roles of convincing the other side that its mission is fruitless; maintaining the morale of the people it purports to represent and that of the guerillas; punishing *pour encourager les autres* traitors or reluctant helpers or those who disobey orders; and, of considerable importance nowadays, attracting the attention and support of world opinion to the particular or pretended cause. As yet, guerilla warfare has only been used in support of political or military objectives, and it is hard to imagine it being used to obtain direct industrial or economic advantage. Strong arm methods used by certain property racketeers to evict 'protected' tenants, by pirate radio organisations, by gambling clubs to enforce payment of debts, are, however, analogous.

It will be seen that guerilla operations—at any rate, modern guerilla operations—involve the use of psychological and military means of persuasion, but it is the psychological *effect* of the military means that is of major importance, usually out of all proportion to their actual military significance.

### SABOTAGE

Sabotage is often a part of guerilla warfare. By secret attacks with explosive or fire as the main weapons on the enemy's vulnerable points, for example, his lines of communication, bridges, viaducts, power stations and distribution systems and so on, it is possible to cause severe disruption of a civilised country or of an army dependent on sophisticated military equipment for its efficiency, at very small cost.

Sabotage has become an important weapon of war. It was probably first used in a big way by the Japanese during the Russo-Japanese war at the beginning of this century, but it did not really come into its own until the Second World War, when it was used extensively by the Allies as a means of disrupting the German occupation of western Europe. The most famous sabotage attacks are probably those against the hydroelectric station at Rjukan[1] in Norway in World War II to destroy the heavy water plant which formed a vital part of the German nuclear research. It also played an important part with aerial bombardment in interdiction in northern France immediately prior to D-Day.

The more urbanised a country is, the more vulnerable it becomes to sabotage. The disruption of New York in 1965 by a short period of electricity failure illustrates this point. Supposing someone had been able to prolong this period to several months and it had been accompanied by interruption of water supplies and telephone and radio communications? Supposing all this could have been repeated simultaneously in, say, twenty major centres of the USA? It is possible that surprise attacks by a few hundred well-trained saboteurs could achieve this without any weapons more potent than plastic explosives and fire. It is theoretically possible to bring a civilised country to its knees by sabotage alone.

### PASSIVE SABOTAGE

In its original meaning the word sabotage signified an act of malicious damage by a disgruntled workman against his employer's property,

1. See Bibliography, *The Virus House* by David Irving (William Kimber, 1967).

but this has been and still is of rare occurrence. There is now a much more popular and more damaging form known as passive sabotage which connotes industrial action such as strikes, go-slows, work-to-rule, and other forms of deliberate industrial disruption, when the purpose is subversive. If such are performed as part of a genuine wages or other dispute between workers and management, the actions, however ill-intentioned, may not constitute sabotage. But if they are performed, whether consciously or unconsciously, in pursuit of a subversive political purpose, e.g., as part of an attempt to bring Communism to power in an unconstitutional way, or are aimed to hamper some legitimate national political purpose such as war or sanctions or vital economic measures, then they may truly be termed passive sabotage. It should not be forgotten that wages, demarcation or other industrial disputes may be trumped up for subversive purposes. Passive sabotage, like active, is often used as part of guerilla warfare with the object of increasing disruption. Again, too, it is much more formidable in highly organised urban societies. Both types of sabotage erode willpower and physical capacity and create conditions favourable to the success of a subversive psychological attack.

Both official and unofficial strikes without apparent political motivation may be subversive if the effect is more widespread than on the employers. A *cri de coeur* of trades unionists who resist the application of policies of wage restraint designed to stabilise a national economy is that incomes are a matter for bargaining between employers and employees, i.e., trade unions. But of course the use of the strike weapon of big or key unions such as the Electrical Trades Union (see Appendix E), the National Union of Railwaymen, the Transport and General Workers' Union, the Amalgamated Engineering Union (see Appendix G), and the National Union of Seamen (see Appendix F), has repercussions far wider than the employers' profits; today it is used as a stick with which to beat the public in the hope that the public will force the employers to surrender to union demands. In other spheres, the process would be called blackmail. If the government, whose responsibility it is to protect the public from the effects of a big strike in a key industry, intervenes before or during the strike, it is accused by some trade unionists of interference in matters which are, they say, the concern only of the union, the employees and the employers. This is of course as true as saying that war is a matter for the armed forces. Even if a large scale strike in a key industry is not subversive when it starts, it will be so long before it ends. The forces of evil will quickly be attracted to the scene like flies to decay; to prolong, to exacerbate, to increase their influences, so that they may in due course impose the will of their small well organised minority on the majority. Thus, as in law malice may be inferred from the act, so may subversion be inferred sooner or later from a national strike in a key industry. In view of the immense damage they do to the country at home and abroad, it is questionable whether such strikes should be permitted by law, any more than is robbery at pistol point. To those who regard the right to withdraw labour as a fundamental human freedom one may adduce the case of the armed forces and the police, who do not have the right to strike on account of the vital nature of their duties. Much of the modern industrial complex is at least as vital to our lives as they are; indeed the armed services could not fight without the power of industry.

Like all the other dark forces, subversion and sabotage, whether passive or active, operate on an espionage type of organisation.

# CHAPTER 5

## *The English Way of Industrial Espionage*

The title of this chapter is something of a paradox for the term 'industrial espionage' has almost certainly never sullied the lips or the *writing paper* of the many English gentlemen who have been past masters of it for years. So subtle is the art as practised that even the perspicacious Anthony Sampson, in his splendid book *Anatomy of Britain,*[1] did not unravel it from the tangle of British industry, commerce, banking and insurance. Yet information, if not the lifeblood of this vast world, is certainly its nervous system. London is a centre of vital information, most of which is there for the gathering, and very few big firms can afford to be away from it for this reason alone—a point studiously avoided in the planners' exhortations to move out. If challenged, these earnest people would no doubt suggest that a small sales office or showroom left behind in the hub would be sufficient, but everybody in the know realises that it is not, unless indeed those left-behind small offices are to contain trained information collectors. For, of course, it is the main body of managers at all levels, through their day-to-day contacts in the pulsating centre, who produce the bulk of the information so necessary to efficient and profitable business operations. How can this be done in an inbred executive canteen in the home counties?

When the Chancellor of the Exchequer decided to tax expense account entertaining, apart from certain export incentives, he was not only aiming at birds on moors and yachts, but also at a major part of the commercial intelligence system. It is of interest to speculate whether information or intelligence expenses, as such, are allowable for tax purposes. There would surely be no objection to the appointment by any company of an Information or Intelligence Officer and staff. Chief Spy as a title may be provocative and bad for security, but it is not yet illegal. However, there is as yet no professional intelligence service in the British business world in the

1. (Hodder and Stoughton, 1962).

sense of the governmental agencies established to safeguard the nation. Of course, a number of big firms such as oil companies, insurance companies and banks, do have information (sometimes called intelligence) departments, and the Board of Trade has recently started an export intelligence service. There is considerable activity in the credit rating field, partly by the banks in the ordinary course of their business, and partly by agencies established especially for this purpose. In the case of the banks, it is possible to get from them a little more than mere credit ratings. There are strong links between banks all over the world and guarded information about other banks' customers is obtainable for bona fide purposes. But the banks do not set out deliberately to discover details of a particular firm's activities and intentions; rather do they pass on in suitable circumstances a discreet account of what happens to be in their files and records. Of course, if a large overdraft is involved, in all probability there will be more detailed investigations. Even then, the research is apt to be rather perfunctory and unskilled to judge by some recent examples.

Where it is necessary to find out more than can be obtained from the banks or from published records, there are several recognised procedures in industry. The first method, and probably the most important, has already been mentioned; nearly all executives have good friends; these may be old school friends, ordinary business contacts, regimental or ex-service friends, club friends, travelling or commuting companions, professional friends, or boardroom friends —executive directors of one firm are apt to be non-executive directors of others. In the ordinary course of English business there are few information problems which can arise at managing director level where it is not possible for the managing director to think of an executive or board colleague with the right sort of contact, who will provide the answer he requires; in which case the executive concerned will telephone his contact and, in pre-Callaghan days at least, propose luncheon or a drink. Usually he will be able to find out what his managing director wants simply by asking, without subterfuge. He will be quite open about his purpose and his preparatory remarks will simply be on the 'Can you help me? The old man wants to know' note.

If this enquiry and other similar contacts produce no result, he will report back to his managing director accordingly. The latter will then be reduced to making more formal enquiries, probably through his firm's merchant bank advisers, auditors or brokers. If all else fails and the matter is of sufficient importance, it would be by no means unusual for the managing director or a senior executive acting on his behalf to make direct enquiries of someone 'in the know', even his opposite number in the organisation or firm about which information is required. After openly indicating his interest, he would put the question and, in the majority of cases, be given a straight-forward answer, or at any rate enough information for him to solve his particular problem. Often there will be an information *quid pro quo*.

It may be difficult for the reader to accept this unless he under-stands or is acquainted with the enormous friendliness of the British business world. Coupled with this are certain very high ethical standards, such as never allowing your sales representatives to run down a competitor's products (which is sound policy for oneself in any case); such as regarding one's word as binding whether it has been confirmed in writing or whether it is convenient or not; which illustrate a way of life and thought in which subterfuge such as deliberate espionage is alien. These ethics apply even where deadly rivals are concerned, although perhaps this is not so true between competing sales forces of the same organisation, where relations are apt to be much more strained.

It does not require a great deal of discernment to see that to a very large extent industrial intelligence, as many other facets of our national life, is tangled up with the 'Old Boy Net'. Like the 'gentle-men's agreements' and similar shibboleths, what is and what is not intelligence cricket, even if not clearly defined or codified, is fully understood and respected by the major part of British industry and commerce.

At first sight this state of affairs and these ethics might appear to obviate any need for a sophisticated intelligence system. But a closer look will show that it has certain snags. In the first place, it is essential-ly haphazard and casual. A managing director will mostly cause enquiries to be made only if something he has heard suggests a need; or useful information may just turn up by luck. But if none of these conditions occurs, he and his organisation may be completely taken by surprise, with serious business consequences. Secondly, because he and his staff are not trained investigators and reporters, they may get distorted, incomplete, inaccurate or misleading information, even when the subject of the enquiry has no wish to deceive; or gossip and rumour may not be clearly distinguished from fact; or reporting may be coloured by the beliefs or wishes of the reporter; or information may be invented through a desire to gain favour or a reluctance to admit failure to find out.

Thirdly, the 'system' only works with those who know and abide by the rules of the game. 'Unsporting' Americans, for example, nourished in a hard school of cut-throat competition, who are out of a job if they fail to pull off the deal, as opposed to being gently transferred to a department specially created for those loyal servants of the company who didn't quite make the grade, may not, and may not wish to, understand the niceties. They would regard the British view of industrial espionage, expressed by no less a person than Sir Richard Powell, Director General of the Institute of Directors, and reported in the *Evening Standard* of 9th April 1963—'We deplore anything of an unethical nature'—as irrelevant to the situation and their needs. Later the same year, however, Sir Richard is quoted in the *Daily Mirror* of 12th June as saying, 'This sort of spying, comparatively new to Britain, is growing to almost professional proportions. Some companies try to suborn employees of rival firms to give away secrets. Others go after the worker who may have the information and is leaving or has been sacked'.

The different American and British approaches to industrial information are clearly illustrated by a *Guardian* leader published on 18th January 1966 entitled *Magnum quid pro parvo quo*. It points out that agreements between the British and American governments for complete exchange of technical information are often one-way traffic unfavourable to the British and cites two examples:

'*For example, there exists an agreement for the complete exchange of technical information on fast reactors with the United States. Much of the research undertaken for the US Atomic Energy Commission is carried out by commercial concerns who sensibly keep a great deal of what they learn very firmly under their hats. Britain has a considerable lead in this particular field, but research is carried out at Government establishments and, in accordance with the letter of agreements involving the peaceful uses of atomic energy, is made available to the United States. With fast reactors the most important future development in the commercial exploitation of nuclear power, and with Britain possessing not a single effective commercially available reactor for sale overseas (except the as yet untried AGR), is such technological generosity altogether wise?*'.

and '*Some time ago the Admiralty signed an agreement, again with the United States, for an exchange of information on fuel cells. The United States already makes use of the British-born Bacon cell under licence, and its basic ideas have been exploited commercially to levels of sophistication which this country will be hard placed to match. Again, because American development is commercial, only a fraction of the important technical information finds its way back. Over here, however, it seems that even when research is being undertaken by a commercial organisation or by a university, it is expected of them that they will openly share their knowledge with official visiting scientists.'*

Experience has shown, the leading article goes on to say, that a visit to 'an American concern, ostensibly for an exchange of information, may turn out to be no more than a lush managerial-cum-public relations tour'.

The underlying reasons for the English industrial intelligence 'system' are matters of history. The Industrial Revolution and the growth of the public schools were roughly contemporaneous. The latter, for whom Dr. Thomas Arnold can be largely praised or blamed according to inclination, were designed to provide leaders with the high moral character and ethical standards inseparable from responsible leadership—leaders for the armed services, for the foreign and home civil services, and for industry. Team spirit of a kind probably unequalled by any other educational system in the world was inculcated on the playing fields and in the 'house', as were a sense of fair play and gallant losing—in fact, all the moral of Sir Winston Churchill's work *The Second World War*—'In war: resolution; in defeat: defiance; in victory: magnanimity; in peace: goodwill'.

It must be remembered, too, that from the beginning of the nineteenth century, for a hundred years or so, British industry lived on a seller's market by virtue of the fact that there was very little competition. At the turn of the century, Great Britain was still the greatest trading nation on earth, although there were disquieting signs that Germany was making inroads into some of her overseas markets, especially in the United States. Nevertheless, there was still no need for salesmanship as we know it today. Added to this seller's market was an unchallenged reputation for quality of product and trading integrity. In such conditions of paramountcy there was no need for organised industrial intelligence, which, if it had been considered at all, would have been rejected then, as it is even today, as 'not done'. During the same period, national, military and political intelligence and security were embryonic for similar reasons; Chambers' Encyclopaedia of 1901 makes no reference to Intelligence or Security. Britain's trade, always a primary defence consideration, was adequately protected by her navy, whose size and quality was, until after the Great War, governed by the principle that it must be strong enough to defeat any other two nations. It was not until about 1910, when the growth of the German navy created a serious challenge to her naval superiority, that Britain began to take intelligence and security seriously again. It is no coincidence that Britain's first formal intelligence and security services had strong connections with and owed much of their inspiration to the Royal Navy. They were the result of necessity created by intense competition.

This may demonstrate a flexibility which many people think the British have lost today, but while that may also be true, the nation's own safety as well as its trading safety was at stake; nothing was taught at public school that prevented reasonable measures, albeit of a slightly distasteful type, being taken in defence of the motherland and her empire. The intelligence and security services were from the beginning run in a gentlemanly way, by gentlemen from major and minor public schools, mostly with Army or Navy backgrounds, as they largely are today. They were and still are generally highly successful. De Gramont says of the espionage side, 'One of the most amusing reasons given for the success of the British in espionage is that they are a nation of hobbyists. In what other country could you find on emergency notice a man to lead you through a mountain trail in the Peloponnesus because he went on hikes there one vacation? Or a man who knew every inch of a French beach because he'd hunted for seashells there?'. George Orwell, quoted by Anthony Sampson, wrote of the 'English characteristic which is so much a part of us that we barely notice it, and that is an addiction to hobbies and spare time occupations, the *privateness* of English life. We are a nation of flowers growers . . . of stamp collectors, pigeon fanciers, amateur carpenters, coupon snippers, darts players, crossword puzzle fans'. Presumably the same characteristics that made the British good at political and military espionage would make them formidable industrial spies—if it were not for that typically English phrase 'not done'.

The public schools, as everyone knows, were and are more than an education; they have become a way of life and what they stand for is deeply rooted in the national character. The old-boy net is not confined to Eton and Harrow, it is layered in our society and has spread to all institutions, professions and government, civil and military services, and even the trade unions. If public schools were abolished tomorrow and the upper classes guillotined *en masse*, it would continue and flourish. Our way of obtaining industrial information derives directly and logically from it. It might serve very well in an increasingly close-knit and competitive world if all the other industrial nations had produced their Dr. Arnolds when we did. Since they did not, it is, whether we like it or not, a pleasant anachronism, whose relevance to the present game of hard industrial competition is much the same as cottage industry to the great cartels.

More important still, since we remain one of the most original and inventive of all nations, we have more than most to lose through the practice of deliberate industrial intelligence by others and, because it is not seriously practised by British industry, it has been innocently thought unnecessary to establish defences against it, except where the immediate safety of the nation is concerned.

# CHAPTER 6

## Industrial Espionage—The Contemporary Scene

By the autumn of 1965 industrial espionage had become of sufficient interest in the United Kingdom for a one-day seminar to be held in a West End hotel by a firm called Management Investigation Services (R. B. Matthews). It was attended by forty or so persons whose names and identities were not divulged, but who were said to be 'mostly senior business executives'. The seminar consisted of five lectures entitled—

Justification for the use of industrial espionage and evidence of current activity.

Methods of penetrating the company organisation.

Likely targets for the industrial espionage agent.

Blue-print for planned defence.

Physical methods of protecting information and material.

Mr. Matthews and his co-lecturers certainly made a good case for the professional protection of company secrets, a service which his own firm was prepared to offer to industry on a fee basis. The actual services offered included—

the running of security courses on clients' premises;

personal coaching and consultation for senior security executives;

security surveys;

the security of company conferences, including 'the examination of meeting rooms and accommodation used by delegates to ensure that listening devices have not been installed . . . and any surveillance that may be necessary';

vetting of individuals: 'Because of their duties, it is important that certain individuals should be vetted thoroughly to ensure that an accurate assessment of their characters is made. The taking up of references in the usual way is inadequate. Personnel Departments are not usually in a position to carry out sophisticated vetting procedures. MIS will carry out the task, including field investigations';

confidential investigations: 'Correct management decisions can only be made on the basis of sound, up-to-date information. Company personnel are unlikely to have the time or the skill necessary to carry out certain delicate types of enquiry. In some circumstances the knowledge that an enquiry was being made could cause embarrassment and indicate a new area of interest. MIS will be glad to help in the collection of information not normally available and will undertake most forms of confidential investigation, including legal research by unorthodox methods'.

Readers of Vance Packard's *Naked Society* and champions of civil liberties may hold the view that some of this firm's business activity falls into the category of unwarrantable intrusion into privacy. But closer examination will show that MIS is a logical reaction to the development of industrial espionage on a significant scale. Certainly, there are no official counter-agencies except in certain very limited spheres where the national interest is directly involved. For example, firms engaged on government secret contracts and in certain other circumstances are given official advice by the Security Service.

Since the law does not recognise industrial espionage as a crime, it would be unfair to expect assistance in countering it from the hardpressed police resources. If, in due course, it is made a crime it is doubtful whether the police could give industry much assistance, either in the detective or protective senses, without prejudicing the already uphill fight against other crime.

For the foreseeable future, therefore, firms like MIS have an economic justification for existence and they may also do good business. In the *Daily Express* of 20th January 1966 a journalist claimed to have met an American 'who has fifty counter-spies working in Britain' and expects to have here '200 agents by 1968'. The report goes on to say that the man concerned 'whose headquarters is in a Manhattan skyscraper, works not in military intelligence, but in the world of industrial spies'. The report also states that in the United States this man is 'head of a multi-million dollar organisation employing 520 operatives'.

Those who would gain a living through industrial security have, of course, a vested interest in industrial espionage and due allowance must be made for promotional exaggeration, but nevertheless there is plenty of reliable evidence to show that it is a reality which must be faced. For example, Sir Richard Powell, Director General of the Institute of Directors, is reported in *The Times* of 13th December 1965 as saying that there was evidence indicating a considerable increase in industrial espionage in the past ten years, particularly in the electronics and photographic fields. He had recently had four examples of firms detailing an employee to get a job with a rival firm

C

and, in the end, return at a higher salary. He knew of another man who had returned late to his office to find the cleaning woman piecing together bits of paper out of his waste-paper basket. She turned out to be employed by a rival firm.

There is no doubt that industrial espionage is most prevalent where there are massive research programmes, and the United States with the largest stake in this sphere is finding the traffic in industrial secrets an increasing problem. The American Society for Industrial Security is pressing for legislative action to help give effective protection to America's industrial secrets. Although some concerns in Europe also spend large sums on research, there are others there and elsewhere whose deliberate policy is to profit parasite-like from the vast American research effort; through espionage if necessary.

A case in point, which is the most important of its kind yet reported, is that of the theft of drug secrets from the *American Cyanamid Corporation*, which was the subject of a trial in New York. The central figure in the case was a Dr. Sidney Fox, who in 1958 was leading a small antibiotics research team at the Cyanamid plant near New York. At this stage he appears to have developed a 'chip-on-shoulder' attitude, which is so often the cause of crime or treachery. Apparently his income was not sufficient to 'keep up with the Joneses' in the neighbourhood of Spring Valley where he lived; it seems that he became unduly conscious of his background; he was the son of a Russian Jewish immigrant tailor.

At first Fox began in a small way—as do so many criminals—by making a few sales of drug cultures and information to a local drug firm known as Biorganic Laboratories, owned by two fellow Jews called Sharff and Salb. According to Fox's own story at the trial, he began to take home cultures and documents, some of which he sold to Sharff and Salb. But Fox soon began to suspect that his fellow conspirators were making very big profits out of which he was not getting a fair share. He then decided to deal direct with certain Italian firms, who he knew were in the market for such drugs. In September 1959 he visited Milan, and there, Dr. Fox said in evidence, he negotiated with the consultant to an Italian company to sell cultures and information, for which he received $55,000.

At this stage, according to the evidence given, Sharff of Biorganic Laboratories attempted by various threats to stop Fox's independent dealings for fear they would affect his profits. To this end Sharff arranged a meeting, at the Dorchester Hotel, London, between Fox and an Italian friend of Sharff's. Unfortunately for Sharff, Fox and the Italian became partners.

Fox now decided to set up a full-time 'marketing' organisation in collaboration with his Italian partner. He resigned from Cyanamid, but arranged for a colleague named John Cancelarich, who remained with them, to continue the supply of cultures and information. As cover for these activities he arranged for another former colleague, an analytical chemist named Leonard Fine, to run a small firm that carried on a legitimate business in laboratory supplies. In Fox's house the conspirators carried out the necessary micro-photography, returning afterwards the original documents to Cyanamid, and stored the stolen cultures in a refrigerator.

From October 1960 Fox and the others negotiated deals with five Italian pharmaceutical companies. These deals included the provision of technical advice and Fox and Cancelarich paid visits to Italy using false names. The cultures were carried in pocket cigar containers.

By the spring of 1961, however, the conspirators began to quarrel and Fox became isolated; Cancelarich, Fine, Sharff and Salb linked up. In the meantime, Cyanamid, who by now suspected a major leakage of their know-how, had begun secret investigations. In February they had sufficient evidence to bring civil actions against Sharff and Fox for about $2m damages, although it was doubtful whether the evidence as it stood would have been sufficient to obtain success. But the newer conspirators, who by this time included another Cyanamid employee, a Joseph Gerace, began to crack. Gerace made a confession and was followed by Cancelarich and Fine. After other legal proceedings had been initiated, Fox finally pleaded guilty.

Cyanamid, who claimed that the development of the antibiotics concerned had cost them $30m in research and development, estimated that its sales losses to Italian competitors as a result of this espionage may have been as much as $100m.

Commenting on the final results of the case, in which six of the conspirators were given prison sentences and others suspended sentences, Mr. Lyman Duncan, Cyanamid's Vice-President responsible for Medical Research, said that they marked a 'firm step towards the continued ability of industry to carry on the scientific work which has contributed so much to technological and social progress'. He also said that since Cyanamid had begun prosecution seven States had passed laws to protect industry's research secrets against theft and that others were considering similar legislation. The United States Attorney, Mr. Robert N. Morgenthau, was reported as saying that the convictions marked the first successful prosecution of industrial espionage in the United States.

An interesting case of industrial espionage, also against a research target, which involved Russian diplomats in *West Germany* was disclosed on 25th January 1966 by the Ministry of the Interior for North Rhine Westphalia. A West German scientist whose wife was living in East Germany had been approached in 1962 by the East German espionage network and induced to work for it on the understanding that his wife would be allowed to rejoin him in the Federal Republic. He accepted the bait and was taken to East Germany and given thorough training in espionage work, including micro-photography. He then returned to West Germany where he was secretly contacted by Russian agents, who included some members of the Soviet Trade Mission in Cologne and two Russian press correspondents. Until September 1965 the scientist continued to work for the network providing sketches and security plans of an important industrial laboratory in the Federal Republic. The laboratory was not named, but the Ministry denied that it was the atomic research centre at Aachen. He is also said to have handed over to the Russians sixteen pamphlets of British, German and American authorship in highly specialised subjects, including Laser technique and plasma physics.

After a year the scientist's wife was allowed to join him in the Federal Republic and for his services he was paid about £500. Although there is no definite evidence to support this theory, it seems fairly certain that the scientist contacted the West German counter-espionage authorities early in the case. Certainly he was under surveillance from virtually the beginning and his activities and contacts had been observed and photographed by these authorities. On 31st December 1965 the Ministry of the Interior was apprised of what had been going on. After consultation with the State prosecuting authorities it was decided, however, that there was no basis for prosecution as the criminal code did not contain any provision for dealing with industrial espionage.

A note of bathos was struck by the Ministry spokesman when he added as a postscript to these facts the information that much of the scientific material, including all but one of the pamphlets, was normally accessible to everybody; some of it was in the library of the Aachen Technical College.

Although the cases of Cyanamid and the West German laboratory were both concerned with research targets, they were markedly different in another way. In the first case the motive was purely personal gain, whereas in the second it was obviously for national purposes—Soviet industry being nationalised *in toto* it is logical that the state should carry out all espionage including the industrial variety. It can be deduced from the interest displayed in the security precautions that further operations were contemplated against the West German laboratory unless, and it would seem unlikely, they were required as a sample of the type of precautions taken at installations of this kind. The identity of the laboratory in West Germany which was the target remains a closely-guarded secret, but it appears not to be of direct military importance, or a prosecution could have been made—unless there are other reasons for non-prosecution. For example, the whole release may have been designed to mislead the East Germans and the Russians; such devices are far from unknown to the 'dark forces'.

The *Merck* case in 1962 is an amateurish example of industrial espionage, compared with the two foregoing, but is of interest partly because it is one of the earliest cases to come to light in contemporary England, and also because the rival firm refused the spy's offer and helped to bring him to book.

In the summer of that year a research chemist at Parke Davis, the well-known pharmaceutical firm, was telephoned by a man who said he was from an agency supplying technical information likely to be of interest to Parke Davis. The research chemist, suspicious of the caller's accent and lack of technical knowledge, but impressed by his knowledge of a rival firm, Thomas Morson & Son Ltd., the British subsidiary of Merck, reported the matter to his superiors, who immediately informed Morson's, who telephoned Merck.

There was considerable alarm, for Merck had invested a large sum in research, and in particular they had spent about £1m on a revolutionary new drug called Aldomet, which reduces blood pressure. Three Merck executives immediately flew to London prepared to pay up to £10,000 if necessary for their own secret. A meeting took place in the Russell Hotel in Bloomsbury between Parke Davis representatives, who brought £500 in £1 notes for a first instalment, and the man who had telephoned. He turned out to be not the representative of a major industrial espionage ring which the Americans, at any rate, had expected, but a former process worker with Morsons who had been sacked for absenteeism. There was no doubt, however, about the worth of what he had to offer; he produced the 'flow sheet' of Aldomet. He asked £50 for it and was eventually beaten down to £30. He was subsequently arrested, tried and sent to prison for six months.

A curious case of industrial espionage at the Central Electricity Generating Board (CEGB) headquarters in Southwark, London, came to light in the middle of 1963. A clerk there who had access to the facts and figures of a large tender for a new power-station from one firm copied them and offered them to another firm for a financial consideration. The latter firm immediately informed the chairman of CEGB, Sir Christopher Hinton, now Lord Hinton, and the clerk was dismissed.

There is no doubt that reconnaissance of a very advanced type is used by organised criminals. The objects of reconnaissance are two: firstly, to discover a target and then, having discovered it, to provide information about its security arrangements and vulnerability to robbery. It is in the second instance that espionage is often used. It may be done by suborning an existing employee with access to the target, or a member or associate of the criminal gang may actually join the firm concerned with the intention of feeding back the necessary information. There have from time to time been reports of special reconnaissance organisations operating independently of the criminals and selling information to them, but there has been no confirmation from official sources nor, so far as is known, have there been any prosecutions for this kind of activity.

*The People* of 29th September 1963 carried a report of an organisation said to be known to the police as 'Spies Inc.', which was alleged to be engaged in this type of industrial espionage. According to the report Spies Inc. had helped by their information criminal gangs in London and the Home Counties to make successful robberies during the previous week yielding £100,000. It was said that the organisation's *modus operandi* was to recruit men and woman of high calibre who would then take key jobs on a suitable project. Those chosen for this work were usually persons without criminal records and therefore well down the list of suspects after a raid. Some of this reconnaissance work was said to be of a long term nature, periods of up to a year of employment being envisaged, as well as a considerable stay with the victim firm after the raid so as not to arouse suspicion. Security firms, government departments and even Scotland Yard itself were penetration targets according to the report.

Such an organisation as Spies Inc., if it exists—and organisations such as this are believed to exist—would not differ in concept and method of operation from typical national agencies. If properly run, with cut-outs to prevent the organisation being identified by the odd failure, they would be extremely hard to defeat. Being in constant if varied employment and having no past criminal record, these operatives might go undetected for many years. There are some indications that an organisation similar to Spies Inc. arranges prison escapes for those who can afford the fee. And of course such an organisation as Spies Inc. would be in an excellent position to carry out industrial espionage against scientific and research targets.

An indication of the difficulty of differentiating industrial espionage for purely commercial reasons from that for national political or military purposes is pointed out by the *Kodak* case. The following account is based on reports in *The Times* of the period.

The Security Service in the course of its allotted task of protecting the nation became aware that a state-run East German firm was attempting to obtain information about certain industrial processes of Kodak. They believed that state security might be involved. At some stage—exactly when is not apparent from the available reports —it became clear that the espionage was not of a kind affecting national security, but was purely industrial in character, and the police took over. Two Kodak employees, Alfred Kenneth Roberts and Godfrey Conway, were accused of conspiring together with a certain Jean-Paul Soupert and a man known only as 'Herbert' to contravene certain sections of the Prevention of Corruption Act 1906 by corruptly accepting sums of money as inducements and rewards for doing acts in relation to the affairs of their principal, Kodak Limited. They were both further charged with, being agents of Kodak Limited, corruptly accepting DM 1,000 (£90) from Soupert as a reward for doing an act in relation to the affairs of their principal, Kodak Limited. During the preliminary hearing which began at Bow Street Magistrates' Court on 31st December 1964, and at the subsequent trial in February 1965 at the Old Bailey, the following story was related by the Prosecution:

As a result of extensive research Kodak had developed for their own use a number of processes which were highly secret and confidential to the company itself. At the relevant time, Soupert had been employed by Diachemie, a state-controlled East German industrial firm, for the purpose of procuring information regarding industrial processes. He was, in other words, a commercial spy. In November 1961 he was sent to London where it was alleged he met Roberts whom he asked to obtain reports concerning various cameras used in certain processes in the photographic business and as an inducement offered to pay Roberts DM 700 (£65). From then on it was stated further meetings took place between the two men and information in the form of samples and reports gleaned from Kodak was supplied by Roberts.

Roberts now, it was alleged, pressed Soupert for more money, saying that he had had to enlist the help of Conway who did a more technically skilled job than Roberts. Soupert realised that Conway would be of more use to him than Roberts and a meeting was arranged, which took place in October 1962 at the Law Courts (of all places). Soupert, acting under instructions, tried to deal with Conway, but Roberts turned up at the meetings and Soupert now had to pay both of them.

By 11th January 1964 Soupert had disclosed the meetings to certain security services, and the Security Service in this country was keeping careful observation on the comings and goings of certain people, including the two defendants, because at first it was thought that the security of the state might be involved. On 11th January Soupert, having previously informed certain people, met Conway in a cafe where he handed him an envelope containing DM 1,000 (£90). They then went to the Regent Palace Hotel where Conway handed Soupert a report in the form of answers to a questionnaire concerning certain work at Kodak. These answers were recorded on 35 mm film.

After this, Soupert returned to the Continent and reported to the man called Herbert, who was apparently to take over from him, and a meeting was arranged in Ostend between Conway and Herbert, who was to be Conway's controller. However, Roberts turned up and handed Herbert toothpaste tubes containing 35mm film and explained what the film contained; this was noted in writing by Soupert. This information was sent on the night express to East Berlin hidden in lavatories.

On 29th November police searched the homes of both Roberts and Conway. In both houses a large quantity of photographic equipment was said to have been found. At Conway's address a camera, tripod and stand of a type used for copying documents was found. When interviewed, Conway freely admitted that from time to time he had copied documents, but he did not admit to copying those concerned in the case. In Roberts' home a diary was found containing an address in East Berlin which Soupert said was to be used if one wished to communicate with the other.

On 19th February 1965 Jean-Paul Soupert, aged sixty-nine, who said he lived in Belgium, gave evidence for the Crown at the Central Criminal Court. Prosecuting Counsel said that Soupert had received an undertaking on behalf of Kodak that he would be paid £5,000 if he would come to Britain to give evidence.

In his final speech, Counsel for the Defence said he would not be putting his clients into the witness-box, nor would he be calling any evidence on their behalf. He said:

'. . . *there was no doubt Soupert was a double agent. He was getting information for the East Germans and at the same time telling the Belgian security authorities what he was doing . . . to save his own skin he made peace with the Belgians . . . then he ingratiated himself with the British authorities by agreeing to give evidence on behalf of Kodak Ltd., who had paid him to do so. He has got £5,000 out of his behaviour. He is to get a bonus when this is all over, no doubt depending on the outcome of this case, and he might have a nice article or two in the News of the World, for which he will receive payment . . . He has not done too badly out of all this, has he?'*

In his summing up, the Judge, Mr. Justice Melford Stevenson warned the jury of the danger of convicting on the uncorroborated evidence of an accomplice:

*'It is my duty to warn you that it is always dangerous to act on the the evidence of an accomplice, and for that reason you ought to look for corroboration of his evidence . . . Soupert is only here, quite obviously, because of the promise of £5,000, of which he has had some. He has been called a double agent, whatever that means, but he is here, and he is here for money. Well now, what is the exact impact of all that on the assessment of his evidence? . . . First, there is no power, legal or otherwise, which would have enabled anyone, Kodak or anyone else, to hold Soupert in this country against his will. Even more important, a subpoena does not operate outside this realm . . . even if Soupert's physical presence in this country could have been secured, it does not follow that he would have opened his mouth unless he had some pretty good reason for doing so, say £5,000. In other words, the hook designed to catch Soupert in the muddy waters had to be adequately baited'.*

After an absence of more than three hours, the jury returned verdicts of Not Guilty on the whole indictment.

According to *The Times* of 3rd March, Roberts said later that he and Conway were going to see a solicitor about the possibility of issuing a writ against Kodak for wrongful dismissal. He added that both he and Conway were members of the Communist Party and that they had both visited Moscow and been presented to Mr. Kruschev. It is to be hoped that Mr Justice Melford Stevenson noted these statements.

According to *The Times* of 22nd May 1965, in reply to a question in the House on 21st May the Attorney-General said:

*'. . . The security aspect of the matter, which he would only mention in broad terms, was that, at the material time, operations were in progress, in conjunction with other allied security services, for the purpose of breaking up a hostile spy ring controlled by the East German intelligence service. It was initially thought that Soupert, who had*

*never been an employee of the security services in this country, might be involved in the acquistion of defence secrets in Britain. That was why he, and those with whom he was connected and was frequently meeting, initially came under surveillance by the security services. After a time, however, the security authorities came to the conclusion that Soupert's interest was in obtaining trade or industrial secrets. At that stage the matter passed from the security services to the police . . . security considerations had not affected the decision not to prosecute Soupert for perjury, or the Kodak company for conspiracy to pervert the course of justice. Soupert's coming here and testifying as to his activities in connection with the East German authorities would have caused him to suffer substantial financial loss by having to forfeit the pension he was otherwise expecting to receive from the East Germans . . . These were not monies paid for the purpose of persuading him to lie to the court.'*

This case has been examined at some length to highlight the following:

the involvement of a state in industrial espionage;

the danger of giving communists access to industrial secrets (this poses the question of how to identify them);

the need to clarify the legal position in regard to industrial espionage.

It is of interest that Jean-Paul Soupert's name was mentioned shortly afterwards in the press in connection with the trial in France of an East German, Herbert Steinbrecker, aged twenty-four, who was charged with industrial spying (the report does not specify the exact charge). Apparently Steinbrecker may have been arrested on information provided by Soupert. If so, these ramifications provide a substantial indication of an international industrial espionage organisation based on East Germany, and therefore presumably in close touch with, if not actually controlled by, the Russians. They add force to Dr. Riester's allegation that East Germany has 'earned millions as a result of industrial espionage' (see Chapter 1, p. 4).

*Beechams*, the large drug and food group who were responsible for the development of penicillin, are believed to have been the victims of industrial espionage in 1964. It was reported in March of that year that police had been called to their research laboratory because an executive had noticed that filing cabinets containing formulae and reports appeared to have been interfered with; a lock had been forced and papers disturbed. Although no papers were missing, an intruder could, of course, have photographed any of them. According to press reports the laboratory secretary said: 'It is true that we have called in police in connection with an irregularity in our research records. But, beyond that, for obvious reasons, I cannot say any more. The least that is said, the better'. Silence on this has been maintained and there does not appear to have been any prosecution. This is the main interest of the case, illustrating as it does the extreme difficulty with which the student of industrial espionage is faced in gathering the facts. Companies are naturally anxious not to reveal the nature of their loss because prosecution and publicity might still further affect their business. This is why the private security firm is often preferred. An admitted lack of security might prejudice present and future government contracts, or damage other interests, or relations with other firms or their image generally.

A manufacturer in a highly competitive industry who is about to launch a new product, or who plans to sell an old product by a new gimmick which he hopes will increase his share of the market, must make an appropriate advertising plan. This is normally done by or in consultation with a professional advertising agency, who must of necessity be given information about the new scheme.

On 22nd June 1964 John Louis Brand, an advertising executive aged 30, was found guilty at the Old Bailey of receiving confidential documents belonging to a firm of advertising agents, knowing them to have been stolen. These documents were held by an advertising agency on behalf of *Procter & Gamble Ltd.*, manufacturers of detergents, including 'Daz'. Prosecuting Counsel said that the documents related to the advertising and marketing plans of this firm and it had been estimated that, if the information contained in them were in the hands of a rival and used wisely, a loss to Procter & Gamble in the region of £750,000 could ensue. 'These documents were dynamite,' he said. After they had been stolen, Colgate-Palmolive, said to be the closest rivals of Procter & Gamble, received a letter from a person who said he was in possession of the confidential documents and would sell them for £3,000. The police were informed.

According to a press report, Brand said in evidence that on 16th March 1964 a man calling himself Robinson had telephoned him and said that he was acting on behalf of Mr. Scott Matthews, managing director of Colgate-Palmolive, and wanted him to do something of a confidential nature connected with security. He said the only way to stop security leaks to Procter & Gamble was for themselves to obtain secret information of Procter & Gamble affairs and to go to them and point out that Colgate-Palmolive could play the same game.

Robinson told him that documents would be sent on to him. He was to make a synopsis of them and to send the synopsis with a letter to Mr. Scott Matthews offering them for sale. Brand said that on 1st April Robinson again telephoned him and asked him to pick up a parcel and send it. He picked up the parcel, which he assumed contained documents, and was arrested.

Sentencing Brand to 13 months imprisonment, Judge Aarvold said, 'Here you are so lowering your standard as to receive stolen property and to use that stolen property to enrich yourself by no less a sum than £3,000. You yourself called it a dirty business and I regret to find that description an accurate one.'

In 1965 Procter & Gamble and Colgate-Palmolive were again in the espionage news. According to the *Sunday Times* of 24th October, earlier in the year Colgate-Palmolive's parent company in the United States was approached by a junior executive of Procter & Gamble. He offered them complete details of the latter's sales and promotion campaign for a new toothpaste, known as 'Crest', for the sum of $20,000. It is said that the worth of the plans to Colgate-Palmolive was $1m. Colgate, having informed the FBI, agreed to a meeting with the executive which took place at Kennedy Airport. Then, in the words of the *Sunday Times*—

'"Mr. Crest" as he asked to be known went into one cubicle; "Mr. Colgate" was in the one next door. Mr. Crest asked Mr. Colgate to take off his trousers with the $20,000 in the pocket and pass them under the partition. This he did; Mr. Crest took the money out, put the plans in, passed the trousers back and fled—straight into the arms of the waiting G-men.'*

All the cases mentioned so far have been of espionage in one of its two common forms—from within by persons actually working in the organisation or its affiliates, or from without, by illegal entry. There is, however, a third form, which was briefly touched upon when Spies Inc. was discussed. This is where a man or woman enters one firm and serves, say, for a year and then joins a competitor. If the person concerned were a scientist or highly skilled engineer, he or she could in the space of a year learn a great deal about a firm's plans, research progress, aims and discoveries; enough, at any rate, to be of immense value to a rival, especially in a highly competitive market. Even if it is an intelligent secretary, the damage could be considerable.

Of course, whether it is espionage or not depends upon the intention. A person who left the original firm simply for a change and then made use of knowledge gained during employment is obviously a very different case from one who joined with the idea of leaving to sell or make use of their employer's secrets once learned. But either might be equally damaging to the original company. Would it be fair or reasonable in the first case to prevent the employee using elsewhere the skills and knowledge he had learned which, it could be argued, are the basis of his earning capacity? Is he in his new job to stand idly by while, for example, his new associates carry out research which from his previous employment he knows to be unfruitful, and which if slightly altered would yield a good harvest? To some extent companies can protect themselves by entering into contracts with their employees, which will prevent an employee, should he leave, from joining another firm in the same field for a given period of time. But the courts will not enforce such agreements if they impose, in their view, an unreasonable restraint on the employee.

Although the case has no connection with espionage, a reserved judgment of the Court of Appeal in *Commerical Plastics Ltd. v Vincent*, discussed in the *Financial Times* of 5th August 1964, shows the difficulty facing employers who try to protect themselves from espionage of the kind postulated in the preceding paragraph. The company's letter appointing the employee had added that 'in view of the highly technical and confidential nature of this appointment, you have agreed not to seek employment with any of our competitors in the PVC calender field for at least one year after leaving our employ'. PVC (polyvinylchloride) can be treated by a number of processes, one of which is calendering—a process akin to mangling, by which the material is put through revolving rollers reducing it to the thickness or smoothness required.

The question the courts had to decide was: did this restraint go beyond what was strictly necessary for the protection of the company's trade secrets? The Court of Appeal decided they could not uphold the agreement, that in fact it constituted an unlawful restraint on trade. They found that the geographical limitation was too wide. And although he undoubtedly gained much technical skill from his employment, this was something the employee could not be prevented from taking away with him—as opposed to his employer's secrets.

The point here is, of course, the difficulty of tying a man down and thus inhibiting or deterring industrial espionage of the kind envisaged, through joining a firm, learning their know-how and then taking a job with a competitor and selling it in one way or another. To ensure successful prosecution under present law, it would almost certainly be necessary to prove 'intention' and then 'conspiracy'.

It is appropriate to round off this sketch of the contemporary scene by briefly examining the case which provoked the public comment referred to in Chapter 1 on the question of making industrial espionage a crime under an industrial secrets act analagous to the Official Secrets Act.

On 3rd November 1965 William Joseph *Downey*, aged twenty, was sentenced to three months imprisonment after pleading guilty to stealing code cards and correspondence valued at £3, the property of the Donald Macpherson group of paint companies.

Prosecuting Counsel said that this was not the simple case of larceny it would appear, but was what was commonly called industrial espionage, which meant acquiring by criminal means trade secrets for the purpose of selling them to a competitor. He hoped this would not be the beginning of an era when courts would have to deal with such matters. At the moment it was not an offence to steal another man's secrets, only the papers they were written on. He went on to say it was perhaps significant that this matter began after a BBC programme on industrial espionage. He added, according to *The Times* report, 'It could be—it is only a matter of conjecture—that that programme implanted a fast-growing seed in the defendant's mind'.

In June 1965 Downey was discharged from Sherwoods, a subsidiary of Macphersons, for bad time-keeping. At Sherwood's Barking factory where Downey had worked they employed about fifty people and carried out a great deal of research and development for industrial and decorative paints. On 22nd September Mr. Harold Day, the chief industrial chemist of the firm of Jenson & Nicholson, proprietors of Robbialac paints, received a telephone call from Downey offering technical information about paints. Mr. Day reported the matter, through his employers, to Macphersons. A meeting was arranged in a Bayswater hotel; microphones were put in the room under a desk and behind a pelmet and the conversation was recorded on tape.

At a further meeting, in response to a request from Mr. Day, Downey produced amongst other things the de-coded formula for a new water paint known as Speedex which had just been marketed by Macphersons. The formula card had been kept locked in a desk in Sherwood's production office; examination showed that a quantity of formula cards had been stolen.

In his concluding remarks, Prosecuting Counsel said to the Barking magistrates:

'*You may feel that some sort of legislation is necessary, so that this sort of thing becomes an offence; the stealing of another man's trade secrets, some sort of industrial trades secrets Act.*'

The Downey case is trivial compared, for example, with the Cyanamid one. He was no defecting scientist nor member of a sophisticated international espionage ring, or he would have used more sophisticated methods, but a disgruntled workman who saw a way to what he thought would be easy money. But the case may mark a turning point in the country's attitude to industrial espionage, and perhaps also to crime generally. It drew attention to the possible influence of television at a time when espionage had become a major programme feature, tending to replace robbery and westerns. And it led to correspondence in *The Times* about the legislative situation (p. 4).

Stealing his research or marketing secrets is not the only way of damaging a competitor. Deliberate leakage of a rival manufacturer's plans for new models may leave him with embarrassing surpluses of current production which cannot be economically disposed of. This form of sabotage actually happened to *Mercedes Benz*, who in 1965 suffered from a world-wide premature announcement of their 1966 range of motor cars. They thought the cost of cancelled orders and cut profits on unsold models could amount to £500,000, and *The Times* motoring correspondent estimated that there were £2 million worth of 1965 Mercedes models awaiting sale in Britain alone at the time.

\*     \*     \*     \*

The foregoing is but a selection of the published cases of recent years designed to show industrial espionage in different forms. There are others recorded in this country and many more in the United States, but even in the sum the recorded cases probably represent only the tip of the iceberg.

# CHAPTER 7

## Industrial Espionage: A Summary of Techniques and Technical Aids

Industrial espionage may be carried out by the following:

*A disgruntled employee*, or ex-employee, may spontaneously decide to sell his employer's secrets for money, and perhaps for revenge. The Merck case of 1962 involving the young man named Kenneth Rees, who had been sacked by Morson's for absenteeism, is one example (p. 51). An employee may also take information from his employers with the object of selling it back to them.

*A 'professional' organisation* operating for profit may be employed to obtain secret information by the firm desiring it, or the organisation may of its own initiative steal secrets which it conceives to have a market value. Very few organisations admit to carrying this out, but a number of private detective agencies are known to do so, and the existence of international organisations established for this and other clandestine, if not criminal, purposes is strongly suspected.

*A firm desiring a competitor's secrets* may try to obtain them itself using clandestine means. The Italian pharmaceutical companies concerned in the Cyanamid case (p. 48) would appear to fall into this category. There is, however, some suggestion that an intermediate organisation may have been used; there is a reference in *The Times* of 13th December 1965 to an Italian Count said to have met Dr. Sidney Fox, the scientist formerly employed by the American Cyanamid Company, in a room at the Park Sheraton Hotel in New York in November 1960. But undoubtedly the initiative came from the firms themselves, their motives being to save so far as possible the massive costs of pharmaceutical research.

*The state espionage agencies* may, as well as carrying out industrial espionage for defence or political purposes, accidentally or deliberately acquire information which will be of use to the national industry. Totalitarian countries such as Russia and East Germany certainly regard this as a normal role for their intelligence services, and if the prediction in the last paragraph of page xii is true, this may become the general pattern. The case of the suborning of the young West German scientist (p. 50) is one illustration, and the Kodak case (p. 53) another.

*A subversive political party* may carry out espionage against a firm or its workers in furtherance of its own subversive political ends and those of a hostile foreign power, for example, to discover where there is, or where it can easily create, industrial unrest which it can exploit to strengthen or maintain its position in trades unions.

The importance of obtaining power in trades unions for the achievement of communist ends cannot be overstressed. Lenin himself said, 'It is necessary . . . to resort to all sorts of stratagems, manoeuvres and illegal methods, to evasions and subterfuges, in order to penetrate the trades unions and to remain in them carrying on communist activities inside them *at all costs*' (author's italics). Once it has taken over the key trades unions, it is then in a position to create the industrial and economic chaos necessary to its usurpation of political power (no communist party has come to power by democratic means).

Industrial espionage for subversive political purposes is a routine function of the political cell. Most communist cells, for example, will include one member (of the cell, not usually of the party—these are too easily identifiable) whose main task is the provision of information. He will be told what to look for and to get it by any means, using espionage if necessary.

### SOURCES

The principal ways of obtaining information are—by stealing or copying documents, through people yielding it consciously and unconsciously, by surveillance from adjacent premises, by theft of a specimen or prototype, and by interception of communications. Of these, documentary evidence is the most sought. It is the easiest to assimilate, tangible from the selling point of view, and usually self-authenticating. Documents include maps, plans, blueprints, charts, graphs, computer tapes, recordings, films, photographs, sketches, waste paper, carbon papers, shorthand notebooks, and in fact any kind of recorded information other than that stored in the brain.

### THEFT AND COPYING OF DOCUMENTS

It is usually a major consideration in espionage that the victim should not discover for as long as possible the fact that his information has been stolen. Obviously, if the loss is discovered quickly, counter-measures can be taken. Apart from the increased risk to the spy which early discovery entails, plans can be changed or patents taken out sooner than would otherwise have been the case. It would therefore be a primary aim of the industrial spy to leave no trace of his activity. For this reason photography is the favourite espionage method of obtaining documented information, and this is best done *in situ*, or during the transmission of documents from one point to another. Access to documents may be gained by stealth; for example, by illegal entry at night or at other times when the premises are unoccupied, or with inside help through the suborning of an employee who has legitimate access, or by planting someone in the organisation for the specific purpose of stealing the information. Copies of documents may also be obtained by remote photography, and, as has been indicated, by interception, including photography, during transmission.

### THE SELECTION OF A SPY

There are a number of reasons why an approach to a person working in a firm may be made rather than attempting photography of documents by illegal intrusion. There may be a requirement for skill as well as, or in preference to, documents, or possibly reconnaissance has shown that the security arrangements to protect the required documents are so effective that grave risk would be entailed in attempting to gain access to them from outside. Or there may be a continuing need for information which could not be satisfied by documents alone, or which would involve a dangerous intrusion frequency.

Before going any further it is necessary to explain that common usage of the word spy embraces two distinct espionage functions, those of the *agent* and the *informer*. An espionage agent is usually a full time salaried employee of an intelligence organisation; an informer is on a piecework footing, that is, he is paid by results. In the Portland naval secrets case. Lonsdale, the Russian, and the two Krogers, Americans, were agents; Houghton and Gee, the two British employees at the Naval Base, were informers. Informers may become agents.

The selection of a suitable agent calls for the highest intelligence skill, and that of an informer skill on the part of the agent. Faulty selection of an agent may bring disgrace and even defeat to the state and of an informer capture or death to the agent. Classes of persons for consideration will include:

*Those who have legitimate and regular or occasional access to the information by virtue of their position.* These will usually be in the scientific, administrative, executive, or technical classes, probably well paid, well educated and, apparently, quite unlikely to be ready to carry out disloyal acts. But the industrial spymaster will know that even amongst people of the highest intellectual calibre there are character weaknesses, such as vanity, greed, sexual aberrations, chip-on-shoulder attitudes, alcoholism, race and class complexes. He may discover similar weaknesses in the potential agent's wife and make his approach through her; he will take care to assess her relations with him—whether she is domineering, spendthrift, ambitious to 'keep up with the Joneses', jealous, discontented, or sex-starved (and therefore open to a sex approach). It will be remembered that Dr. Fox, in the Cyanamid case (p. 48), was probably unduly conscious of his racial origins and also desirous of improving his lot to keep up with the Joneses of Spring Valley.

*Those who have legitimate regular or occasional access to the vicinity of the information.* These may include employees in adjacent offices or workshops, and, often more important, mobile workers, cleaners, electricians, telephone engineers, tea-trolley attendants and others who visit the target area in the course of their duties, and therefore do not attract unwelcome attention. These are favourite occupations for industrial spies whose motive is a subversive political one.

MOTIVES AND INDUCEMENTS

The industrial spymaster, be he a member of a 'professional' organisation or of a state agency, may then use any or combinations of the following inducements and motives and weaknesses to achieve conscious co-operation from the intended espionage agent or informer:

*Money.* That every man has his price is a principle of espionage. In certain state-controlled operations, the required information may be of such importance that money may be no object, although there is obviously a limit to what industrial firms can pay for information and still make a profit. But the suborning of a person by money is usually a diminishing expense. After the initial 'capital' investment, which is usually a down payment with promises of 'more to come' or 'more on results', the suborned becomes compromised, that is to say, he is in the power of the spymaster by virtue of the fact that he has accepted money for illegal purposes. Even if these purposes are not technically illegal, they are certainly sufficient to deprive him of his job if they become known by his employers. Professional spymasters are at considerable pains to compromise their informers as soon as possible. From then onwards, money becomes only part of the inducement; the other part is threats of what will happen to his career if he does not provide the further information required, or become a full time agent.

*Blackmail.* Instead of being the accompaniment of the second stage of suborning by money, this may be the first with or without the money inducement. The spy or spymaster, having discovered the vulnerable point of his potential victim, will exploit it. For example, if he or she is involved in an extramarital love affair, or if there is some matter, such as a criminal record or sexual perversion, of which they are ashamed and which, if revealed, might be prejudicial to them, he will try to obtain co-operation by threat of revelation, perhaps sweetening the pill with appropriate quantities of cash and promises of more to come.

There are no available examples in the industrial field, but the case of William John Vassall, who was convicted of political and military espionage at the Old Bailey on 22nd October 1962, illustrates the point well. The Russians compromised Vassall, whom their observations had shown to be a homosexual, by taking him to a party in Moscow and photographing him in compromising positions with other men. From then on, according to John Bulloch, 'Vassall was kept loyal to Moscow through fear of exposure and through regular payments', and 'he was entrapped by his lust and thereafter cash kept him crooked.'

*Intimidation.* The spy or spymaster may try to inspire his victim with fear by suggesting that if he fails to co-operate he, or possibly a member of his family, may be injured or killed. In two recent cases of intimidation (not concerned with industrial espionage), the victim was told that unless he co-operated his wife would have a bucket of acid thrown in her face. Intimidation is not usually a very satisfactory form of inducement; many men and women are courageous enough to defy intimidators, although the threat of injury to a beloved child or wife can undermine the courage of many who would accept the risk of violence to themselves.

*Ideology.* The ideological motive might be used in state-inspired industrial espionage and in industrial espionage for subversive political purposes. An interesting example of the ideological spy in the politico-military field is George Blake, a senior member of the British Foreign Service, who in May 1961 was sentenced to forty-two years in prison. He was Vice-Consul in Seoul when it was over-run by the North Koreans in 1950 and was a prisoner of the communists for three years. According to John Bulloch, 'He was not brainwashed, but the constant reiteration of communist propaganda, like the drip of water on stone, gradually wore him down and when he returned to England in 1953 he had become convinced, as he later admitted, that the communist system was the best and that it was eventually bound to triumph'.

Blake's defection was one of the worst disasters ever suffered by British intelligence. As a senior British agent himself, he knew the identities of others and from 1953 for nearly eight years wreaked havoc in British intelligence. When he was arrested as a result of a tip-off from an agent in East Berlin, as Bulloch says,

*'The intelligence officers questioning him were appalled. Blake had compromised dozens of British agents. They suddenly realised the cause of some mysterious disappearances and the unusual silence of some of their operatives.*

*'Top priority messages by wireless and by courier went to every M.I.6 man known to Blake, telling them to get out immediately. Many of them did; four did not move quickly enough.*

*'At a crisis moment in the Cold War much of Britain's foreign intelligence organisation had to be dismantled and built up again from scratch.'*

Blake's escape from Wormwood Scrubs Prison on 22nd October 1966 showed the pitiable state to which prison security had been reduced by years of neglect. On the reasonable assumption that the escape was organized by his Soviet masters, it was also encouraging evidence to potential spies that they are good employers.

No doubt brainwashing techniques could be applied to and should be reckoned with in considering espionage against industry, especially that connected directly or indirectly with national defence. Since the strength of a political system rests to a large extent on the prosperity of its economy, espionage against its industrial secrets could be another way of weakening it. Thus, industrial espionage performed on ideological grounds might well accompany the other forms of weakening such as passive sabotage and subversion generally.

*Spirit of adventure.* This is sometimes a motive in political and military espionage, and as life gets less exciting and supported more and more by the welfare state it may be an initial reason for some people to take up industrial espionage. It seems unlikely that it would be done wholly without the money motive. In any case, the spymaster wishing to compromise his agent so as to bind him to his service would probably nourish the spirit of adventure with money.

*Sex and Character Weaknesses.* In military and political espionage the sex motive seldom plays a significant part, although many contemporary espionage fiction writers would have it otherwise. Mata Hari was more important for her beauty and her favours than for her espionage activities. As Ronald Seth[1] says, 'Except in the case of the Japanese . . . sex as a weapon of espionage has rarely been used on any scale'. This is not to say, of course, that women have not been extremely successful spies. On the contrary, they have been amongst the most successful, but in the majority of cases this is not because they used their attractions as the main weapon. 'Cynthia', the code name given by British Intelligence to Amy Elizabeth Brousse, a highly successful spy of the Second World War, is an important exception; she appears to have had quite extraordinary physical attractions, which she used to good espionage effect.

There is no doubt that Ethel Gee, who was sentenced at the Old Bailey in 1961 to fifteen years in prison for her part in the Portland naval secrets case, was the mistress of Houghton. But the Lord Chief Justice addressing her before sentence said he did not think it possible that what she had done had been out of blind infatuation. 'Having heard you and watched you I am inclined to think yours was the stronger character of the two; I think you acted for greed.'

There are, of course, many cases in which sexual promiscuity on the part of the spy has led to his discovery, and illicit sexual relations are often a means of compromising a spy or an agent.

It seems possible that sex, especially in a context of emotion and marriage prospects, might play a more important part in industrial espionage. Men and women in the civil and military services who are given access to military and political secrets are usually long term public servants, carefully chosen for their security reliability and trained in the security arts. They are taught to guard against the sex approach by spies and their agents, and are not usually given access to vital material until they are sufficiently mature. But in industry quite young girls are apt to reach important secretarial positions, sometimes for the reason that they are young, but also because good secretaries are in short supply. Very few of them, if any, are given real security training at any stage. For all these reasons they might be vulnerable to apparently innocent questions about their work from good-looking men who appeared to be marriage-prospects. Middle-aged spinsters, unhappily married women, or divorcees, may be vulnerable to the purely sexual approach if they have not been thoroughly indoctrinated with security. Any person with tendencies to sexual aberration or perversion is a particularly good prospect from a

1. *Anatomy of Spying* (Arthur Barker, 1961).

spymaster's point of view; on two counts: firstly, such tendencies offer a possibility of compromising them so that blackmail can be used; secondly a sympathiser or co-pervert who may be able to gain their confidence and extract the information can be produced.

*The Sunday Times* of 24th October 1965 relates the story of a young secretary in the market research department of a large consumer goods firm who encountered a young man, apparently by chance, whilst she was on holiday with a girl-friend. Later it became clear that this was a deliberate encounter on the part of the young man, but eventually to gain his favour and because she thought it would do no harm she agreed to show him some confidential market surveys of considerable value. She had by this time fallen in love with him, but soon realised that he was taking advantage of her affections. Eventually he told her that he was 'working for an organisation from Paris'. The girl decided to have a share in the proceeds and she was given a new Mini which arrived with an envelope containing £300. According to *The Sunday Times'* story, the girl later decided to work for the same firm as her male friend and went to another job 'serving two masters and drawing two pay packets'.

Here we have an example of a girl who gave away her employer's secrets to a young man with whom she had become involved, hoping, no doubt, for marriage. When she saw this hope was not likely to be gratified, she thought she might as well reap such financial benefits as she could. But here again emotion and the prospect of marriage were probably the original inducements.

So far we have dealt with people as conscious sources of information, that is, those who for one inducement or another decide to take part in deliberate industrial espionage. But industrial espionage, like its military and political counterparts, may also employ unconscious sources. An employee in possession of a secret may as a result of excessive enthusiasm, drink, or vanity, talk carelessly about it in public and reveal it without meaning to do so, and without knowing that he has done so. He may be tricked into revelation by clever questioning, or simply 'conned'. Drugs may be employed to this end, or the eavesdropping may be done remotely by technical means. He may then become compromised and used as a conscious source with money or blackmail as the inducement.

*Chip-on-Shoulder Attitudes.* A man who in some way feels inferior to his fellows, e.g. his colleagues or neighbours, or if he is dominated by his wife or perhaps his mother, may store up a general resentment against society, which can be taken advantage of by a spymaster. Apart from dominating him, his wife may, by continual harping on

some inadequacy such as his earning ability compared with neighbours or his sexual powers, drive him to crime, including industrial
espionage.

*Patriotism.* This was once a common motive for spying for political
and military purposes but it has been largely replaced by ideology.
In certain circumstances it might be an industrial espionage motive,
for example in a state-inspired operation.

There are other motives and inducements, but enough has been
said to show that industrial espionage feeds mainly on a diet of
corrupt practice and moral deterioration, which evils it also causes.

### SURVEILLANCE

It would be possible to watch processes in a laboratory with powerful
binoculars from a nearby building, or cameras with telescopic lenses,
similarly positioned, could be used to photograph processes, prototypes, or documents on desks. These ways of obtaining information
are certainly far less risky than others and there is little chance that
they will be detected unless they are suspected which, in this country,
in the present state of lack of awareness of the threat, would be unlikely. On the other hand, it is probable that this method could only
be used in a minority of cases and it could be defeated by the simplest
precautions, such as curtains or frosted glass.

### PROTOTYPES AND SPECIMENS

In certain circumstances it may be possible to steal a prototype or a
specimen of the particular product of which information is desired. In
the Cyanamid case (p. 48) actual cultures were stolen by Fox and sold
to the Italian pharmaceutical companies. Of course, a specimen
alone does not always provide the information required. It is one
thing to see it, but it may be quite another to determine how it was
produced.

### INDIRECT ESPIONAGE

Up to now we have been concerned with direct theft of documented
information or products, or direct approaches to employees, but
oblique methods such as that used in the Brand case (p. 57), which
involved documents held by a firm of advertising agents on behalf of
Procter & Gamble Limited, may offer good prospects. There is a
whole spectrum of persons and firms who perform services for other

firms in the nature of which they gain access to confidential information. In addition to advertising agents and public relations consultants there are management consultants, market researchers, engineering consultants, auditors, solicitors, patent agents, medical consultants, merchant bank advisers, banks, overseas selling and service agents, associated and subsidiary companies, caterers, architects, surveyors, and others besides who might be in possession of information which would be of use to a competitor of the firm on whose behalf they were engaged.

INTERCEPTION

Interception of communications is a highly developed branch of political and military espionage. It is countered mainly by enciphering sensitive information, but this is hardly practicable on any scale in the industrial sphere. The main communications of industry are telephonic and postal, and both are vulnerable to interception. Technical devices to intercept the former are certainly obtainable in the United States and probably in the United Kingdom as well. According to the *Daily Sketch* of 5th April 1966 the Sales Manager of the Telephone Manufacturing Company did not disagree with an estimate that 4,000 to 12,000 telephones a year are being tapped by unauthorised people. Interception of mail needs access either at the dispatching end, the receiving end, or during transmission. It is difficult, but by no means impossible, to intercept mail whilst in Post Office hands; suborning of a sorter or delivery postman are obvious ways. But postal dispatch and receiving sections of firms, where the most junior or lowly paid staff are apt to be employed, would usually be more rewarding targets. Firms often assist interception by marking the envelopes of important letters 'Private and Confidential'.

SYNTHESIS AND SIMPLIFICATION

An intelligence organisation of high quality almost always has many sources of information, both overt and covert in nature. In many of the problems with which it is confronted, much of the answer may be deduced from careful piecing together of existing information. What is often lacking are details of time and place; for example, when and where the particular plan is to be implemented, or the intelligence process may have shown that there are only a few courses of action open to the subject of the investigations. In this situation all that needs to be known is which course, and perhaps when.

The espionage task is then greatly simplified, as its whole effort can be concentrated. Secret future intentions may be revealed by observation of quite simple acts—a sudden journey or meeting may of itself indicate a subsequent course of action. The following is a not entirely hypothetical example from the political sphere.

The Governor of a certain colony, in which the forces of law and order were trying to contain nationalist subversive activity accompanied by considerable violence, had to decide which of two important political moves he would make. The intelligence organisation of the subversive forces, which were supported by a foreign power, knew from various sources that there were only two courses open to the Governor, but did not know which he would take. They and their foreign masters considered it vital to know this in advance so that the necessary political countermeasures could be taken. They also knew that one course had already been approved by the home government and that the alternative needed further consultation; that the Governor would fly home if he decided to advocate this latter course. The subversive intelligence agency was able to intercept a secret message detailing a military aeroplane to fly the Governor home. As a result, his enemies had several days' notice of the course which the Governor had decided ought to be, and which subsequently was, adopted.

Similarly in industry, provided the general circumstances were known, a careful study of the movements of key figures, the log-books of their motor-cars, their visitors, might easily reveal merger intentions or marketing plans.

TECHNICAL AIDS

The point has been made elsewhere that all technical aids to espionage are extensions of the senses. Most known development in this sphere has taken place in the USA where, according to many authorities, spying devices are rapidly becoming a public menace. On his return from a tour of the United States, HRH The Duke of Edinburgh was sufficiently put out by the prevalence of eavesdropping and other devices that he made a now famous vernacular comment. When questioned about this comment at London Airport on 26th March 1966, he said, 'They have these great listening devices . . . we have had the long Peeping Tom cameras for some time, now we have the eavesdropping microphone . . . This eavesdropping is a dreadful imposition. They have a tendency to do this all over the place.' No doubt His Royal Highness's use of the adjective 'great' was for purposes of emphasis rather than a description of size, because it is the small size of eavesdropping microphones which makes them so formidable an intrusion into privacy.

The main technical developments of interest to the industrial spy are remote listening devices, including recorders, and remote seeing devices. These are of two kinds: firstly, those which are pre-positioned in the area of the conversation or scene it is desired to hear, record or see. The second kind comprise long-range directional microphones and cameras. Provided that access to the desired premises can be obtained to implant whichever kind of device is appropriate to the occasion, or that the scene can be overlooked from nearby, there is no doubt that any meeting, any conversation, any action or any scene in theoretically private premises can be overheard or observed. The listening devices can, of course, be concealed in property such as a briefcase or handbag which some person who has legitimate access to the premises carries in inadvertently.

Miniaturisation in the field of electronics has greatly aided the spy. Equipment for eavesdropping can now be made as small as a fingernail and disguised as is appropriate to the occasion. Combined microphones and transmitters can be fitted inside a lipstick tube or a ball-point pen, or be made to resemble a lump of sugar. Other forms of miniature listening devices include wrist-watch microphones, tie-clip microphones; it is said that there are detector capsules which can be inserted into food to be swallowed by the intended victim, and that for some hours afterwards everything that person says can be received by a distant listener.

In the United States, according to Vance Packard,[1] at least thirty companies are now involved in the manufacture of electronic eavesdropping equipment. 'One of the larger companies, Solar Research Inc. . . . claims that in 1962, for example, its sales increased fourfold within a year.' Packard says that he saw 'on display in the window of an electronics shop on 43rd Street in New York City a device that automatically starts a tape recorder when a telephone conversation comes onto a line.'

The *Daily Mail* on 29th November 1965 revealed that a device called a 'microbug spy transmitter' could be bought in some TV and radio shops in the UK. This is said to fit easily into a matchbox and can be hidden in an office, house or car where it will transmit conversations into an ordinary radio up to one hundred yards away. This device was bought by a *Daily Mail* investigator for £185 and he was told it could have been hired for £20 a week. He took the device

1. *The Naked Society* (Longmans Green, 1964).

to the GPO's Radio Services Department and their verdict was 'Terrifying; its efficiency in picking up even whispered conversations as far as 20 feet away and transmitting them a distance of 100 yards is alarming. It can only be described as an evil device designed for sinister purposes.' The supplier said that he had sold between two and three hundred already and could provide them in various disguises— hidden in pens, inkwells, brooches, compacts, picture frames, desk lamps, or to customers' special orders. The model bought by the *Daily Mail* used a battery smaller than an aspirin tablet, which was said to have a life of four hours; but according to the report the supplier said, 'Give me twelve hours' notice and I will modify it to make it work for a full year, twenty-four hours a day, every day.'

*The Daily Mail* investigating team drew attention to the possibilities of these devices for such purposes as criminal planning and industrial espionage. They pointed out that there was nothing in the law to stop such devices being sold, although a GPO licence was necessary for operation.

The following day the Postmaster General ordered an immediate investigation and said, 'I have studied reports on this evil from the American Bar Association and the US Senate. It is a very important problem indeed and one that urgently needs looking into in this country.' Subsequently sales were stopped.

A report in *The Sunday Times* of 6th March 1966 on the well-known Italian private detective, Tom Ponzi, drew attention to a directional microphone to be used in conjunction with a telescopic camera. This microphone is in the form of a long tube which can be aimed like a rifle and mounted on a tripod, and is said to be able to pick up conversations as much as three hundred feet away. It is more precisely aimed by ear through headphones and includes filtering devices to exclude side noises such as traffic. Mr. Ponzi also had a wrist camera worn like a watch. It was said to be able to take twenty-eight pictures, making only a faint noise which could be disguised with a cough.

There are recent reports of microphones which can be attached to teeth by means of some device like a bridge. These are powerful enough to enable a conversation between two people to be heard and recorded from some distance away.

In addition to the *Daily Mail* revelations, the author has seen letters from firms calling themselves electronic consultants advertising such services as 'surveillance and interception'. There have also been recent moves by some American companies to sell 'antibugging' devices of both detecting and neutralising types in this country which shows that they, at any rate, consider there is already a market for such things.

* * * *

To sum up on techniques; the industrial spy will usually attempt to gain the information he requires by stealing or copying the relevant documents, often employing an agent for this purpose. Alternatively he will achieve his purpose by suborning an employee or an associate of the firm whose secrets he requires. An actual product may be stolen.

The principal technical aids which the industrial spy may employ are those which facilitate observation and hearing from a distance. These are often supplemented by other devices which record a particular scene or conversation.

The clever spy will always take the easiest and cheapest course. He will find out all that he can from overt sources such as press reports and careless talk and by observation, and only use the more risky and expensive clandestine methods when the required information cannot be obtained by other means. The amount of difficulty, risk, time and expense which his operation necessitates is governed directly by the strength and skill of the security defence established by the target organisation.

*The Arena*

# CHAPTER 8

## The Acutely Anomic Society

Professor Leon Radzinowicz, in his recent book *Ideology and Crime*[1] described a theory of Emile Durkheim in the following terms:
*'Since there were no natural limits to human desires . . . society alone had the moral authority to impose such limits. He was thinking here not of the criminal law, but of the duty of society to decide, first, what degree of comfort and privilege was appropriate to those fulfilling different functions in the community, second by what means individuals could legitimately attain to the various functions and their corresponding benefits. If a society was to retain its stability it must be able to decide both of these questions in a manner generally accepted as just.*

*'Abrupt social change was likely to cause a failure in this kind of regulation. Traditional rules broke down, people and classes no longer knew where they stood, ambition was perpetually stimulated but never satisfied. This condition Durkheim called acute anomie.'*
There are some indications that this country is moving towards this condition of a breakdown in social regulation.

The experience of two world wars and history generally has been that a balance between liberty and a rule of law based on public consent is the strongest social system—much stronger than autocratic, racialist or despotic societies of any kind. That liberty is on the march in the western world cannot be denied. The great danger is that it has become confused with licence. Attempts by the forces of law and order and government to control licence and material appetites are genuinely regarded by some people and wilfully misinterpreted by others as infringements of liberty. And law and order has now to face additional hazards.

The new threats posed by espionage and subversion occur in the order vacuum which appears to be resulting from the accelerating withdrawal of the great social binding force of feudalism and its more liberal developments of recent times. Integrated village life under its hereditary squire, the class structure, disparity of wealth.

1. (Heinemann, 1966).

strongly upheld parental authority, were undoubtedly undemocratic; they were also forms of order which in Britain have not yet been replaced. Concurrently, as has already been pointed out (p. 30) there are those among us who seek to undermine our established system of values without putting anything in their place. They are sixth columnists, ideological saboteurs, busy with mindless acts of demolition. For example, the television satirists who beggar the meaning of the word by sneering at ways of life such as Christianity and marriage, held dear by many decent folk. Such satire transmitted to millions by modern mass communications, reaching adults and children, some of whom are not intellectually fitted to cope with it or to take a balanced view, is one more contribution to the order vacuum.

Although there have been setbacks the post-war period has seen the establishment of the affluent society—a society from which want of the economic kind has been largely removed—and the welfare state. This same period has seen the triumph in the United Kingdom of liberal doctrines of penal reform culminating in the virtual abolition of capital and corporal punishment.

Instead of 'a social state of ideal perfection', as Utopia is defined in one dictionary, which many people sincerely believed could result from the implementation of such policies, there is a totally different situation. In his inaugural address on 2nd November 1966, the Honourable George Chubb[1], Chairman of the Royal Society of Arts, said, 'We live in an age of barbarity—of merciless violence against young and old—of pillaging on a frightening cartel-like scale.'

Notwithstanding the valiant efforts of those who try to stop crime at its source by improving human behaviour, it continues and flourishes in our affluent society. Miss Kathleen Smith, a former assistant governor of Holloway prison, in an article in *The Spectator* of 17th January 1964, said: 'Crime is now an economic investment for those who fancy big returns with some small risk: exciting to plan, thrilling to commit, sordid but sensational when found out, richly respected when not . . . Prison is now less a place of horror and more an economic factor in criminal reckoning—a sentence is the "period of risk" between "investment" and "maturity"'. Many recent annual reports of Chief Constables have carried similar warnings.

Radzinowicz refers to the 'dark figure' of crime. He makes what he terms an inspired guess that 'Crime brought fully into the open and punished represents no more than about fifteen per cent of the total. At every stage the total is increased; offences go unnoticed or

1. Now Lord Hayter.

unreported and offenders go undetected, unprosecuted or uncon-victed', and he goes on to speculate, 'Who can say what our attitude towards the criminal—in emotional terms as well as in terms of practical policy—would be if the whole, or at least a large segment, of the dark figure were brought to light and thus, to refer to England and Wales, another three or four million indictable offenses were added to the recorded figures'. Perhaps in such circumstances in a democratic society the criminal, if he were prepared to pay taxes, would be accorded the rights of a political minority with representa-tion in Parliament! And how long would he remain in a minority? The estimated value of money and property stolen in 1965, which was £42m, of which about £8m was recovered by the police, is based on losses through known indictable offences only. It does not take into account the amounts lost by the public, industry and commerce through pilferage and other wastage or the 'dark figure.' According to the *Security Gazette* the grand total may be £117m, which is more than three times the turnover of the entire British security industry.

In a three and a half-hour television documentary put over the air in New York in August, 1966, gamblers, mobsters, drug addicts and crimi-nals involved in protection rackets gave frank accounts of their activi-ties. There was evidence about crime syndicates, police corruption and the penetration of big business by gangsters. It was asserted during the programme that the Mafia turnover was then about £17,000m a year, which is more than the entire American military budget.

Radzinowicz says there is nothing transitory about the dark figure: *'I am inclined to believe that the delinquent of today is more likely to remain with it than his predecessor of some twenty or fifteen years ago. The evolution of society, demographic and social, seems to favour him in this as in so many other ways. As society becomes more anonymous, more mobile, so do its criminals . . . The growth of the sheer bulk of crime has been accompanied by changes in its proportions. It may even be true to say that new frontiers of crime have been opened up by the affluent society and the welfare state. Has contemporary crime assumed a new physiognomy? I can discover eight features which may be regarded as prima facie evidence that it has.*

*'First, the growth of motiveless destruction, hooliganism. Second, certain other kinds of violence. Third, expansion of new forms of steal-ing, such as automobile thefts and very lucrative robberies. Fourth, a shift towards disintegrated, asocial behaviour and drug consumption. Fifth, a spread of occupational crime, white collar or blue collar criminality, or of illegal conduct by those generally presumed to be law-abiding. Sixth, a stronger contingent of offenders from the middle*

*strata of society as compared with the working classes. Seventh, an increased proportion of crime by the younger and the young-adult groups. Eighth, the influx of first offenders and their relatively greater share in crime as compared with recidivists.'*

Crime is now a capitalised industry of its own. Not only does it plough back money to finance its future operations but there is evidence to suggest the existence of a sort of cradle-to-grave welfare system which arranges escapes for and cares for the relatives of those who fail. It is said that it is possible to 'insure' against operational failure. The premium has not been stated but criminal 'actuaries' might well consider the risk to be low.

All serious crime today, of which the Great Train Robbery is a classic example, is planned in detail at least as great as many major business operations, which is of course what modern criminal operations are and for which the rewards are very great indeed, especially as profit before tax is the same as profit after tax. The meticulous planning demands precise information, and for this reason elaborate espionage networks are built up. These networks, like others of their kind, provide not only the information necessary to criminal planning but the means by which traitors (e.g., police informers) are punished, jurors, witnesses and agents intimidated, prison escapes arranged and any other devilment necessary to those who choose to live on the wealth of honest men and women. If the unparalleled crime wave is a symptom of social de-regulation, of appetites stimulated beyond true earning power and work capacity, so too is the endless round of wage demands. The industrial scene today is characterized by demands for more pay for less work, perhaps too for work less well done. Productivity agreements are often empty charades of promises which both sides know will not be kept, to enable employers and unions to by-pass Government economic policies.

Hitherto in our society the professional and upper classes have provided an immense stability. With high ideals of social responsibility, patriotism, leadership, self-sacrifice, went a concept of duty to pay taxes in full without question and to support law and order regardless of personal interest. Today the aristocracy have become business men commercializing their titles or country houses so that they may enjoy the standard of living they regard as their right, and consequently many have neither the time nor the money nor indeed the incentive for any form of social duty. Even more significant is the increasing avarice of the professional man defending himself from the taxative exactions of the welfare state and the workshy. Both aristocrat and professional man regard the chartered accountant as a sort of inverted Robin Hood.

The growth of material appetites has been fostered by advertising and continuous mass communications, through television and glossy magazines, of how the wealthier half live or should live.

Society has become more mobile and more anonymous. The motor car has made us mobile and urbanisation and industrialisation tend to make us anonymous. The family is becoming a simple conjugal unit with the aunts, uncles, grandparents and cousins spread throughout the land or living in twilight homes; hitherto, the larger family in frequent or daily contact in the village or small provincial town had been a considerable stabilising influence in society. There is a tendency today to herd and classify people in mutually distrusting age groups—e.g. teenagers, pensioners and so on. Horizontal social groups are unnatural and unstable. Vast masses of people live in anthills of identical flats, and land-owning, a great stabiliser, is becoming more corporate than individual. The criminal has also become more mobile and more anonymous, and if he continues unchecked the same will become true of property. Naturally the mobility and anonymity of society is reflected in the police, whose local character is diminishing with amalgamations. The police preoccupation with the mobility of society, especially mobile man and his motor car, has made their image more prefectorial than paternal. The segregation of the police from the people and the extinction of their paternal role will be completed with their nationalisation which many authorities regard as inevitable. When they are nationalised they may well be indistinguishable from military forces.

In former times most men worked in the same area and environment in which they lived, in all the community and friendliness of English provincial life. Today most men and many women are commuters and the anonym of the anthill becomes too often the cipher of the corporation. The sanction of what the neighbours think diminishes when there are no neighbours in the old sense of the word. In days of declining and in some cases almost nonexistent parental authority, the factory or the office may be the only place where the individual encounters discipline after schooldays. Today's industrial manager controls most of the property and wealth of the country and employs most of the people and he should be for all these reasons the logical inheritor of the squire's mantle as a social binding force; in general he is very differently regarded by much of society today.

Shining brightly out from the murk of materialism and social flux are the steadily advancing qualities of an increasing humanity and tolerance towards delinquency. Rehabilitation has become more important than punishment. These qualities, which are surely right in principle, do nevertheless at first glance deprive society of some of its security weapons; especially they appear to weaken the power of deterrence. No more may criminals be shackled or birched, mantraps be set, lethal weapons be used to keep intruders out or prisoners in, nor a life be demanded for a life. But at each successive stage of humane advance, security should be modified to meet the new conditions. It seldom if ever is even considered, and it therefore, to the accompaniment of pained official surprise, breaks down.

Closely connected with the stability of human society is the right of privacy. The mental processes which have enabled man to rise from the jungle nearly to the moon need repose just as much as do his muscles. An Englishman's home is no longer his castle. Not only has a host of officials the right of entry without warrant, which the police do not have save in exceptional circumstances, but millions of homes are invaded continuously by noise, the adverse mental consequences of which have not yet been fully assessed—they are probably considerable. There are few homes in Britain today that do not suffer from the roar of the motor car, motor cycle, moped or aeroplane.

There is another current social phenomenon which can well be placed alongside the foregoing selection of intrusions into privacy and that is the habit, apparently condoned by many people who ought to know better, of gatecrashing parties: a harmless little pursuit practised in some of the best circles. Of course, it is theft and trespass of a kind, but 'he can afford it' and 'he won't dare to turn me out' are apparently justifications. Gatecrashers number among their brethren even young Guards officers—the author's own house in Cyprus was gatecrashed by several of these young 'gentlemen.' And the situation was sufficiently serious for the head mistress of Sherborne School for Girls, Miss Diana Reader Harris, to have circulated parents at the end of the Christmas term 1965 as follows:

'*Many parents must already be thinking ahead about the parties next holidays at which their daughters will be either hostesses or guests. I hope you will not think me presumptuous if I mention one or two points which seem to cause some girls anxiety or uncertainty and sometimes even fear. So often young people persuade their parents to go out and leave them and their friends to run a party on their own without realising the problems they may have to face. Gatecrashing for instance may bring to a party unknown visitors whose standards of behaviour are not those of their hosts or hostesses and who can spoil the evening for everyone. Without their parents or other adults the young hosts and hostesses don't know how to cope with the uninvited guests who quite often arrive in large numbers, news of a party having got around. There are, moreover, changing social customs among adolescents which present risks and temptations for which girls may be unprepared and which they may find it hard to cope with in the absence of any adults in the house. May I quote two such customs as examples? The first is the increasing tendency of some young people—even as young as fourteen or fifteen—to bring with them to a party bottles of wine or even spirits. The second is the custom of turning down the lights and allowing everyone the run of the house. It is not easy in either of these situations always to present the standards one believes to be right, and I think that sometimes we lay an intolerably heavy burden on the young and on girls in particular in underestimating the difficulties that some parties present to them.'*

Mr. Tony Geraghty related in *The Guardian* on 1st January 1966, under the heading 'Ungentle art of gatecrashing' the experience of a Hampstead parent, who was the victim of a particularly massive 'break in'. He quotes the parent as follows:

'"*We invited thirty people*" he said. "*It was a party for my son, you see. Just in two rooms on the first floor. But 300 turned up. Three hundred, mark you. One opened the door and they just swept one aside. And the damage! They were all over the place.*

"*About half an hour after the party started the ceiling began to bulge. Then the neighbours called the police because they could not stand the noise. My wife, who is a woman of spirit, helped to clear them out.*

"*In forty-five minutes it was all over. I went down to the off-licence to console myself with a bottle of whisky. On the way back I met a gang of yobs who asked me the way to my address. They said something about a swinging party. I told them the police had stopped it . . . but others kept arriving from as far away as Kent and Essex until the early hours.*"'

Apparently another Hampstead victim lost his electric fire, his record player, his *au pair* girl and also his staircase: 'The crash could be heard for miles'.

There are other teenage activities, which, in the grossness of their immorality, are probably far more significant than the ordinary follies of youth. There are the young 'troglodytes' of the Peak District in Derbyshire, whose way of life is completely parasitical, and the beatniks of West London. According to the *Evening Standard* of 6th May 1966, 'Today Richmond and Twickenham are crawling with beatniks. They pack into derelict houses, dossing down on the floor.'

Apparently, although they wander the length and breadth of the country searching for something new, they all end up at weekends at a club on Eel Pie Island, in the middle of the Thames at Twickenham. One twenty-year-old beatnik interviewed by the *Evening Standard* reporter said, 'I have had fifty jobs since I left school nearly five years ago. We are nearly all banned from the pubs around here, but we would never get chucked off the island.' Membership of the club, which functions at the Eel Pie Hotel on the island, was said to run into 'thousands'.[1]

The problem of debauched youth is not confined to the United Kingdom. Elsewhere in Europe and in the United States there are similar groupings. The *provos* of Amsterdam have been very troublesome to the Dutch police. Originally it seems they were an anarchical movement, against authority but not organization. But as with other similar movements, the rabble have been attracted and today the provos are mostly dirty, unkempt, idle hangers-on.

Our democratic society is thus being devoured by excesses and abuses of the very liberty which it gives us; by motiveless destruction of property; by invasions of privacy; by mindless demolition of established values; by organized crime becoming a way of life; by widespread intimidation; by the tolerance and subsidising of the workshy; by beatniks and troglodytes. These forces of disintegration represent natural primordial tendencies of individual groups which if unchecked fulfil their physical desires and private ambitions by direct action without the rule of law and at the expense of the common interest. Order is also being weakened by attitudes of hostility towards authority generally which are being increasingly engendered by a spreading and proforma'd bureaucracy and by the progressive weaving around us all of a taxation cocoon many times more complex and constricting than that which helped to bring about the fall of Rome. Many of those who would formerly have upheld the law publicly and privately may now be amongst Professor Radzinowicz's dark figure. A view of the Russian revolution expressed a few weeks before it occurred in a letter to the Tsar from the Grand Duke Alexander Mikhailovich, is relevant—

'*In conclusion I will say that, strange as it may appear, it is the Government which is preparing the revolution. The people do not want it; but the Government is employing all possible means to increase the number of malcontents, and it is perfectly successful. We are watching*

1. A subsequent report said that the organiser of the club was a sociologist and that from the start the club had been run as an experiment in reaching and helping disturbed youngsters.

*an unwonted spectacle, revolution coming from above, and not from below.'*

We may fittingly end the chapter with some applied Pavlovian theory. In the same twenty years as has seen dramatic internal social change Britain has experienced equally dramatic international transformation. For example:

from being the strong head of a powerful and united empire to being the weak co-ordinator of a commonwealth which could at any time fly apart from centrifugal force;

from being the saviour of Europe she has become a rejected applicant for membership of the European Economic Community;

from being the manager of a powerful reserve currency she has become responsible for the largest unsecured overdraft in the world;

from being through her island state comparatively immune from military attack she has become one of the most vulnerable of all nations to modern weapons.

These international factors have served to add pace to the process of disruption of nervous stability brought about by internal social deregulation and to increase the confusion.

Thus is the abandonment of the restraints and binding forces of former societies leading to their replacement not, as many had hoped and believed, by liberty and cultural bonds, but by licence and unbridled material philosophies. The overwhelming importance attached to worldly success and independence undermines the social and industrial regulation necessary to their attainment.

This is the law of the jungle.

*The Defence*

# CHAPTER 9

## The Science of Security I: The Survival Discipline

Security is a whole science which has been forgotten too soon by a society whose liberal attitudes and material progress have outstripped its moral capability.

It is imperative for our government and managers to realize that organized crime, espionage, industrial espionage, subversion, sabotage, and prison escapes are not only based on like and in some cases the same systems and organizations, but are also and for that reason defeated by similar methods applied simultaneously from an overall concept. For example, it may be no more realistic to consider prison security in isolation than to examine railways alone when the problem is one of transport.

The selection of a distinguished military man—Lord Mountbatten—to lead an urgent enquiry into prison security as a result of the Blake[1] escape was nevertheless an important landmark for the security philosopher. While it is more than doubtful that it was so intended, it serves as a reminder that what are regarded by some as three separate sciences—military, police and security—have a common origin and purpose. All are concerned with the protection of man and his property from the wickedness of other men.

Like any other branch of knowledge, these sciences can be prostituted, but we are concerned here with them in their role of defence of the legitimate interests of a law-abiding nation. Broadly speaking, there are two types of attack which can be made against these interests: from without and from within. Defence against externally-mounted attacks is a military responsibility; the preservation of internal law and order being regarded as the duty of the police and public, aided if necessary by military power.

This has certainly been the case in the United Kingdom since 1829, when the Metropolitan Police Force was established. Although it was

1. George Blake, the spy who in 1961 had been sentenced to forty-two years imprisonment for spying for Russia, escaped from Wormwood Scrubs gaol on 22nd October 1966 (See p. 67 of Chapter 7).

not the first police force in Britain, the date of its founding may be held to represent the final division of the police science from the military. Hitherto, most serious policing had been performed by soldiers, of which the forces of Cromwell's major-generals are an important example. The famous baton charge of the Metropolitan Police on the occasion of the Lord Mayor's Show in 1830 was the first time a dangerous mob had been dispersed without military assistance. Thus the proud military and police professions began their separate development.

The armed forces developed staff colleges and other seats of higher learning, such as the Imperial Defence College and the Royal United Services Institution, whose influences played a major part in enabling the country to survive with distinction in two world wars. The Royal Military College of Science has recently asked the Council of Academic Awards for permission to confer degrees, and there is little doubt that it will be granted. Most of the institutions are non-exclusive and there is interchange between the armed services; civilians attend and lecture, particularly in the higher spheres. There have been plenty of military intellectuals. Many members of the armed services continue to play important roles after retirement in industry and commerce, in their communities, as teachers, writers, and even as professors, bringing the contribution of their distinctive culture to a wider society.

The most influential institution founded by the police is the Police Federation, which is in effect a trade union, although it does not have the right to strike. The Federation was constituted under the Police Act 1919 and consists of all members of the police service below the rank of superintendent. Its principal statutory purpose is to bring to the notice of police authorities matters affecting police welfare and efficiency, but not including questions of individual discipline or promotion. Many if not most of its public utterances are concerned with promoting increased police pay and maintaining a closed shop. The power of the Federation will increase with amalgamations, and the attitude to nationalization is significant. During its 1966 conference a resolution was passed accepting the inevitability of a national force and insisting that no action be taken to hinder progress in this direction.

These remarks must not be taken out of context. For many years the top positions in the police force were filled by distinguished persons from other spheres, particularly the army. It was natural that this should be deeply resented by the career officers and the formation of the Police Federation was a logical consequence. Lord Trenchard's

Hendon College should have been and was intended to be the nucleus of an eventual police culture, but its progress was interrupted by the war. In 1945 the Police Federation was able to persuade the government of the day that Hendon was undemocratic because of its direct-entry system, although direct or rapid entry to the managerial grades after gaining high educational or professional qualifications is a characteristic of most professions, however democratic.

Much has since been done to broaden the police base. The Police College, for existing members of the police, has been re-established. It was announced in May 1966 that the age limit of recruitment of the Metropolitan Police had been raised from thirty to forty, and in special cases forty-five for men from the armed forces. This is a clear indication of a crisis of leadership, since the appointment of army officers to senior posts in the past was a major source of discontent in the lower ranks of the police. Inevitably there was a swift and adverse reaction from the Police Federation, who were at the time holding their annual conference at Blackpool.

According to *The Daily Telegraph* of 27th May 1966, 'Officials of the Federation made a bitter attack on Sir Joseph Simpson, Metropolitan Police Commissioner, and the Home Office. Mr. Reginald Webb, Chairman, called the decision "disgusting and sickening"'. He was followed by Sergeant Peter Joiner, secretary of the Metropolitan Police Federation Branch, who said, according to *The Daily Telegraph*, 'We have been stabbed in the back by our police authority and the Commissioner'. It should be added that the Police Federation seized the opportunity of their conference and public anxiety about the present state of crime to make what was described by *The Guardian* of 25th May 1966 as a 'blunt pay demand'. The Chairman, Mr. Webb, according to *The Guardian*, told the Home Secretary who was present at the conference, 'I cannot impress upon you too strongly the plain truth—that the entire service is looking to the September pay review as evidence of the good faith of the Home Secretary. If any attempt is made to fob off the police at this time of crisis with a diluted pay award in which we are the sacrificial lambs on the altar of an incomes policy, no one in (sic) this platform will be prepared to take responsibility for what will happen to the police of this country.' This is indeed in accordance with the policy of some trade unions, which status the Police Federation does not officially have, at any time of high bargaining power—for example, the National Union of Seamen.

There will be many people who feel that a uniformed and disciplined (and sometimes armed) service should not get itself into a situation where the rank and file can describe their most senior officer as one who stabs them in the back. Such attitudes as this, coupled with 'blunt pay demands', which one hopes were not strike preliminaries, can hardly further the cause of crime prevention.

No doubt the Police Federation can make out an irresistible and conclusive case for more pay, as can anyone else in similar circumstances. According to *The Guardian*, Mr. Jenkins, an experienced politician, told the conference that, although it would be premature to say anything at present on pay, the Home Office fully recognised its high priority. He added: 'These negotiations can begin soon. I don't want them constricted by inadequate time'.

The real point is that it is illusory to think that a mere increase in pay will restore the situation. Much deeper thought has to be given to the whole concept of policing. The present one, in the opinion of the author, is out of date and irrelevant to modern problems. Because the rank and file of the police feel but do not understand this, they make their protest in the form of a demand for more pay, believing like many others in this day and age that this is the cure for all ills.

### FRAGMENTATION OF A SCIENCE

The national failure to create a police culture has meant that no one has properly and continuously investigated what the true scope of police activity should be. No one has determined what police perfection is and how to make it prevail. Among the many consequences of this is that a large and vital part of its role of prevention and detection of crime has passed beyond police dominion, and in some cases outside its sphere of influence.

For example, the crimes of espionage and sabotage are prevented and detected much more by the Security Service, which was sired by the armed services, than the police, whose counter-espionage role is mainly executive. The control and disciplining of traffic along the highway is becoming increasingly the responsibility of traffic wardens, who must now be regarded as the nucleus of an eventual traffic corps. Again, the prevention of the crime of escaping from gaol and the detection of attempts to do so is the responsibility of the prison authorities. And, in many people's minds, insurance has become an alternative to security.

The prevention of crimes against property is to a large extent the responsibility of the owner, who for some time has relied largely on the safemaker or locksmith for guidance as to protection. To these industries must be added today a growing complex of commercial security services providing guards for premises, armoured cars for the secure movement of valuables, and burglar alarms. These latter are detective in nature and increasingly linked to commercial central alarm stations. There is probably more protective security know-how in the security industry than anywhere else.

A new profession of security advisers and security officers is developing rapidly which performs a function analagous to that of the police. On management's behalf it holds sway over large areas of private, industrial and public property. Its professional body, the Industrial Police and Security Association, has 2,100 members.

In many cases this fragmentation of work is necessary and advantageous to society. The dichotomy of the Police Special Branch and the Security Service is a safeguard against the creation of a gestapo; the moral obligation of the owner to protect his property should save much police effort and expense if it were carried out—and insurance has in the past been a strong disincentive.

But the other result of no culture, the fragmentation of the science, which in fact has meant its disappearance as a branch of knowledge, has been little less than a disaster. Its loss accounts in large measure for the wave of successful crime against property and the state of prison security today.

Since so much of what may be termed security is now outside the police and military spheres, it is clear we must evolve a separate security culture, and revive and modernize its lost science.

ORIGINS OF SECURITY

Security probably began as a survival discipline invented by nature to ensure the continuation of the species, and it is most highly developed in mammals. Originally intended for the preservation of life, it was later extended by man to preserve the power and wealth brought to him by his brawn and brain. It would seem to be older than the military science, which, being concerned with the deployment of formed bodies of men, could not have existed until man organised himself into groups.

The pattern of early security was a partnership of man and barriers for the purpose of protecting him and his family. It was defensive in character, but not static, because early man was nomadic. (See Appendix H for information on early security organisation.)

Feudalism and the immediately preceding social systems, the German mark and the Roman emphyteusis, changed the pattern of security. These systems resulted from the discovery of land cultivation, and in broad terms the concept of feudalism was that of a land-holding society coupled with the duty of military service to defend the lands of the tribe or the nation from external aggression. By now, the main enemy was not the rigours of climate and wild animals, but man. The idea of security as the linear defence of land reached its climax in the war of 1914-18, of which the 1939-45 war was essentially a continuation.

There are many signs that the beginning of the nuclear age also marks the final demise in Europe of the feudal system and its replacement by a society in some respects analagous to the nomadic one from which it developed. Since this change coincides with the development of economic strength and subversion as major instruments of foreign policy, the effect on security is profound.

CHAPTER 10

*The Science of Security II: A Technology for Today*

Security's original purpose of helping to ensure man's physical survival in primitive times against the dangers of wild animals and the rigours of climate was successfully accomplished. In its military form security has become progressively more internecine in character, the logical end of which is Armageddon. The lucky accident of nuclear balance (due in part to acts of espionage) has given society a breathing space in which to discover better ways of achieving political ends. The East appears to be choosing subversion and propaganda; the West except the CIA seems to prefer economics and public relations.

THE GREY JUNGLE

Today's struggle of man against man takes place mainly in the jungle—not the green jungle of uncontrolled vegetation, but the grey jungle of conurbation. As opposed to the tiger or the snake of the green jungle, the preyer of today is at first glance indistinguishable. This means that he always has the initiative. And he carries on his nefarious trade under the guise of legitimate activity.

The best example is the subversive agent operating in a work force, who pursues the wants of rogues under the label of the 'rights of man'.

Let us look now in more detail at the four principal preyers.
*The spy*: He appears in several forms in today's jungle society and in each of these forms there are two types: the willing and the unwilling. The willing one works for money, 'kicks', or ideology, and mostly for money; the old patriotic, semi-glamorous spy is almost extinct. The unwilling spy is the one who has been blackmailed or intimidated. The spy, willing or unwilling, may be acting in pursuit of subversive activity, robbery or theft, including theft of information. Usually the spy needs to obtain access to documents or a person in possession of the knowledge required. He may use technical aids, particularly remote listening or remote seeing devices, but the importance of

these is exaggerated by those who wish to sell them or make money out of defeating them. Most really valuable information is obtained by the suborning of an employee or someone with easy access to the required information.

*The robber*: This is the organized criminal who carries out robbery in conformity with a master plan constructed after a painstaking reconnaissance which nowadays often takes the form of espionage.

*The mind-bender*: There is a growing number of great persuaders in our society—people who for subversive political purposes or financial gain (often both) bend others to their will. Such people are to be found anywhere from Mayfair to the factory floor. They usually operate in secret or in an aura of mystery. Physical violence is not used in the build-up stage, but may be used later for disciplinary purposes to punish deviationists or traitors. Drugs, particularly of the halucinogen group, may be increasingly employed. (See Chapter 4, p. 32.)

*The intimidator*: Intimidation is used in pursuit of espionage, robbery, revenge, or in subversive activity to restore failing psychological discipline. The intimidator bends people to his will by threats of violence against persons or their families. Death, acid in the faces of loved ones, beatings-up, are promised if a person will not hand over keys, provide the requisite information, perjure himself in the witness box, bring in a verdict of not guilty when a juryman, promise to avoid reporting adversely in the press, and so on.

TECHNOLOGY OF SECURITY

In the whole history of man's struggle for survival there is no example of victory being won by purely defensive means. Unless the criminal of today can regularly be hunted down before he strikes there is no real hope of arresting the crime wave and its attendant evils of espionage, subversion and intimidation. Equally, were this alone to be done and protection neglected, success would be as probable as for an army which practised but one of the phases of war.

Security has been developed by man from the original combination of his senses and muscles to guard himself. Today, in addition to having the further responsibilities of guarding his mind and his possessions, security must be translated into a technology of specialized human and technical functions appropriate to the society in which we live. The following paragraphs suggest and attempt to classify into eight phases the resources which should form the basis of a modern security technology.

*Phase I—Scientific method:* No technology, no science, no art can develop to meet society's changing needs in the absence of detached thought. There are no faculties of security in Britain but there is a considerable area of thought devoted to criminology—which is like having a good intelligence picture of enemy forces without studying strategy and tactics. The subsequent seven phases should be studied as a whole science.

*Phase II—Prophylaxis:* This consists first in trying to ensure freedom of the individual from material or psychological want, of which the latter is the more important. This is not merely a matter for government—it is a primary responsibility of management. There should be mild paternal influences and definite stimulation of cultural as opposed to material interests, with the aim of preventing defection and encouraging resistance to, and reporting of, criminal activity.

Secondly, there must be security education. Just as the young child of primitive man was taught to protect himself against the other denizens of his jungle, so should our youth today be taught how to defend his body, his mind and his possessions in today's area war.

Thirdly, potential criminals must be made to feel that crime does not pay. This is not only a matter of obtaining a high detection rate, but of engendering a belief that failure, which is more than detection, is the most likely result.

There is no doubt that a strong police presence in society, provided that it is felt that they are 'with us' and not 'against us', both reassures and deters. But an image of the police as trades unionists or as prefects trying to catch us out with radar cameras is immensely damaging.

There are also possibilities, insufficiently explored so far, of deterring the owner from being careless with his property, by insurance or other sanctions; and of deterring manufacturers and architects from producing insecure cars or buildings. There would not be much future for them if their designs let in the rain or the wind—which are less damaging to society than the criminal.

*Phase III—Detection:* Since the major part of all the criminal activity with which we are concerned here is planned, the opportunity for detecting it and preventing its taking place is greatly increased. It is one of the biggest failures of our present system that, in spite of this, the bulk of detection, if it takes place, takes place after the event. Since espionage is a common denominator of all the major threats of today, the logical answer is a counter-espionage organisation. The police themselves are not really constituted or organised for counter-espionage work, which may seem rather strange, if it is accepted that organised crime employs espionage methods.

The fact is that the Criminal Investigation Department is recruited from the uniformed branch, whose minimum physical standards are very high. They are trained to have a fine bearing, encouraged to form habits of dress and attitudes which mark them as members of a uniformed and disciplined service, whether they are wearing uniform or not. If it is desirable that the CID should wear plain clothes as they do, it is presumably desirable that they should not be easily identified as policemen. Yet, in addition to the hall-mark of their calling, they have their offices in police stations, wear uniform on ceremonial occasions, and drive in and out of police stations in their cars which may quickly become known to the criminals. No doubt some live in known police quarters. They are often involved in the publicity surrounding arrest and trial.

Moreover, from his earliest days in the force the policeman is brought up in an atmosphere of high principle and morality to believe that the very first loyalty of his calling is to the law. It is not perhaps generally known that a constable is not obliged to obey the order of his superior officer to effect an arrest. The constable is the judge of whether arrest is justified, and it is he who will be held responsible for the arrest by the law. Most true counter-espionage operations have to be carried out from rather different moral and legal standpoints. If they became the responsibility of police officers, painful conflicts might occur in men of such high calibre and high ideals as are the vast majority of police officers. If actions of doubtful legality or morality were associated with the police, serious damage might be done to their public image.

In the cases of espionage against the state and subversive activity, responsibility for counter measures is split between the Special Branch of the police and the Security Service, where anonymity is more important than dominance, and whose members are un-uniformed and un-uniform. This Service is a highly professional civilian counter-espionage organisation. Its members have no special powers; if arrest or search is necessary, they must so persuade the police, usually the Special Branch. In short, while the Security Service has most of the knowledge, the police have the power; this situation is at once a safeguard against tyranny and, as results have shown, an efficient system of operation.

There is a sound case for extending the responsibility of the successful partnership of Special Branch and the Security Service to include the countering of other branches of criminal activity which are based on espionage, including organised crime. The CID could then concentrate on the work of investigating crime that is individual, localized and spontaneous, as opposed to grouped, nationwide and planned, and on reducing the success of petty crime, so often the seedbed of major crime.

On the reasonable assumption that nevertheless a considerable proportion of crime will not be detected at the planning stage, it is necessary to ensure that the earliest possible warning is received of an actual attack. This means the installation of burglar alarms around important targets wherever these are practicable.

The third facet of detection is that of investigation after the crime, which is properly the responsibility of the CID, jointly, if necessary, with such counter-espionage service as there may be.

It must be stressed that detection is but one of the phases of security and only of real value in a balanced whole. There are many who erroneously regard it as the panacea. The Home Secretary said recently:

*'I don't believe any of us yet knows the root causes of crime; what makes some individuals criminals and others not. So I move to the next stage, which is that of deterrence. The most effective deterrent is to increase the chances of detection—and detection means the police.'*

With respect to Mr. Jenkins, the most important single prophylaxis of crime—the factor which more than all else deters a man from committing a crime—is a virtual certainty of failure. This is not quite the same thing as increasing the chances of detection. Failure may, it is true, occur as a result of detection, but not always; detection of robbery after the fact, for example, followed by a light sentence for a first offender, followed by a term of years spent in increasingly congenial surroundings at public expense, followed by maximum remission, followed by release to live on the loot, is not failure at all and is not much of a deterrent either. Failure may occur without detection; for example, the security defences may be too strong and clever for the robbers or spies.

If Mr. Jenkins' efforts to improve detection were to be successful it is to be wondered whether he would like the result. If Radzinowicz's figure (p. 80) is reasonably accurate, and the rate of detection increased to say eighty per cent of the dark figure, there might be another three or four million indictable offences to prosecute and try. There would also be a need for much extra prison capacity.

These points are not in any way intended to suggest that detection by the police is not of fundamental importance. Rather is the intention to stress that we must not rely on this alone, or even place too great a significance on it; to do so would be fallacious and unfair to the police. Nor is detection solely a police responsibility, as might be inferred from what Mr. Jenkins said. The public have a duty to report crime they detect, and in many cases nowadays detection of crime occurs through burglar alarms installed by them.

The assumption that a drastic improvement in detection by the police is the panacea is not only inaccurate, but is also ingenuous. More than anything else detection depends on information, and since more information comes from the general public than from any other source it is to a large extent governed by factors outside direct police control.

Just as military attack presupposes defence and a firm base so does detective security depend for its success on protective security.

*Phase IV—Protection*: This is one of the few highly developed crafts within the technology and among its products are ingenious barriers which range from perimeter fences to massive strongrooms. The best protective system is a harmonic of appropriate barriers and alarms in depth invigilated by trained guards. Protective security also includes measures to prevent the admission of undesirables into a work force, or indeed a home.

*Phase V—Justice*: It is very important in the deterrent sense that guilty men should be found guilty and sentenced according to the law. The gravest threat to justice of today is intimidation. There has already been a number of cases of attempted intimidation of witnesses and jurors, one of a press reporter, another of a distinguished QC and member of Parliament.

The main deterrent to intimidation, which is usually ultimately based on threats of death, was capital punishment. Protagonists of the abolition of capital punishment are apt to defend it at times of stress, such as the recent occasion of the murder of three policemen, by saying that since abolition here and elsewhere the number of murders has not increased significantly. This is, of course, irrelevant. From society's point of view murder is a trivial crime. Intimidation is a cancerous crime of first importance. When a man with a gun says 'Do my will, or else', what can the victim say? He cannot reply, 'If you kill me you too will die'. Quite apart from the low detection rate at present, this is simply not true. The criminal may well point out that in no circumstances will he be called upon to forfeit his own life, and that even if caught for the murder he may well be able to enjoy the fruits of his crime within a decade or so in present conditions; that dead men in any case make bad prosecution witnesses.

The problem posed by increasing intimidation is one of the most difficult in the whole field of security, and there is no experience to fall back on. The introduction of majority verdicts is only palliative; it merely means more intimidation or intimidation of a different kind, say against police, magistrates, judges and their families. Since intimidation, like subversion and all major crime, for example, that of the Mafia, is always based on an espionage-type of organisation, the answer probably lies in skilled counter-espionage work. It is also essential to create a new offence to take care of those kinds of espionage activity which are not yet unlawful.

*Phase VI—Imprisonment*: This has two purposes—to ensure that the sentence of the law is carried out, and the reintegration of the criminal into society. In modern penology, this means that security is virtually confined to the outer perimeter. A psychological element can be built into the defence by security means which will serve the two purposes of assisting rehabilitation and discouraging escapes. There is no technical difficulty in constructing a perimeter system, at reasonable cost, that is virtually impregnable from either side.

*Phase VII—Restitution*: A security system must ensure that the criminal's debt to society is paid in full, and that neither he nor his family benefit from other people's losses, either during imprisonment or after release. This is an essential corollary of humane treatment.

*Phase VIII—Insurance*: Accumulated insurance funds are the treasure store from which unwonted loss may be replaced. If insurance is to fulfil a security role in society, as it should—as everyone should— it must not subsidise the continually careless owner and thereby indirectly assist corruption by making things easy for the thief. It is not only a question of actuarial justification but also of social justification; and in any case, is not the condition of society an actuarial consideration?

The first message of these two chapters is the wholeness of security and consequent inter-dependence of each phase of the technology. Until the millennium arrives men will be tempted to commit crime. They are less likely to do so if failure is virtually certain. Failure means detection, defeat by security defence, completion of the punishment laid down by law and no prospect of ultimate financial gain through crime. Detection must be likely at all stages. Protection must be strong, skilled and co-ordinated—that which protects must itself be protected. All phases must be in, and remain in, balance; for example, technical advances in protective equipment may require modification to alarm devices which, if not carried out, will result in weaker security overall.

Secondly, security, humanity and rehabilitation are not anti-pathetic; they are sympathetic. But just as it is wrong to introduce new security measures without first considering humanity and re-habilitation, so must the security implications of advances in their techniques be weighed and translated into advance action. Equally, it must be remembered that humanity will usually help rehabilitation, which in its turn will help security by reducing criminal recidivism and escape attempts. Among the many there are two particularly unfortunate examples of failure to appreciate the need for continuing balance in this sphere.

The first is prison security. The object when most prisons were built was cell security. High risk prisoners spent much of their time in the cell under lock and key. The penal reformers suggested that re-habilitation prospects would be considerably enhanced by giving them greater freedom of movement within the prison.

Not until a large number of significant escapes had been made and considerable sums of money spent on building prisons which relied on old security concepts was it realized that new security concepts were needed to match new concepts of penal reform. Although something can be done to convert to perimeter security a prison designed for cell security, it can never be really satisfactory.

The second example of failure is intimidation already discussed in detail under Phase V. An obvious consequence of the abolition of capital punishment was a rapid increase in intimidation, but no security action was taken in advance. Intimidation has now obtained a serious grip which it never would have done if security experts had been consulted in the planning stage of abolition.

It is not necessary to gaze into the crystal ball to predict the next major crime form. In an increasingly cashless society, forgery and financial fraud and theft of valuable documents (£2 million worth of airline tickets in the past two years are admitted by the airlines) will be major criminal preoccupations. And no doubt in the future many people will be expressing surprise and shock at vast swindles 'which could not have been foreseen'.

\*   \*   \*   \*

This book is of course mainly concerned with the technology of security in the context of espionage and subversion in industry. But it is of the utmost importance for the manager to appreciate that the various courses advocated and techniques described in the suc-ceeding chapters for the countering of these threats within his domain, important though they are, will only be truly effective if the remainder of the technology is correctly applied to the gamut of criminal activity. It therefore becomes management's direct interest to give all assistance and encouragement within its power, particularly to the government, the police, and the law to ensure that this is so.

# CHAPTER 11

## The Communal Task of the Manager

Subversion has much in common with dry rot. It does not flourish in the light of day, but seeks conditions where there is lack of ventilation and general neglect. It grows particularly well, as does dry rot in the dark and is at its best, as is dry rot, if the surrounding unventilated air is warm and damp, as in Malaya and Vietnam; but this may also be because these climatic conditions produce the green jungle which provides the concealment and camouflage so necessary to its operations. Similarly, it chooses the grey urban jungle as a lair for its 'peaceful' disruptive activities in tactical support of its strategy of rotting the fabric of whatever order it is attacking so that the political organisation, whose weapon it is, can take over in the chaos of collapse.

There are two communities which are the concern of the manager, the ambient and the internal. However skilled and energetic his internal operation may be, it will never be wholly successful if the surrounding circumstances are adverse. As each one of us has a responsibility not merely to the immediate family but also to the community, so has the manager. But since corporate responsibility and influence are more than individual ones, the manager's role in the community should be of considerable significance. We are an industrial society, and a considerable amount of Parliamentary time is taken up with measures directly affecting industry. In one session alone of 1966, Parliament fixed the rate of corporation tax, introduced a direct tax on employment, changed the system of investment incentives, suspended free wage bargaining, made new proposals for nationalising steel and instituted the toughest credit squeeze for many years. It could reasonably be expected that management would be well represented in central and local government.

No accurate figures are available but some generalizations can be made. According to John Nott, MP for St Ives, writing in *The Times* of 29th September 1966, not more than ten young industrialists had entered Parliament in the past few years. He pointed out that the trade unions were heavily represented as were most of the professions except management. Although financiers and family businesses were well represented, career industrialists as opposed to those whose political lustre adds gloss to boards, were conspicuous by their absence.

No doubt the fact is that today the manager is precluded by our taxation system from building up the capital which would enable him to take the financial risk which forsaking a steady job for the vicissitudes of political life entails.

Certainly, large firms should give serious consideration to the possibility of sponsoring members of the managerial profession in Parliament. Nott suggested that the Confederation of British Industry could well help in this respect, as do the trade unions. Then could the manager influence decisions and policies which affect his performance, and especially his relations with the labour force. To avoid divisiveness it would be useful to sponsor members to both the major parties. In days when these parties are steadily becoming indistinguishable except at the extremities, the danger of bringing politics into the firm is not very real.

In most cases the need for a managerial presence in local government is of almost equal importance.

As regards his internal social responsibility, the famous Hawthorne experiments showed, and a number of eminent industrial sociologists such as Professor Tom Lupton have repeatedly stressed, 'that the task of management is not just a technical one. It is also a job of creating a social organism in which everyone can participate to the greatest possible degree and with which everyone can feel a sense of close identification'.

This book is only concerned with industrial relations in so far as they are responsible for subversion and industrial espionage and no exhaustive treatment of the subject is possible or desirable here. But since industrial harmony would resolve most of our problems and, not least, subversive activity, a treatment of the subject in some depth is necessary.

Seen from a distance the problem of industrial relations seems to be one of attitudes and values. The manager's aim is profit, and the worker's aim is wages at least sufficient to pay for the goods and services which he now regards as his due: house, car or cars, holidays, washing machine, television and other items. The possession of a Morris quickly leads to the desire to own a Jaguar, unless there is some compensating factor which creates contentment at a certain level.

Apart from winning the pools or similar good fortune, there are three theoretical ways by which this escalating aim may be achieved: one is by sheer individual effort leading to promotion; the second by combined effort which raises productivity so high that Jaguars are within reach of everybody. These are real. The third, which is illusory, is by uniting and demanding the necessary wages by threat of strike or other industrial wrecking; which is analagous to the ipisto or sword-point of the robber barons and is a modern version of piracy, the obtaining by force of what a man has not the energy or the brains to obtain by other effort. An eventual aim of such attitudes—not necessarily an ultimate one—might be moon-going Jaguars for all! But of course this lunatic process must be self-defeating long before such a state is arrived at, and it is hard to see how it alone could bring any interim or ultimate contentment.

Contentment is the nub of the problem. The philosophy which was expressed by 'We must be content with our lot', or 'We must be thankful for what we have got', or 'God bless the squire and his relations, And keep us in our proper stations', is no longer valid in our time, described recently by the Minister of Labour as 'the Age of Grab'. Those devoted philanthropists who have worked so hard in the past hundred years or so to redress the wrongs of the Industrial Revolution certainly can never have contemplated or desired this spirit which appears to rule today. And they did not see any need to replace the 'unconscious simplicity of traditional feudalism', which provided the stability of our agricultural and earlier industrial societies, with any other form of order.

How, then, is contentment to be achieved? At least the old philosophy described above was practical and realisable, and probably brought in its wake more contentment that 'What's in it for me?' 'Never had it so good!' 'Couldn't care less!' These philosophies, endemic in industrial society today, can only stimulate the maw of further demand. They ignore the need for cultural and spiritual satisfaction, and, unconsciously missing it, both management and workers are apt blindly to seek fulfilment through material satisfaction as a tangible substitute, forgetting that 'great men are they who see that spiritual is stronger than any material force, that thoughts rule the world'.

It is pertinent to look at the Japanese industrial success of the last ten years. While it would be a mistake to draw too exact a parallel between Japan and Britain because of certain fundamental differences between the Orient and the Occident, it does seem clear that so far the Japanese have not forgotten the value of culture and broad education in industry. Mary Crozier, reviewing in *The Guardian* of 6th May 1966, a BBC programme 'Made in Japan', said—

'*It is not only Japanese will to work, Japanese co-operation, and Japanese skill, but a fundamental attitude to life and work (which produces Japanese industrial success) . . . She does not . . . become a soulless civilisation. The Japanese family bonds, the passion for education and the ability to live a cultured life, seem to give a deep impetus to all the technical prowess.*'

Many other reports of Japanese ability to reconcile industrial and cultural, material and spiritual needs flow in from business men and casual observers. By accident or design it seems many heads of big companies are men of taste who fill their buildings with excellent paintings, sculptures and other works of art.

The Japanese group, Jissen Rinri Koseikai, amusingly described by Nina Epton in *The Times* of 7th May 1966, is but one example of Japanese determination to avoid complete materialism. This group apparently has more than a million members and describe themselves as 'a moral culture educational group'. Their meetings are held during working days at 5.0 a.m.; this is the main virtue preached— that of early rising. The meeting begins by singing the morning pledge in unison: 'All day long today we will work willingly without forgetting about the three blessings (of society, teachers and parents). We will not talk of other people's wickedness, or of our own goodness. We will promptly do whatever we should do. We will not get angry, or feel dissatisfied. Eliminating the three wastes (of things, time and mind), we will live a new life.'

After this, the devotees go one by one to the platform and give a 'potted confessional autobiography' for ten or fifteen minutes.

This means of getting their attitudes and values right is unlikely to appeal to British management or labour, but the fact remains that Japan's exports have gone up fifteen per cent each year for ten years. She is now the fifth-ranking country in the world in exports and the first in ship-building, and the British performance in the same period compares most unfavourably. Here, in Britain, overtime has become a way of life and the main object of shorter hours is to gain more money. The pace of work is adjusted so that management has to allow overtime to get the job finished and all sorts of devices are resorted to to ensure this: taking longer over a cup of tea, or a smoke, starting a few minutes late, and so on. There was a case quoted recently in the press in which a 'blue' film was shown during a night-shift in a factory. There are also some examples which have come to light recently where certain services such as hair-cutting, book-making, unofficial shops for selling such items as razor-blades, have been set up by the workers themselves within the factory. No doubt these services help to make for overtime.

Anyone who does not conform or objects may be dealt with by illegal courts, as at Cowley, and there are many other methods in common use, such as 'sending to Coventry', and bullying.

It is of course pertinent to ask what management is doing while these activities proceed. Is it that they do not go on night-shift with their workers and therefore do not know of them? Or do they know and are indifferent? Are they afraid for the safety of themselves and their families or of strikes which intervention might produce with even greater damage to production and profit than the activities themselves? It seems that, in several cases, such matters are thought better left to security officers and works police, which is about as sensible as believing that military action alone will produce peace and success in Vietnam. The men themselves might answer, if questioned, that the management had their expense accounts and Soho strip clubs.

These are but a few illustrations of an enormous problem, which at its worst results in strikes, like the seamen's, which may cause economic disruption and damage on such a scale as to cripple the nation and therefore make the strikers themselves worse off.

Although, no doubt, the vast bulk of the men and many of the leaders genuinely believe that they have grievances which cannot be solved except by striking, it would be idle to pretend that subversion is not at work. It is there all the time, festering, fomenting, agitating, aggravating, seeking to prevent settlement for as long as possible, and to effect the maximum possible damage, not only economically, but by promoting bitterness between men, management and government. This is communist policy and wherever there are communists subversion will also be—let there be no doubt about this. If there is subversive activity not communist in origin, communism will fasten upon it to its own ends.

The theme of this chapter is therefore that to prevent and defeat subversion something must be done to create in our industrial society the same conditions of contentment and mutual confidence which once existed in our liberalised feudal agricultural society. The leaders of that society were taught to be leaders from an early age. There were servants at The Hall and tenants in the village with whom the young squire mixed from his earliest days. If we are to believe the literature of the time, he was not a god and might well have his ears boxed below stairs if he went too far. The relationship between squire, servants and tenants was a well-balanced one, by no means dictatorship on the one side and servility on the other. According to Trevelyan, 'It has been observed that when the ensign (joined his regiment and) was handed over to the respectful care and tuition of the colour-serjeant, the relation of the two closely resembled that to which the younger man had been accustomed at home, when the old gamekeeper took him out afield to teach him the management of his fowling piece and the arts of approaching game.' Very few of the leaders of today are given this early chance to understand the arts of leadership and human relations, and they therefore need to be taught.

It is not of course to be inferred that the relationships between leaders and led should be the same today as they were centuries ago. They have changed and will continue to change, but the basic ingredients of leadership have not and will not. In the present age some of the qualities of leadership required are more subtle than ever before; instead of inducing obedience through inherent authority it should induce co-operation through knowledge and professionalism. But the need for humanity, warmth and suchlike remains constant.

Trevelyan also said, 'Agriculture is not merely one industry among many, but is a way of life, unique and irreplaceable in its human and spiritual values.' In the eighteenth and nineteenth centuries there were intimate relations between agriculture and industry and commerce. These had been established even as far back as Elizabethan times when it was the custom for younger sons of the manor house to be apprenticed into industry. Much of the capital employed in industry at the time of the Industrial Revolution came from the accumulated wealth of the land. In its turn this land was recapitalised by the profits of industry, partly no doubt because of the inherent desire of the industrialist to 'have a place in the country'. In some cases this may have been for reasons of snobbery, but it was mainly because of the interconnection of the two spheres. Good communications between town and country were not confined to the managerial or proprietor level. In days before the great conurbations, country was within walking distance of the factory and many of the workers still had families in the villages with whom they kept in touch. Later of course, as the conurbations became vast like London and the south-east, communications broke down and touch was lost, particularly of course at the poorer, i.e., shop floor, levels.

Those who believe, as does the author, that the split between town and country is responsible for at least a part of the indifferent

E

industrial relations of today may derive some comfort from the advent of motor cars for the masses and the Location of Offices Bureau. The efforts of the latter to reduce and prevent traffic and living congestion in the cities by moving industry to the provinces may well bring about a reunification of industry and the countryside, if indeed the planners are able to leave us with any countryside. The motor car makes it possible to work in the town and live in the surrounding country, if the conurbations are properly planned and not allowed to become too large.

An investigation by a team of psychological research workers of forty senior British business executives during a search for an incentive scheme to make them work harder supports this belief. The head of the investigating team, Mr. William Schlackman, who was born in America, said that the results had come as a shock to him. More than half of the executives had only one ambition: not to work at all. 'They would rather retire as gentlemen farmers if they had the means than end up as chairman of the group, in effect rating a sporting squire superior to a captain of industry.' Apart from this, the serried and mostly stationary motor cars full of families packed together like their conveyances to be seen on the main highways at weekends and holiday time are pathetic evidence of the desire of all classes to escape from their urban boxes and be reunited with nature. What is needed is a balance between urban and rural life.

It is suggested, therefore, that any manager who needs to improve his industrial relations could do much worse than investigate the possibilities of linking his industry and his workers with the countryside. If this is not possible, there is no reason why an industrial society should not achieve stability and contentment through the establishment of its own values and culture, if it can be understood that these will be self-defeating if they are wholly material; that the race for pelf has no end, no ultimate or interim satisfaction if it is that alone. It has of course a part to play, for it is an important incentive to much useful progress.

Although we are not here deeply concerned with the technical efficiency of management, it must not be forgotten that this in itself makes a major contribution to happiness and contentment. The creation of wealth and economic strength is impossible without it. What is avowed is that it is very far from enough. If management and men comprehend this and act upon it, the resulting technical performance will be far better. This is not as cynical as it may sound; there is nothing intrinsically wrong with good technical performance.

A need for two types of mind in management was postulated by

Professor G. L. S. Shackle of Liverpool University in a presidential address to the economics section of the British Association meeting in Nottingham in September, 1966. One type was the truth seeker or scientist. Management had been deeply and rightly sold on mathematical methods. Programming even himself as if he were a computer, the trained manager of this type could see ahead of him 'the one right answer'. But industry also needed the poet-architect adventurer who saw a landscape inexhaustibly rich in suggestions and materials for making things, whether business, history, or 'the complex, delicate, existential system called a business'. The radial as well as the axial type of mind was needed in industry. Technical efficiency must not therefore be the only value. If every man and woman is to be judged solely by this standard those who do not match up to it will either fall by the wayside and become burdens on the state welfare services, or criminals, or will unite to protect themselves, which union will include many of those who are technically efficient. The atmosphere of insecurity will bind them together. At best, they will act as a brake on the efficiency of the state as a whole; at worst, all will become subversive.

The fact is that there are very few people who are not able, properly handled, to make a contribution. The sloppy shorthand typist whose spelling is indifferent, whose punctuality is the subject of frequent rebukes, who is nevertheless the active leader of the division's drama club, may have a value to the company's morale and cohesion which quite outweighs her typing errors. The elderly little clerk, who is always in a muddle with his invoices, henpecked in the office as at home, may be the company's staunchest supporter in the local pub— the only place where he feels 'big.' Knowing his weaknesses, and at the same time that the company will always look after him, he may do more for its public image than the consultants whose retainer is £10,000 a year.

Humour is highly antipathetic to all forms of subversion, including communism. Who ever heard a communist laugh, except in the sense of *schadenfreude*?

A man's (or woman's) life does not begin and end at the office, but it is strongly linked with his home and other activities. His reward from it dictates in most cases the kind of home he lives in, the way his wife and children are clothed and the latter are educated, the holidays they have and the car they drive in, the friends they can afford to mix with. Likewise, the attitude to and support of the family in his work will have an important bearing on his efficiency and success. An extravagant or socially ambitious wife may drive a man not only to technical inefficiency through worry and debt, but to alcohol and crime at the firm's expense. In the case of a working wife, the co-operation of the family, their help with the housework and encouragement, will sustain her in the office. The invaluable secretary's fiancé is also of interest to the office. It is, after all, partly his attitude which will determine whether she stays on after marriage and returns after childbearing.

There is, therefore, a considerable interdependence between office or factory efficiency and home and social life. The one can play a vital part in the success and well-being of the other. It is not therefore logical that they should be entirely segregated, as they so often are in the larger industrial organisations.

It is postulated, then, that office and private life are not and should not be separate organisms, but sections of one. It follows that the manager's interest should not be confined to the man's technical performance in the office, for this may depend on outside factors and difficulties, which he can influence and rectify by advice and help, including financial help. The fact that he takes an interest in the man beyond his mere performance will of itself be valuable, provided of course that it stops short of inquisitiveness, or undue material coddling which can be no substitute for the spiritual security which is usually what is really needed.

The point here is one of the importance of taking a healthy interest in employees. As a 1966 report of the Ministry of Labour entitled *Attitudes to Efficiency*, published by HMSO, says:

*'One of the outcomes of the well-known experiments conducted in the 1930s by Elton Mayo[1] was to show that improvements in the output of some of the groups studied were not related to improved physical conditions (e.g., better lighting) but simply to the fact that the workers concerned knew that they were being studied and that this gave an interest to their work which was otherwise lacking. The moral of this seems to be that managements should take a real interest in their employees and what they are doing, and let it be known that they do.'*

The manager ought to know, and if he does not he must be taught it, that the establishment of good human and industrial relations is also inseparable from culture, that 'the great aim of culture is the aim of setting ourselves to ascertain what perfection is and to make it prevail'. This is not only a matter of works cricket teams and piped 'Music While You Work', but also the encouragement and development of artistic gifts and talents in his workers, of being himself

---

1. The Hawthorne Experiments. See also p. 107 of this chapter.

well-read, well-informed. Not every manager has the time or inclination to become a student of the classics or a part-time opera singer, but he can learn to be sympathetic to and even appreciative of those who have such talents and wish to indulge them. He may be able to encourage the formation of appropriate groups by allotting money for such things as libraries, record players and the like, but he must remember that money alone for these activities is not enough; he and his colleagues must also take an interest.

When management, staff and workers live close to the factory it is no great burden for management to take part or take interest in extramural activities, or to meet in informal circumstances the men and women who work for them, and their families. But this becomes much more difficult in such commuting places as London, where employees may live sixty or seventy miles apart or away from the factory or office. Drama groups and the like, after an initial burst of enthusiasm, tend to wither away for lack of support and managerial interest. It is easy to understand. After a busy day the middle-aged manager, for example, is apt to be tired. He may have as much as an hour-and-a-half's journey home before him. He may see little enough of his home in any case, due to travel around the country and overseas. But the importance of communal activity in an office or factory of a kind not related to the particular job, where management, staff and workers meet on different terms, must not be underestimated. The difficulties are just an additional challenge; removal to the provinces may provide an answer in some cases, lunch-time activities in others.

So the manager must be much more than technically efficient. He must have a high sense of responsibility for those who work for him and this must be complete and not partial. To this end he could conceive of his office and factory as a kind of second home for those who work for him and of himself as a kind of father figure, to whom trivial and serious problems can be brought with and in confidence. Whether these are personal or directly concerned with the office is irrelevant, because both will affect performance. Personnel and welfare departments can be of great assistance in these functions, but these are, or should be, advisory services and the final responsibility is that of line management alone.

What is asked of a manager is, in effect, a high sense of duty towards those whom he manages. He must be prepared to share their hardships (such as night-shift), partake in their activities, and be a man of broad humanity.

This may seem to be asking a great deal of an already overburdened profession. But such dedication as is demanded will surely save more problems than it creates. A manager is entitled to some cushioning against the wear and tear which it demands; a better income, a higher standard of living, perhaps a chauffeur-driven car, are reasonable rewards for the burden he carries. But it must never be forgotten that a primary purpose of such cushioning is to give him more time and strength for his job, which includes the wellbeing of those whom he controls and should also serve.

The communal task of the manager in countering espionage and subversion is to care for and care about his employees in much the same way as did the good squire and his wife for their tenants and workers. This means the creation of a healthy and happy social atmosphere in and around his domain. And this cannot be achieved without his influence amongst the workforce, in the families, and in the decisions and policies of local and national government. In this way the personality of the manager, of management, becomes reflected in the workforce and a distinctive ethos is created. Thus are laid the foundations of a culture. Provided that the manager and his firm are technically efficient, such attitudes will also result in greater productivity, which is in itself a further counter to subversion. When he hears his employees are turning down other jobs, saying 'Of course, the money's better, but I'm happy here and don't want to change', he will know he has succeeded in his job, and, more important, for the nation.

Such espionage and subversion as are not strangled at birth by the vitality of the organism must be discerned and prevented by application of the appropriate techniques, and these are discussed in the next three chapters.

# CHAPTER 12

## Intelligence as a Management Aid

'Intelligence is the soul of public business', said Daniel Defoe in his *Scheme for General Intelligence* which he sent to Mr. Speaker Harley in 1704 (Appendix I). He was of course referring to its importance in the art of government, but what he said applies today with equal force to the complexes and corporations of an industrial society, on which most of us rely for our livelihood and Britain depends for her survival as a great power.

For the manager to carry out the task which his calling lays upon him, especially in regard to the communal responsibility discussed in the previous chapter, he must know what is going on. Unless he does he will be unable to detect the insidious approach of subversion or espionage, or prevent the development of conditions which favour their growth.

If a manager's career in industry were planned along the lines suggested by Management Selection Limited, there would be three stages in his development which would bring him, if he were worthy of it, to the top position. The first stage, which can be taken as being roughly from the time he joins a firm on leaving school or university for about ten years onwards, consists in the acquisition of experience in depth of one discipline. In this time he is learning one or other branch of the management trade, and if he is wise, trying to be better at it than the next man.

The second stage, which may last seven or eight years, is the diversification of this discipline into other interdependent fields. For example, had his first period been concerned with sales, the second might be in sales or service management or advertising. The third stage would perhaps be marketing, a co-ordinating function, leading to his translation into the general management sphere and ultimately to consideration for the highest positions, including managing director.

To some extent a junior manager can perform his job adequately with little knowledge of the world outside so long as he is master of

117

his particular craft. If he is a salesman, he must know his product and how to sell it, and perhaps how to service it; at this stage he would certainly not need to know much about the world outside his sales parish. Even if he became a home branch manager in the second stage, he would still only need to be locally orientated, although if he became an export representative or manager during this time he would obviously need to know a great deal more about the world outside.

At the marketing stage, he would certainly need rapidly to broaden his outlook and this might be a great deal easier if he had acquired the habit earlier. It is apparent that, in fact, very few young men and women do this in our age of increasing specialization; how many of them really read the papers properly, and include a weekly journal or two, or go to public lectures or night schools with the object of developing their knowledge of the world in which they live and work?

It is, however, when he is on the threshold of general managership that the breadth of his knowledge and powers of leadership will determine whether or not he is to be numbered amongst the great. If he is to be, he must take cognisance of political, economic, social, technical and financial trends and events and be able to estimate their likely consequence to his business.

For example, it could be argued that the following are some of the more significant trends which affect the manager of today:

*Full employment.* The main political parties are in general committed to a policy of full employment which, however desirable socially, has amongst others these effects: higher wage levels; the manager's position in labour negotiations is weakened; he may be coerced into employing more labour than he really requires; modernisation may be delayed.

*A decline in authority.* This is in part due to full employment and also to social change over which the manager has very little control, but it means a new attitude on his part to those under him, whether in the office or on the shop floor, if he is to extract the greatest possible productivity, maintain a good service and keep to delivery dates.

*The growing influence of consumer associations.* Nowadays a business can be seriously damaged if its products receive adverse reports made impartially by such associations.

*The increasing rate of technological change.* This can affect the whole policy of a business, for with it comes quick obsolescence; thus it may strike at the basic security and concept of what was hitherto a comfortable and steady progression along tried and proved lines.

A general manager who was not aware of or did not understand the significance of such trends and developments would almost certainly be unable to form an accurate judgment, which is the basis for correct decision. He must, therefore, be well informed and in close touch with government thought and actions; what happens today in now less remote China may easily affect his business tomorrow. Professor Tabatoni, the French management expert, in an address to the British Institute of Management several years ago, contrasted the British manager unfavourably in this respect with his highly success-ful French opposite number, and suggested that this was a major factor in Britain's continuing economic weakness.

He must above all things, then, be *au courant*, that is, he must know what is going on in his business and in the environment of its activity which, for practical purposes today in a business of any size, is virtually the whole world, and he must continue to know it.

To be *au courant* in a world glutted with information of all kinds, in many forms and of vastly different degrees of reliability and accuracy, implies an intelligence process.

\*     \*     \*     \*

It has already been pointed out that journalism and espionage perform roughly the same task (p. 14). It would perhaps be more accurate to say that the reporter and the spy perform a similar service, i.e., collection of information, by basically different means, but often in similar circumstances, e.g., without the consent of the owner. At editorial level part of the task is similar to the intelligence process—sifting, assessing, collating. But here real differences emerge, too. The final presentation of newspaper news must take into account the editorial line; the news must appear in print next day; it must not offend the law of libel, or the precepts of the Press Council. The intelligence officer must ensure unbiased accuracy and the careful separation of fact from comment and opinion; the grading of sources according to past reliability and so on. He does not normally publish his information, there are usually less severe deadlines, and his papers are often privileged.

It is generally agreed that in addition to his appreciation of the value of intelligence as such, Harley was one of the first statesmen to understand the power of the press both for its delving and influencing abilities. He used Defoe not only as an intelligence agent, but also as a public relations officer to put over the government angle, and the latter's periodical reports show considerable assiduousness on his part in this regard. Defoe's versatility was further demonstrated after he had ceased to work for Harley and the Tories were out of office;

he succeeded in making peace with the Whig leaders and they found a job for him which only he could do. It was a new kind of secret service work and a good account of it is given by Professor James Sutherland in his pamphlet *Defoe* published by Longmans Green & Co.:

*'Although the Tories were out of office, and the Jacobites in a hopeless minority, their various newspapers were still an active source of annoyance, and even of some danger, to the new government. What Defoe now did, with the approval of the Whig Secretary of State, was to pose as a Tory under the displeasure of the government, and get himself a job, as a translator of foreign news, on the most virulent of all the Tory papers, Mist's Weekly Journal. As this experienced journalist became more and more necessary to Mist, he appears to have got the running of the paper into his hands, and to have used his position to tone down its asperities, or, as he put it himself to 'disable' and 'enervate' it, 'so as to do no mischief, or give any offence to the government'. This remarkable piece of double-crossing appears to have worked successfully for several years'.*

The foregoing is of course an excellent example of subversive activity. It is as if left-wing sympathisers secretly infiltrated the editorial staff of the *Daily Express* and insidiously negatived its policies.

*     *     *     *

The main essentials of any system of intelligence are covered by Defoe's scheme (extracts from which are quoted in Appendix I). He considered both external and internal intelligence. At that time, 1704, central government had not been fully accepted, even in England, and in the extremities—in Scotland, for example, there was considerable restlessness: the Act of Union was not ratified by the Scottish parliament until 1707.

Defoe's first point, and every intelligence officer would agree with him, was that there must be adequate money. As he points out, too little means in effect that nothing is done; 'the money which is given for it is lost'.

Next, the service must give wide coverage—'The Secretary's office should be an abridgement of all Europe'. Europe was in those days virtually all that mattered in the external intelligence sense. For internal purposes Defoe's first requirement was that there must be sound records of the interests and character of all persons of significance in town and country, of clergy and of laity. In particular as regards the clergy, there must be records of the Dissenters, that is, clergy who, in 1662, two years after the Restoration, left the Church of England rather than submit to the conditions of the Act of Uniformity, and those who sympathised with them, and who represented a considerable political problem in Defoe's time. It is noteworthy that in regard to the clergy Defoe, himself a dissenter, thought that the records should include a statement of their morals—always a factor in security. There must be also records of political parties, of their strengths in each area and their activities. The records should include the names of people throughout the country who could be trusted if necessary in an emergency. It is again of interest that Defoe considered men of great personal estate were more likely to be amongst the most trustworthy—a realistic if cynical view.

In extension of the foreign intelligence aspect, Defoe stresses the need for equally adequate records of important persons, including favourites, of every court in Europe; of their military strength and military personalities, financial states, methods of government and, very important, 'so just and authentic and regularly amended as alterations happen that by this he (e.g., Harley) may duly estimate their strength, judge of their interests and proceedings and treat with them accordingly'. In addition there should be regular demi-official correspondence with opposite numbers and the other people of standing throughout Europe. Defoe thought that £100,000 per annum should be spent on this item. He also thought that good intelligence could contribute much to good relations with Scotland and said that he would like to submit further suggestions on this point. Defoe also refers to a Turkish book on espionage, which the author has so far been unable to trace, which suggested to Defoe an espionage network in France based on Paris, Toulon, Brest and Dunkirk. He concludes this important passage by reminding Harley of the great importance of security and illustrating it with references to his own experience and to the merit of Cardinal Richelieu in this respect.

It must be borne in mind that Defoe's main overt purpose in this brief was to show how a man, particularly Harley, could gain and maintain a position of political power, but there is little doubt that this is a remarkable document by any standards and a sound guide for any intelligence purpose.

\*     \*     \*     \*

A main function of business intelligence today is to discern the present truth from the imbroglio of printed paper and statistics with which the modern manager is confronted and assaulted, and which may inhibit his proper functions. For this reason alone, a number of large organisations now boast intelligence departments whose principal job it is to sift the mass of information and disentangle and deduce that which is relevant to the conduct of their business.

An interesting case in point is the Greater London Council, whose task is to administer ten million people living in a concentrated metropolis. The Royal Commission which recommended the setting up of this authority fully appreciated the complexity of its function and said in its report: 'The first requirement of all is that the Council for Greater London should set up a first-class Intelligence Department'.

Section 71 of the London Government Act, 1963, implementing this recommendation of the Royal Commission imposed on the council the obligation of establishing 'an organisation for the purpose of conducting, or assisting in the conducting of, investigations into, and the collection of information relating to, any matters concerning Greater London or any part thereof, and making, or assisting in the making of, arrangements whereby any such information and the results of any such investigation are made available to any authority concerned with local government in Greater London, any government department or the public.' The General Purposes Committee of the Greater London Council in its Report Number One said that these functions corresponded to the Royal Commission's summary of the tasks of their proposed 'Intelligence Department' as being to collect, collate and disseminate information relevant to the purpose of local government functions in Greater London.

The General Purposes Committee envisaged that the intelligence unit to be formed would not be a department with executive responsibilities, but rather 'an academic service organisation working in a field closely related to policy'. The General Purposes Committee stressed the importance of the standing of the proposed intelligence unit and said, 'the director of the unit and the unit itself must be recognised outside the council service as of the highest standing'. They were concerned also that the director of the unit should be in a position where his voice would be heard, and they therefore recommended that during the formative period, at any rate, the unit should be attached to the department of the Clerk to the Council and should, through him, be responsible to the General Purposes Committee. They suggested that for the initial period no detailed definition of the unit's precise function should be made, and indeed that the director of the unit should be 'appointed and charged as a first task with surveying and assessing the field within which the unit should work'.

They saw three functions for it. The first would be to establish a library of statistics and information about Greater London and publish a regular series of London statistics. From this would emerge the second function of being fully informed about past and current research fields in which research could be usefully undertaken and possible agencies through which research should be carried out. The third main function would be to be expert in statistical and research methods. The unit would then be able to advise on how investigations should be tackled without itself necessarily undertaking them.

They also foresaw an important liaison function, whereby designated research officers might be placed in the service departments with the responsibility for maintaining contact with the intelligence unit.

Any large business today, it is suggested, needs a similar organization to that set up by the Greater London Council if it is to function with the maximum effectiveness and economy. Failure to have accurate and up-to-date information will often result in deployment of the wrong resources in the wrong place at the wrong time. In the majority of firms today, intelligence is a haphazard affair. How many of them make continuous studies of all the factors that relate to their business and, having done so, co-ordinate them so as to produce a coherent picture from which the managing director can take the right decision and carry his board colleagues with him?

The bulk of the information needed to build up an intelligence picture comes from the press. Many executives read one paper fairly thoroughly, but experience shows that it is necessary to read at least four to obtain a complete and balanced coverage. The popular press is often the first to get really 'hot' news.

To supplement casual reading, companies often employ press cutting services, but these, excellent though they usually are, can only operate to specific briefs. A managing director does not always know exactly what he wants; a particular idea which he could develop for the good of his company may be sparked off by some apparently irrelevant triviality which simply could not be covered by a brief to a cutting service. But a trained intelligence staff officer well and truly in the mind of his managing director, as he must be, would be able to ensure that everything conceivably relevant or of interest was brought to notice, having been properly collated.

Technical intelligence is far too serious a business to be left to the technicians. Technical research and development, as the government and the aviation industry have found out, absorb enormous sums of money and are apt to become ends in themselves and proceed regardless of their true purpose or economic viability. They are also apt to be concerned with producing, say, bigger and better oil heaters without ever concerning themselves as to whether oil heaters are going to be needed at all in the future. If the managing director is to ensure that the company's financial resources are correctly deployed and the greatest advantage taken of technical development, he must ensure continuing conceptual analysis. For this he must be broadly aware of technical development generally, not only of that within his own firm, and he has not the time or perhaps the skill to study the technical press himself. The intelligent layman can keep abreast of the most important scientific developments by reading *New Scientist*. This excellent journal performs for him much the same function as Professor Lindemann (later Lord Cherwell) did for Churchill: 'Lindemann could decipher the signals from the (scientific) experts on the far horizons and explain to me in lucid homely terms what the issues were'.

As far as associated companies (which term includes subsidiaries, trade investments and consultants) are concerned, the managing director will, of course, get periodical information from his opposite number, but this will not always give him what may be described as the 'feel' of the firm concerned; to get this he needs lateral contact at lower level rather as described in the GLC concept. An example of the importance of this form of intelligence occurred when a substantial company employed engineering consultants. These, as is often the case, were called in for a long period to advise on particular problems and were given access to the firm's factories and information. In the meantime, the chairman of the engineering consultants was appointed to a non-executive seat on the board of the firm's principal competitors and, although it is not suggested that anything improper took place, there could be a very great temptation for the chairman to make use of information acquired through consultancy. In any case, no interest was declared and the matter only came to light through good intelligence. Similar situations can occur with overseas agents who may quite legitimately act also as agents for competitors, either in the same place or in different places. They will not always openly declare this and there is probably no reason why they should; the information is, however, relevant and will only be discovered accidentally, unless deliberate intelligence is used.

The need for market intelligence is on the whole recognized, but except in a few very large concerns this is apt to be haphazard for long periods, until some special need arises when outside experts are called in. It would be far better for business for continuous watch to be maintained as well by the firm itself. This should indicate exactly when to exploit the resources of professional market research agencies, whose experts can operate more efficiently from the intelligence base provided. Indeed, as is clearly brought out in *The Marketing of Industrial Products*, edited by Aubrey Wilson and published by Hutchinson of London in 1965, a better return will be obtained from the money spent with the market research agency as the internal researcher or intelligence officer is in a position to isolate the true research needs and to provide a detailed research brief. If he undertakes the desk research, the agency can concentrate on field interviewing, which it is not normally possible for the intelligence officer/internal researcher to undertake.

The importance of continuous watch as a market research indicator is illustrated in the article entitled *Marketing Myopia* by Theodore Levitt, a professor of the Harvard Business School, in this same book: *'The railroads did not stop growing because the need for passenger and freight transportation declined. That grew. The railroads are in trouble not because the need was filled by others (cars, trucks, aeroplanes, even telephones), but because it was not filled by the railroads themselves. They let others take customers away from them because they assumed themselves to be in the railroad business rather than the transportation business. The reason they defined their industry incorrectly was because they were railroad-oriented instead of transportation-oriented; they were product-oriented instead of customer-oriented.'*

Customers and clients are really part of the firm just as much as shareholders. The wise managing director will be continually aware of the way in which they regard his firm. If some of them are discontented through bad service, bad deliveries or indifferent products, the managing director is usually the last person to be told by those whose fault it is. When he learns, it is often too late to make the necessary changes.

Internal intelligence may be regarded by some as controversial; people are apt to think of it as internal spying. But the spread of the civil service, the recent involvement of virtually the whole population in military and government spheres, and the advent of larger companies has encouraged a belief in the use of set channels of reporting, stage by stage, up and down the management ladder. This system does not always produce the truth, which is apt to be varnished or garnished at every stage; the meaning of the final product being often quite different from the original. Anyone who doubts this is advised to try the old nursery game of passing a reasonably involved verbal message through, say, ten well-educated adults and then comparing the original and final message. The result is usually astonishing. It can be made more so if each person is allowed to add his or her comments on the substance of the message. If this happens in a game where the participants can be expected to be detached, it is not difficult to imagine the distortions which occur when there is, as there often is, subjectivity at some or all of the reporting stages. Personal ambition, fear of passing on unpleasant truths damaging to the person who does so, malice, preconceived ideas, may result in unconscious as well as deliberate twisting of the facts. This problem is well known to those who work in large institutions where it has been described as 'The Rule of Ten', or, less elegantly, 'The ten times "fiddle"'. It must be stressed that in the Civil Service this problem is well understood and there is an exceptionally high standard of re- porting, between highly educated, highly trained and highly princi- pled men and women. To this day, Her Majesty's Ambassadors sign their dispatches 'With the highest regard for the truth'. Nevertheless, as has already been pointed out elsewhere in this book, great men often use direct lines; the 'J' Service of Field-Marshal Montgomery and the 'personal representation' system of Sir Winston Churchill are examples.

A good intelligence officer will by communications like those en- visaged in the Greater London Council plan ensure that his master has an accurate internal picture of the firm and there is no need for it to be done secretly. It can be made palatable to the 'usual channels' by tact, the establishment of good personal relations, and by demon- strating its usefulness to them as well. If they have nothing to hide they have nothing to worry about, and if they have, an intelligence service is even more justified. Its existence will encourage the truth.

A system of intelligence can be a major management instrument for the prevention and detection of espionage. Whilst it should not be involved in the employment of counter-spies, it should be able to give early warning of subversive activity in any trade unions which have members in the company—careful collation of press re- ports will often indicate this, as for example that in the Amalgam- ated Engineering Union (see Appendix G)—and to detect significant internal unrest, which is often the early stage or breeding ground of espionage-borne subversive or criminal activity.

It may be argued that line management or personnel departments might perform this latter function equally well. But often subversion, for example, only becomes apparent from the picture obtained by knitting together small scraps of information by a mind trained in the intelligence art. Both line manager and personnel officer have im- portant operational and administrative tasks, and intelligence like security is in the end a whole time occupation. Personnel officers engaged in the staff and labour relations fields could not be associated in any way with intelligence, or for that matter, security, without severe prejudice to their real work, which would seem to many to be mere cover for spying (see also Chapter 14, p. 143). This is not to suggest that the information they glean in the course of their proper activity will not be of high importance to the intelligence picture.

How far should intelligence go in its pursuit of information about competitors, their plans and processes? This question was put (in relation to market research) to Aubrey Wilson (see p. 125) in a recent broadcast interview, and his reply sums up the position (see also Appendix L):

'*Interviewer—Peter Darling*

*Firms in the market research field are occasionally approached with somewhat sinister propositions which would involve over-stepping the line from the legitimate to the downright dishonest. Most can spot such a customer a mile off. Mr. Aubrey Wilson, Managing Director of Industrial Market Research Ltd., gets about half a dozen doubtful enquiries a year.*

*Aubrey Wilson*

*Very often, people ask questions, in all innocence, "can you tell us", this is a very tricky question, "what the turnover of such and such a company is?" Now these figures are not published and they are usually one of the most highly kept secrets within a company. We would not attempt to go out and get this information, except by asking the company itself. The company almost certainly would refuse to give it. On the other hand, you can make some jolly good estimates by numbers employed, by the types of products which are made; you can even do it sometimes by the number of lorries they have. There are good correlations which will enable you to make deductions which are absolutely legitimate: but to go and get it, if you like, out of the Chairman's top righthand drawer, would be absolutely illegitimate. But, I do want to make the point that of the enquiries we get, which we would regard as "espionage", almost all of them are innocent in themselves. They have not realised that this sort of information just cannot be got.*'

The correct answer to the information problem of management (as was suggested in Chapter 1, p. 7) may be the combining of the intelligence and public relations functions as Defoe did. Unfortunately PR itself has an indifferent public image. In the minds of many businessmen it is almost irretrievably associated with princes and pop stars, plush Mayfair offices, and an eternal round of champagne and caviar, the entree to the latter being a retainer measured in thousands of guineas, which is, they think, but a sample of the final cost.

The true role of PR should be commercial diplomacy, and if it had got off to that sort of start, with ambassadors of the calibre and integrity of professional diplomats, its image might be far better than it is. It should be adduced that a cardinal function of an ambassador in the Foreign Service is the provision of intelligence about the country where he exercises his functions. Here, then, is an example of successful combination of the diplomatic and intelligence functions.

Considerable pressure has been brought to bear in recent years to make the British Foreign Service more commercially minded—a necessity perhaps if our economy is to be strong. It is suggested that a corresponding move to make business public relations more like an embassy in both the diplomatic and intelligence senses would mark an even greater advance.

The whole business intelligence process could be materially improved if the City of London were to modernise and centralise its market information mechanism. It could attain a new dominance by becoming the world centre of economic and financial intelligence, and be a main means by which Britain regained her influence and prosperity. An interesting step in this direction has been taken by a firm called Centre-File Limited. This organisation employs a computer and is an information bank for use by stockbrokers, to whom it is connected by direct line. In this stockbrokers can store their information and withdraw it at will. This development was described in *New Scientist* (Vol. 32, p. 366) by David Fishlock. This article and an accompanying editorial pointed out the dangers which would arise if such an organisation fell into the wrong hands. The combined information of the principal stockbrokers on the stock market as a whole might be worth many millions of pounds to speculators. It is also true that such a collation could be used for political purposes, including subversive political purposes. No doubt the future will see a growth of computerised information banks which properly controlled could be of immense service to industry and commerce.

One approach to the problem of control would be to consult ASLIB, the independent but Government-sponsored information organisation. This is the principal British source of authoritative information and advice on the systematic acquisition and use of specialised information, and has a worldwide clientele and reputation for efficiency and comprehensiveness.

Finally, and of more immediate relevance to this book, it must again be stressed that an intelligence-cum-diplomatic service should be of immense value as a counter to subversion. In the first place, it should be able to detect subversive influences within the firm. Secondly, it can help to demolish them by exposing them to the light of day and the assault of the facts—precisely as Defoe did in his embassies for Harley.

# CHAPTER 13

## Twenty-one Principles of Defence against Industrial Espionage

Although security is a science it is, like economics, a practical one and thus the principles which guide its various branches are not scientific laws, whose observance produces a definite result, nor are they like the rules of a game, failure to comply with which brings a certain penalty. They illustrate methods and ideas which have been successful in many cases, and in general provide sure foundations for the establishment of a security system. Ignorance or disregard of them is apt to be dangerous, and will often be unnecessarily expensive in time and money.

*First principle: protective measures must be so designed that when documentary information is stolen or copied or photographed without authority the fact becomes known as quickly as possible.* Most of the techniques which an owner may use to protect cash and jewellery are also appropriate to the protection of secrets. But when cash, for example, is stolen it is usually missed very soon afterwards; a hue and cry can quickly be raised and it may be recovered in whole or in part at any time after the event.

This is not necessarily true of the loss of information. A document can be secretly photographed *in situ*, or it may be removed for external photography and returned later without the owner's knowledge. The first an owner of information may know of its loss is the appearance of his new idea in a product manufactured by a rival company. Even then, he may not suspect espionage, for it is perfectly possible for another firm's research and development to have progressed independently along the same lines as his own. Perhaps the first espionage indicator will be falling profits.

There is another difference: almost all cash risks are insurable, but loss of information usually is not, mainly on account of its incalculability. And if the loss is not detected, there is obviously no possibility of a claim.

*Second principle: the initial breach of security of information occurs when it becomes known that a secret exists.* The existence of a large cash target cannot usually be disguised. Cash is needed for wage payments at specific times on specific days; banks always keep cash reserves, as do post offices. But secret plans are not necessarily self-advertising. While a board of directors may discuss many confidential subjects as a matter of routine, it only occasionally has plans whose premature revelation or leakage to rivals could be classed as a disaster. It is at such times, however, that some boards tend to take special and all too obvious precautions; an air of mystery pervades the office; a file normally held in open registry is impounded by the managing director and locked by him personally in his safe; or a mysterious folder is passed round from director to director by hand of director; the meticulous secretary who attempts to tidy the folder away is sharply rebuked by a boss who has 'never spoken to me like that before'; the chauffeur who normally couldn't care less where he drives the chairman is told not to mention where he has been, or even to make a wrong entry in his journey book. By these and other means attention is attracted; it becomes apparent that 'something is going on,' and speculation begins. Thus is an espionage target identified and the spy's task simplified.

*Third principle: protection of information is the responsibility of the owner.* It is important to state the responsibilities. While the taking of measures to detect[1] criminals is the responsibility of the police, although in cases of political crime they will be assisted by the Security Service, the protection of property is a primary responsibility of the owner. He is expected to lock up his valuables and secure his home against intrusion.

*Fourth principle: the best person to organize protection against industrial espionage is the owner of the information.* As a corollary, efficient security is closely connected with maximum interest and the person who has the maximum interest in security is the owner. There is therefore a limit to the amount of security delegation which is permissible. It is not enough to buy a good safe, to install a good burglar alarm, or to engage a good guard company, and leave it at that. The owner in the end knows best how to protect his property and permissible degrees of interference with operational efficiency. He can achieve the best results by getting sound professional advice from security experts in the various fields, but only he can say what is the right system having regard to the whole situation, and only he can

1. Burglar alarms are, of course, detective in that they are designed to give early warning of illegal intrusion. But they are principally protective since their main purpose is to summon help to protect the property or information with which they are concerned. For this reason and because they must be sited within his premises they are the responsibility of the owner.

make it work continuously which, of course, it must.

*Fifth principle: security measures should be commensurate with the threat.* The amount of time, effort and money which may be justifiably spent on security is governed by the risks to which the target is likely to be exposed. This assessment of the threat is a highly professional matter. Suffice it to say here that it is generally compounded of the value of the target, its marketability, its accessibility, and the nature, extent and skill of criminal and espionage activity. If security is carried to an absurd degree it can have effects more adverse than the loss of the information or property it was designed to protect. At the same time, inadequate measures may be dangerous (compare the ninth principle).

An immensely important extension of this principle therefore is that on no account should information which can be released or published without damage to the concern (or the state) be subjected to security measures. Not only will this be unnecessarily irksome to staff and thus tend to give security a bad image (see the eighth principle) but free exchange of as much information as possible is vital to human progress. Neither science nor art can grow in secrecy. An excess of security zeal might spread rapidly in industry and be injurious to legitimate commercial information services such as ASLIB (see Chapter 12, p. 128). It would promote espionage rather than discourage it.

*Sixth principle: concentration of risk.* In pursuit of the foregoing principle and also of security efficiency, vital information and material should be concentrated into as small an area as possible. There are two facets: the first is the classification of risks; this will show where maximum security effort must be made, and also where no security effort can be justified. The second facet is the creation of a secure area within the premises. This, in addition to making physical protection more economical, enables restrictions of access to be reduced as far as possible.

*Seventh principle: the criterion of access is need.* This principle is often expressed vernacularly as 'the need to know and the need to go'. What 'need to know' means in the context of this chapter is that no one should be given secret information unless it is necessary for the purpose of their duties. Put another way, secret information must be confined to as few people as efficient operation allows. The French have a saying, '*secret de trois, secret de tous,*' which means that no secret can exist if more than two are privy to it. It is clearly impossible in many cases to restrict secret information to two people, but it is a fact that the likelihood of a breach of security increases out of all proportion to the numbers who know it. No firm rule as to the maximum number can be made, but experience shows that after twenty know it a secret becomes extremely difficult to keep. Nevertheless, in highly disciplined organisations, secrets have been kept when known by many more people, sometimes by accident, as the following illustration will show.

It has never been revealed how many allied persons directly concerned had to be told the details of Operation 'Overlord'[1], but in the scale and nature of the operation it must have been necessary for several hundreds if not thousands to know. The secret was, however, very well kept except that the plans did reach the Germans via the British Embassy in Turkey through Operation 'Cicero', in which the Ambassador's valet was able to photograph Foreign Office documents giving the full details of 'Overlord'. It is hard to see how the duties of Ambassador in Turkey required him to know the exact detail of the plan, especially in regard to where the landings were to take place, and if *principle seven* had been obeyed by the Foreign Office the loss could never have occurred. Luckily, German Intelligence believed the information to be a 'plant' and in the result nothing was lost.

The second part of the principle—'the need to go'—is that in addition to being denied information which they do not need to know, people should not be given physical access to the area where the information is stored, produced or worked on. To get near the information is half the battle for the spy. The author recalls an occasion on which it was his duty to inspect the physical security of a certain cipher office. He was accompanied on his inspection by a very high-ranking service officer. The corporal in charge of the cipher office had a list of five people who were allowed regular access to that office. The author's name had been added for temporary access, but not that of the senior officer, whose duties did not require such access. The corporal allowed the author access, but was adamant, even under heavy pressure, in his refusal to admit the senior officer, for which he rightly received commendation in the inspecting officer's report. Need, not rank, is the criterion of access.

An important corollary to this principle is that those who do need to know or who are likely to find out, or who do come close to finding out, must be told the secret. Security is as likely to be breached by not telling persons in these categories as it is by telling some who do not need to know. Failure to observe this corollary may lead to widespread and possibly accurate speculation amongst people who may

1. The code name for the Allied landing in Normandy in 1944.

not understand the need for secrecy because they have not been told the reasons.

*Eighth principle: security must have a good image.* In a democratic society security is apt to be regarded as something sinister and un-welcome, savouring of totalitarian regimes. It is at its most effective in a democracy when all concerned in the organisation understand the reasons for such measures as are necessary and co-operate in the establishment and maintenance of those measures. If security is seen as the spy system of a mistrusting management, it will be almost bound to fail in its purpose. It must therefore be as sensible and open as possible and people must be encouraged to participate in making its working effective.

*Ninth principle: it is not one measure that will give security, but the sum of all practicable and possible measures.* Another way of stating this principle is 'defence in depth', but it is not so exact, as security at its best is not purely defensive. What it means is that all the *proved* security aids and techniques known, provided they are applicable and justified, should be used. It is evident, for example, that the greater the number of obstacles interposed between a potential in-truder and his target, the more difficult will it be for him and the more time will it take him to gain access. If in trying to negotiate them he unknowingly sets off an alarm bell which rings in the police station, he may well be caught in the act of intrusion. If there are alert guards, the risk of detection is increased or, at any rate, more time for, and care in, negotiating the obstacles is required. This is an important deterrent. At the same time, the number and type of aids which are used must be governed by practical considerations and obedience to the fifth security principle.

But not only should these various forms of protection be used, they should be co-ordinated so that they are mutually supporting and protective to each other in accordance with the *tenth principle—that which protects must itself be protected.* One interesting application of this principle is the anti-tamper system which is now a feature of sophisticated burglar alarms; another is the emergency re-locking de-vice fitted to high-quality safes—if the safe door, its lock or its bolts are attacked an additional set of locks automatically operates to jam the door in its frame. Burglar alarms can also support all types of barrier, and will often need barriers to protect them from inadvertent operation or interference.

This principle is similar to the military one of mutual support to prevent defeat in detail.

*Eleventh principle: a security system is as strong as its weakest link.*

This corresponds to the military principle of all-round defence. It is very little use fitting a good lock on the front door and an inferior one on the back door; or protecting every possible entrance to a building except a cable tunnel or air-conditioning duct, through which a man can crawl. Similarly, a target which moves from point to point must be adequately protected during the whole cycle—while in storage, ... use and in transit. It is pointless to keep an extremely valuable document in an excellent safe for part of the time, and at other times send it through the ordinary post to a place where it is kept in a wooden drawer.

*Twelfth principle: all security systems should contain an element of surprise for the spy or thief.* Nothing is more disconcerting to a carefully rehearsed intrusion plan than the unexpected. Frequent but irregular changes of routine may upset the spy's calculations, as may changes in positioning of equipment and changes of locks and combinations. Security is essentially defensive and the use of surprise is a means of wresting the initiative from the spy or illegal intruder.

The practice of this principle includes cover and deception plans, which are calculated stratagems designed to mislead or deceive the spy.

*Thirteenth principle: quality is more important than quantity.* A few good, well-trained guards are worth far more than any number of indifferent, untrained nightwatchmen. Similarly with equipment; cheap locks and safes are immediately noted by the skilled intruder and are just so much waste of time and money, for they serve to indicate a target rather than to protect it. High quality equipment in such depth and strength as is appropriate to the task in accordance with the ninth principle, concentrated on that which really matters, will produce the best answer. In security as in other spheres one usually gets what one pays for.

*Fourteenth principle: co-operation.* Security is considerably increased by co-operation with others who may be concerned. First and foremost there should be close liaison between those responsible for the security of an installation and the police. Protective security is complementary to the work of the police force—not a substitute for it. Most police forces have crime prevention departments or sections which offer impartial advice to corporate and individual owners of property on how to safeguard it against theft. The advice is skilled and free. Because industrial espionage as such is not yet a crime in the United Kingdom—it now is a crime in most states of the USA—the police crime prevention department may not be able to give specialised assistance in this field. But, as has been stressed already, the

F

techniques of protection of information differ very little from those used for the protection of cash, and therefore the advice will be of considerable value. The police are usually able and willing to put the owner in touch with reliable commercial specialists in any field of security. Alternatively, the British Security Industry Association[1] will assist.

Another instance where co-operation will increase security is through liaison with neighbouring firms and this is particularly true of firms sharing the same building. It is extremely difficult to protect part of a building when the remainder is in different ownership or occupation, and an overall security plan for the whole building will be more efficient and more economical. There are many examples in the history of theft where successful attacks have been launched from adjacent premises.

There should also be co-operation with the insurance company. Although the latter may not be directly concerned with the security of information, they will be interested in the security of valuables or property, much of whose protection will fall under the same system. Many insurance surveyors are skilled in the art of security and can assist in the construction of an effective overall security plan.

Responsible trade union officials may with advantage be brought into the security picture and can be of assistance in ensuring the co-operation of the work force.

*Fifteenth principle: maximum complicity.* Wherever it can be, the security system should be so designed that successful espionage will require the collaboration of two or more employees. This principle is intended to increase the difficulties of —

(1)   *the internal spy*—if he, for example, needs the collaboration of a third party before he can deduce the *whole* secret or before he can enter a given area, security will be greatly enhanced;

(2)   *the external agency*, who would attempt to subvert staff loyalty. It is often comparatively easy to persuade one man to be disloyal; it is much more difficult to find two in the same organisation, and any system which means that access to information cannot be gained without the collaboration of four people presents a most difficult target.

*Sixteenth principle—guilt must be pinned.* No security system can ever be perfect, but a good one will in the event of loss enable the responsibility for loss to be narrowed to a very small area, and a very few persons—preferably one or two. In addition to affording important assistance to those who investigate a loss, it will be a

1. 14 Tottenham Street, London, W.1.

strong deterrent to those who might contemplate taking part in espionage.

*Seventeenth principle: security tasks are usually irreconcilable with others.* The point of this principle is to stress that operational security duties do not easily mix with others. One often hears the argument put forward that when men are working at night in a particular installation there is no need for physical security measures because the building is occupied. The fact is that a man who is employed on some other duty is hardly likely to be alert on security matters. Likewise, a security guard or a security officer who is regarded as a general factotum to stoke the boilers or make the tea is unlikely to be effective in the security sense, and not the least of the reasons for this is the diminished status of security which these extramural duties imply. Another reason is that such routine duties usually have to be done at specific times and ill-intentioned persons will know that the security person is otherwise engaged at these times.

This principle is not intended to be applied to the security problems of departments or offices where the nature of the security duties is largely planning and advisory and the threat is not great. Part-time security officers or advisers are permissible in these circumstances.

*Eighteenth principle: while the strongest barrier should be that closest to the target, the most effective burglar alarm is that which gives the earliest warning.* High-quality protection is extremely expensive and it must therefore be concentrated on the target itself. It is the last line of defence, and when it has gone there is none other. It is quite impossible to construct an outer barrier of the same strength as a safe. At the same time, the sooner a burglar alarm is alerted, the sooner will help arrive, and therefore the best burglar alarms will be sited at some distance from the target with the idea that help will arrive before the last line of defence can be breached.

*Nineteenth principle: the effectiveness of delaying devices such as barriers should be measured in terms of the delay in time which they inflict on an intruder,* and the object should be to inflict a minimum of thirty minutes' delay. Experience has shown that the risk of detection increases with the time spent attacking a well protected target in roughly the following progressions: up to thirty minutes, an arithmetical progression; after thirty minutes, a geometrical progression. In other words, if barriers can be constructed to ensure at least thirty minutes' delay, the risk of detection and consequently the deterrent power of the obstacles are then very great indeed.

This principle may be viewed with some surprise by those who have read of weekend raids on banks when thieves secrete themselves in adjacent premises and can proceed to attack (often unsuccessfully) their target at leisure for 36 hours, or more at bank holidays. The fact of the matter is that to leave a bank safe or strongroom unprotected by supporting devices is utterly wrong in principle—quite contrary, for example, to the ninth, tenth and twelfth principles. Of course, high quality safes and strongroom doors do stand up to attack for much longer than thirty minutes, but a sound security system ought to ensure that no piece of physical equipment is left unsupported by any other security device for more than this period of thirty minutes. On the assumption that burglar alarms are used, as they should be, this gives rather more than adequate time for the police to arrive.

*Twentieth principle: the security system must be designed to prevent reconnaissance of the target.* It is impossible to make a sound plan for intrusion without detailed knowledge of the defences.

*Twenty-first principle: security measures (of whatever kind) must ultimately defer to the concept of human freedom.* There is no doubt that by the use of Gestapo-type methods a very high degree of security efficiency can be attained, but what is the use of this if the way of life that security is trying to protect is itself destroyed? Man-traps, poison gas and other potentially lethal or injurious methods cannot therefore be used in security.

These principles have been drawn up in relation to the security of documentary and verbal information, but they also apply, where the context allows, to the security of information in the form of models, samples and prototypes.

This list is not exhaustive; there are others of a subordinate nature, although, in special circumstances, the subordinate principles may assume a greater importance.

# CHAPTER 14

## Management's Defence System against Industrial Espionage — Part I: Physical

The Radcliffe Committee set up in 1962 to consider security of information procedures in the Public Service said—

'. . . *nothing is more important to effective security than the basic measures of physical security if well planned and consistently carried out. Safeguarding premises, documents, and cyphers and eliminating carelessness are of first importance.*'

\*     \*     \*     \*

When a managing director becomes conscious of a need for security of information, often as the result of a loss, his first thoughts may be of equipment—safes, locks, strongrooms. But a moment's reflection will show him that the finest of these are no use if someone forgets to lock them, or if the keys become compromised through carelessness, or if the information is stolen while out of its container or in transit.

There are far more losses of information or, for that matter, cash due to lack or failure of system than there are due to failures of good quality equipment. The first point therefore that management must understand is that the security *system* is of paramount importance; that the right equipment is a vital part of the security system, not a substitute for it.

There is no ready-made answer to a security of information problem and every system has to be tailored to the particular case. But the essential elements of all security systems, whether devised to combat theft, sabotage or espionage, are similar and are based on the principles enumerated in the previous chapter. They fall naturally into two parts— physical security and security of personnel. The latter is discussed in the next chapter.

PHYSICAL MEASURES

Control
Planning, advice and co-ordination
Security officers, men and dogs
Classification

Physical and documentary security: barriers
                                    gates and control of access
                                    locks and keys
                                    documents
                                    car parks
Intruder detection:                automatic alarms
                                    cameras and closed-circuit
                                      television
                                    security lighting
                                    technical intrusion
Installation and maintenance of equipment

CONTROL

Security is a technical advisory service and its control is therefore a responsibility of line management. The managing director is responsible to his board for the security of the firm. It is his duty—
to assess the threat
to appoint the necessary staff
to allocate sufficient resources
to approve the security system
to supervise personally the maintenance of psychological security

Security is an expensive and apparently unproductive overhead. However carefully planned and organised, it is an inconvenience. For these reasons it will not work efficiently without the managing director's strong and continuous support. It is often salutary to make it known that breaches of security discipline will be dealt with by the managing director personally.

PLANNING, ADVICE AND CO-ORDINATION

This is the first security function within management: to provide expert advice.

The most important task of a *security adviser* is to assist the managing director to formulate security policy. He should also guide and assist management at all levels in the implementation of that policy.

This is the most important security appointment in industry. It would not, except in very special circumstances, be at board level, but at one or two levels below. The security adviser should be able to talk to heads of departments and works managers or general managers on at least equal terms.

It is important not to confuse this appointment with that of security officer, whose job is operational. The security adviser is a planner, thinker, theoretician, giving his specialised technical advice wherever it is needed from the position of a staff officer to the managing director.

The assessment of the threat is a matter calling for the highest professional competence and the security adviser should be of the greatest assistance to the managing director in this task. He must also help him to ensure that it is reviewed from time to time in the light of changing situations. Once the threat assessment is agreed, the security adviser should design an appropriate security system for the approval of the managing director. For the better achievement of this the security adviser may consult other people concerned, including any or all of the following:

*Heads of Departments and Factory Management within the Firm.* In addition to assisting in the final assessment of the threat, these officials can be invaluable in helping to determine what is and what is not practicable. To enlist their assistance is likely to ensure their co-operation.

*Police Crime Prevention Branch.* This, as has already been mentioned, offers skilled and impartial advice on systems and equipment to protect property. Here again, consultation will ensure co-operation.

*The Firm's Insurance Company* will usually be able to provide experienced surveyors with a sound knowledge of protection. They may be involved in cash and fire risks, and will probably welcome an opportunity to help tighten the security system. The British Insurance Association is the insurance world's principal advisory body in the security field and produces books and films of value to security against theft and fire.

*Industrial Security Companies.* Reputable companies who supply security equipment and services have considerable know-how about the tactics and strategy of security, in addition to knowing the capabilities of their wares. The British Security Industry Association will supply names of suitable companies from which a selection can be made.

*Adjacent Firms.* These may be consulted about a security plan and mutual help may well at once increase security efficiency and enable significant economies to be achieved. There must be regular liaison to ensure continued and progressive co-operation.

*Architects, Designers and Building Contractors.* Liaison should be established with these so that they will appreciate the need for consultation in any construction work they may carry out.

It will be evident that the security adviser has considerable responsibilities and needs to be a capable man, skilled in his art. The question may be asked: Where is such a man to be found? There are no recognised security qualifications and no professional body is acknowledged as a natural source of security expertise. This is partly due to the nature of the profession, whose members tend to prefer obscurity, and partly due to the reluctance of a free society to admit the necessity for such. Ultimately, and to judge by the crime figures, the sooner the better, a security profession will be necessary. There will be a need for a thinking area in security as in other professions. In the meantime, retired police officers (especially crime prevention specialists) or service personnel may provide the answer. Although ex-police or service officers may make excellent security advisers, there are many cases in which the contrary is true. Their background usually fits them better for the job of security *officer* which is discussed below. It must be stressed that security adviser is a managerial type of appointment: the nature of the work calls for a sound academic background, administrative and industrial experience, with considerable powers of written and verbal expression.

In some cases the best answer may be to have a suitable member of the existing staff specially trained for this post. Pending the time when the management schools and technical colleges can accept this commitment, basic training could probably be arranged through the security industry.

It should be remembered that the image of security will to a large extent depend on the security adviser; on the way he goes about his business, his relations with other managers and with all employees with whom he comes in contact, and the contribution he can make to the efficiency of the firm.

It is important that the security adviser be kept as far as is possible in the picture of management's future intentions. If new premises are to be constructed, security can be incorporated in the design and will be both cheaper and more efficient than if it has to be added after completion. It is strange how often this truth is disregarded, yet the subsequent alterations, apart from perhaps doubling the capital cost of security, will also cause unnecessary dislocation of work and weaken such security as there may be, for the period of the alterations. Builders and architects also have some responsibility in this matter; they should certainly question customers and clients as to their security needs when discussing specifications and plans.

When the board has a highly secret plan, the security adviser should be told and asked to advise on the maintenance of security—a highly specialised function. He may well advise a cover[1] plan.

Large organisations may require more than one security adviser, but generally the function at lower or operating level is an executive one.

A word of warning: neither the security adviser nor any other security person should be located in or associated with personnel department. The main reason is that the very nature of security work tends to engender a certain amount of hostility and suspicion, both of which are inhibitory of successful personnel work; in a short time personnel officers are seen as security spies.

The security adviser, with the managing director's help, should encourage the establishment of a security organisation in depth. Each department and factory carrying out secret work should have a trained security officer, full-time or part-time according to need. Their work will be much more effective if it is co-ordinated and this may best be done by the establishment of a security committee, which should be chaired by a senior executive—the company secretary is ideally placed for this duty—representing the managing director. The security adviser should be the committee's principal expert.

## SECURITY OFFICERS, MEN, AND DOGS

Having looked at security in its advisory role, the next step is to consider its operational or executive function, which like the former is a service to management. This is essentially supervision and guarding.

*Supervision.* A security supervisor is usually known as a security officer. His main duty is to ensure the day-to-day working of the security system, that guards are alert, equipment in working order, and security procedures carried out. He should have a close technical relationship with the security adviser, but he should report to and be under the control of the head of department or factory manager whose installation it is his job to secure.

*Guarding.* This term is used here to describe a wide range of security tasks which are performed by men, or men aided by dogs, gate control, patrolling, manning of vulnerable points, key control, checking of security equipment (i.e. that safes and doors have been shut and locked), the secure transmission of documents and other property and so on.

1. A cover plan is one which is usually quite different from the actual plan and designed to give a false picture to mask the real intention. It is not deliberately calculated to deceive a particular rival—that is a deception plan.

Many security officers prefer to employ guards provided by specialist commercial organisations. If reputable companies are used this is usually the most satisfactory arrangement for a small or medium size firm, where facilities for training guards and guard dogs and for providing reliefs for sickness and leave might be inadequate. Guarding is a highly skilled branch of the security art and specialist companies have acquired a great deal of know-how about such matters.

Modern technology is producing excellent mechanical and electronic devices which enhance man's security efficiency and at the same time reduce the number of security men who need be employed to guard a particular target. But he will be needed for the foreseeable future, because only man (and his dog) has the ability to distinguish friend from foe, to arrest and actively resist attack.

Well-trained dogs, usually Alsatians or Dobermann Pinschers, can be a valuable aid to security men. In addition to their alerting and deterrent powers they can take and guard a prisoner. They are a considerable comfort to a guard or patrol in his lonely and dangerous job—in many ways more useful than a human partner and a good deal more economic.

CLASSIFICATION

The classification of risk is the means by which security priorities are allocated. There is no standard system in industry by which this is done, although it is well known that the government classifies its information on a system which controls the handling of every document, whether in storage or in transit. Apart from firms engaged on direct government work, who will be given advice on this point by the authorities, there is probably no need for any elaborate form of classification in industry. It is suggested that there might be three classes of information, as follows:

| | |
|---|---|
| COMPANY SECRET | Information whose unauthorised disclosure could cause serious damage to the shareholder's interests. |
| CONFIDENTIAL | Information whose unauthorised disclosure could damage the interests of the shareholders or be administratively inconvenient to the management. |
| STAFF CONFIDENTIAL | Information about members of the staff or work force concerned with their personal administration, families, promotions, salaries, whose unauthorised disclosure would be embarrassing either to management or the individual concerned. |

The purpose of classification is to determine how the information is handled, where it is kept, under what security conditions it is worked upon, and how it is transmitted from point to point. Specialist advice should be obtained on the detailed handling of classified documents, but in broad terms—

SECRET documents when not in use should be stored in a good quality modern record protection cabinet incorporating a coffer designed to resist all known methods of attack. The coffer should be secured by a keyless combination lock. A high quality modern burglar resisting safe may also be used. They should be worked on only in a secure area or keep (see p. 146). Special care should be taken over their transmission —the ordinary post and registering procedure may not be suitable.

CONFIDENTIAL and STAFF CONFIDENTIAL documents should be locked up in a good quality record protection file secured by a keyless combination lock when not in use.

One of the greatest dangers of any system of classification of information is that it is apt to become debased by over-classification. Use of the classification 'Secret,' for example, may be thought by small-minded people to be a status symbol of their work and used by them where a lower classification would do. Management must be on its guard against such debasement and censure should be more severe for over-classification than the other way round. Apart from debasing the security currency by making the higher classifications so common-place that people treat them casually and carelessly, over-classifica· tion can be exceedingly expensive; since secret material should be kept in a safe or coffer, which are inevitably costly, obviously the more there is the more safes and coffers will be needed; more letters may have to be sent by registered post or by safe hands, more staff will be needed, and so on.

The same principles and procedures can be applied to material objects which need security protection and to areas where documents and material objects are housed and worked on.

Classification is, therefore, a system of security priorities which governs virtually every type of security priority. In the words of the Radcliffe report, 'Thus it determines whether a paper is to be locked in a cupboard fitted with this type of lock or that, whether it is to be despatched in an envelope, a leather pouch, or a locked box, whether the staff who are permitted to handle it are to be vetted, and so on.'

PHYSICAL SECURITY—BARRIERS

In this book the term 'physical security' is used to describe, firstly, the material barriers which may be erected to prevent an illegal intruder gaining his target; secondly, the gates and doors in those barriers which allow access to those persons authorised by the owner; thirdly, locks, and fourthly, key control.

It is quite obvious that the more barriers and the stronger each one is, the greater the delay and difficulties which will be inflicted on the intruder, which is indeed the main object of all security measures. Usually the maximum number of barriers used in physical security is four:

*Perimeter barrier.* Many buildings are sited in their own grounds and if the target is important the perimeter may form the first barrier. Although moats and hahas can be effective outer barriers, those in most common use are walls and fences of which the latter are in almost all cases immeasurably superior for security purposes. The main fault of a wall is that it offers a covered approach to an intruder and the defence is blind unless it is prepared to construct watch-towers, which tend towards security inflexibility—e.g. the location of the guards (or some of them) is known. Guards should be silent and see but not be seen. A high (twelve feet or more) chain link fence of strong construction properly buried in the ground, of small mesh and with barbed wire overhang, is a far better proposition and much cheaper than a wall, especially a wall with watchtowers. A classic example of a defence failure due to the use of walls was the escape of the train robber Ronald Biggs together with three other prisoners from Wandsworth prison in 1965. A furniture van was parked outside the wall, masked by it; from the top a ladder was lowered into the prison and the escape took place in a fast car.

*Building.* The walls of the building may well form the second line of defence, and provided that walls, windows and doors are or can be made sufficiently strong; that good locks are fitted, that ceilings, roofs, floors and other possible means of entry such as cable and air-conditioning ducts are sealed, that the means by which it may be scaled such as gutter pipes or trees are removed or lopped, a building may be a useful barrier to intrusion. Slippery paint on the surfaces of the building may add considerably to an intruder's difficulties.

*Keep.* Within a building a room or group of rooms may for security purposes be physically isolated from the rest of the building; or within a group of buildings one centrally placed may be chosen as an inner security area. In both cases this isolated central area is commonly known as a keep, named no doubt after the place of final retreat in a castle when the garrison is hard pressed. But while the keep may have been the last line of defence in a medieval castle, which was chiefly concerned with the safety of people, it is not the case where the protection of documents is concerned.

The main use to which a keep is put in the security of information context is to provide a secure working area. Secret documents cannot be stored in high security equipment the whole time, but must be worked on or taken out for reference. If at such times they are scattered about desks in open office areas which visitors, cleaners, tea-ladies and others pass through, offices which are probably left unoccupied and unlocked during the lunch-hour, the opportunities for a spy are obviously considerable. A small keep with access confined to those who need to enter, cleaned under supervision, with tea sent through hatchways, and so on, which would be impracticable and too expensive to do for the whole installation, will obviously greatly increase the spy's difficulties.

The keep concept is also applicable to areas in which secret processes are carried out, e.g., secret laboratories and workshops. Temporary keeps may be constructed to contain (in the security sense) temporary encroachments such as building alterations.

*Safe or Strongroom.* One or other of these is normally the last line of physical defence, although in certain circumstances of very high risk a safe may be used *within* a strongroom. It is often advisable nowadays to secure safes to the ground, as mechanical lifting devices are readily available to the criminal.

It is important to understand that there are two types of safe: those which are designed to protect the contents from fire and those which are designed to resist theft. To the untrained eye they may look alike but their construction characteristics are or should be vastly different. Full technical descriptions of the two would be inappropriate here, but the most significant difference between them is that fire-resisting cabinets[1] have as little metal in their construction as possible and thief-resisting safes as much as possible[2]. Metal being an excellent heat conductor is obviously unsuitable as an insulator; on the other hand,

1. It is sound practice to use the word safe only in connection with equipment whose primary purpose is protection against theft.

2. Certain types of glass may in future offer the best protective material, particularly for strongrooms. It is reported that Russian scientists have discovered a way of obtaining tungsten crystal threads of diameter 0.000001 of an inch. These crystal 'whiskers' are said to be ten times stronger than the strongest steels. It is possible that these could ultimately be incorporated into glass or plastic to give transparent protection of a much higher degree than, say, steel. Transparency might offer additional security advantage in that remote surveillance of the inside of the strong room would be possible. It is for this reason that many people including the author consider that a safe is often better placed in a lighted shop window than in a dark concealed basement.

it can be made to offer most formidable resistance to the tools of the thief. In theory, and to a large extent in practice, the two requirements are not reconcilable in the engineering sense. In many cases, this irreconcilability is of no great importance. Statutory documents and other records of business transactions must be preserved from destruction by fire because the firm probably could not run if they were lost. (It is said that more firms go out of business after a fire because of loss of records than because of loss of manufacturing capacity.) Such records would not normally need protection against theft. Similarly it is usually more important to protect cash and valuables from theft than from fire; charred or burned notes can be replaced, and other valuables, such as precious stones, will survive even very intense heat.

Where documents of interest to the thief or spy are concerned, and in some other cases, it may also be a consideration that the documents should be protected against fire. In this case a record protection cabinet offering tested and certified protection against fire, incorporating a coffer (see p. 145) is the best-known form of multiple defence. Clearly, documents and cash in the coffer will be protected against both hazards; documents vulnerable to fire only can be kept in that part of the fire-resisting safe not occupied by the coffer, which takes up only a proportion (usually less than half) of the internal space.

The construction, siting, design, employment, maintenance and selection of all kinds of barriers call for a high degree of professional skill. Nowhere is this more true than where safes and strongrooms are concerned.

### PHYSICAL SECURITY—GATE AND GATE CONTROL

Obviously, every security barrier must have a gate or door to permit access and egress of authorised persons. It must be stressed that the fewer gates there are the better, both on security and cost grounds. Gates are more expensive than barriers and usually easier to circumvent, if only for the reason that they can in certain conditions be opened by foe as well as friend and have no intrinsic power to differentiate between the two.

In practice it is often impossible to have but one entrance. Fire regulations almost invariably demand fire escapes which, unless special precautions are taken, offer easy access to intruders as well as emergency staff exits in case of fire. Busy factories may well need several gates to allow a large mass of workers to enter simultaneously without queueing, and it is often necessary to have separate vehicle entrances.

Although much can be done on outer perimeters to discourage illegal intrusion, not too much faith should be pinned on their efficacy by day when there must of necessity be considerable coming and going, not only of staff but of other traders and their vehicles. Vehicles, especially lorries, offer good concealment for intruders. By night, however, an outer perimeter can be made reasonably secure when all the gates are properly locked, and especially if the perimeter can be patrolled by men or, better still in most cases, men with guard dogs.

It is in the keep area that the main hope of effective control of access lies. Here may be postulated a few offices, self-contained administratively, where twenty or so managers, clerks and secretaries are engaged on security classified work. Entrance to the keep could be confined to one door and control of access exercised by a receptionist. Visitors would not ordinarily be permitted to enter the keep, but should be interviewed at reception, or in a special office outside the security area reserved for that purpose. Admission of staff would be on a recognition basis, which is easily the best. In larger keeps a pass-system might be necessary, but passes, like keys, can be lost or stolen or fall into wrong hands.

Visitors' books may be a security risk. A person signing can see who else has been into the building and this may reveal a plan. If it is desired to keep a record, a small card which is completed by the visitor will at once serve as a record and a pass, and it reveals nothing about any other visitors. The cards should, of course, be filed and locked up in a safe place. Visitors should normally be escorted in and out and should not be left alone inside the keep; there should be visitors' lavatories in the reception area outside the keep.

The air lock method of access control is most useful in high risk areas. This consists of an isolated space or corridor between two doors; the outer door cannot be opened unless the inner one is shut and locked and vice versa. The would-be entrant identifies himself by talking over an inter-communication system to a receptionist on the far side of the inner door. The receptionist, if satisfied that the entrant is *bona fide*, opens the outer door by remote control (usually electric); when it has closed automatically the visitor is surveyed by means of a panel or viewer and, if approved, is admitted through the inner door, the outer one of course being closed. The operation of this can be facilitated by the addition of closed-circuit television, which enables the visual inspection of the entrant (and his identity card) when he is outside the outer door. The main advantage of the airlock is that it prevents the keep being rushed.

For control of access systems to work, directors and senior executives must set the example. If a senior executive forgets his pass or is not recognized, he must not get impatient or rude or force his way past, or the receptionist may become too frightened to do his or her job. The author recalls an instance of how not to behave from his Cyprus experience, when he accompanied a certain Colonel to GHQ. The Colonel's entry pass was out of date and this the sentry on the gate noticed. Instead of congratulating him, the Colonel became very angry and threatened the sentry with terrible punishment if he did not let him through. In the end the formidable Colonel completely destroyed the sentry's morale and strode into GHQ. The author, a civilian security adviser to the Government, was happily able to take remedial action later.

The main task in control of access procedure is to ensure that only authorised people have access to classified premises, and at authorised times. Authorised people seeking access to documents at unusual times should be viewed with suspicion. This is discussed more fully under Document Security later in this chapter.

### PHYSICAL SECURITY—LOCKS AND KEYS

The selection of the correct lock for a particular task is a matter for an expert. The best of these are usually to be found on the staff of a reputable manufacturer of *security* locks, which are as different from *non-security* locks as grain from chaff. Amongst the various types the lever lock is as yet unsurpassed for strength and reliability; it is invariably used to secure high risk equipment such as top quality safes and strongroom doors.

The keylock suffers from certain disadvantages. The key is apt to be lost or mislaid, it can be copied, and there is of necessity a keyhole in the face of the lock which permits the insertion of instruments and the tamping of explosives. And once the key is compromised[1] there is no alternative but to change the lever combination and have new keys cut. This is a skilled job and may mean that the lock is out of use for a time. Of course a new lock may be obtained but in the case of high security locks this will involve considerable expense. The key is

1. A key which has been mislaid, even for a short time, or has been exposed to hostile or potentially hostile eyes, is said to be 'compromised'. It takes only a short time, a few seconds, to take an impression of a key. Really well made keys, where tolerances are very fine, are difficult to copy, even for the skilled man, but with a high risk one should assume compromise in the circumstances described.

easy and quick to use, and for these reasons most people prefer it.

The care and control of keys is an aspect of physical security of considerable importance. In principle, exactly the same care should be taken of the key of the safe or strongroom door as should be of the target itself were it away from its container. A key book should be kept showing the issue and receipt of keys and their duplicates and triplicates. Spare keys, that is, keys not in use, should be kept either in the bank or in a safe of equivalent quality in the custody of some authorised person. The spare keys of a number of safes should not of course be kept in one but should be equally dispersed. The key book should at all times show who is in possession of a particular key, who has master keys, and so on; it should itself be kept under lock and key and, where high risks are involved, in a safe. To be able easily to identify target keyholders may help the spy. Wherever possible there should be no *key* key, the possession of which would start a chain reaction of opening, but where such is inevitable the last key should be behind a keyless combination lock.

A safer lock (in most circumstances) than the key lock is the key-less combination lock. In this the opening and shutting is controlled by a numbered exterior dial linked by a spindle to the lock mechanism. The dial has to be set against a setting mark on a numerical code chosen by the owner himself before the bolt or bolt-work can be moved. There is no key to copy and, provided the owner does not reveal his selection of numbers by carelessness such as writing it down in a prominent place, or by choosing easily deducible numbers such as family birthday dates, the lock cannot easily be compromised. If by chance the combination becomes known (and this comes to light), or if the employee who legitimately knows it leaves the company, the numbers can be changed and full security restored. Of course compromise can also occur if the dial is overlooked by an unauthorised person when the safe is being opened. But good quality keyless combination locks have anti-observation shields and, with these, overlooking is almost impossible. The combination lock has no aperture for the insertion and tamping of explosives. It is better not to record a combination—it should be remembered. But if a record is required it should be treated in exactly the same way as spare keys. For the record, the modern high quality combination lock is not susceptible to those gimmicks beloved of fiction writers, the stethoscope and sandpapered fingers.

There comes a time in the protection of an attractive target when compromise should be assumed. A keyless combination lock can be easily re-set, for the combination is set by the owner in any case;

about every six months is the usual frequency for change, but it should be varied so that the date of change is not predictable. The combination should also be changed when custody of the container alters; this costs nothing except a few minutes of time. Changing the levers of a keylock is a more involved operation which has to be done by an expert; the suppliers or makers should be consulted on this point.

Where padlocks are used it is sound security practice to keep supplies (in safe storage) and change them over at frequent but irregular intervals.

The most secure lock of all is the time lock. This is a clock mechanism fitted to the inside of the door of the safe or strongroom which permits its opening only at a predetermined time, which may be hours or days ahead. Once it is set and the door closed, no one, not even the owner, voluntarily or under duress, can open it until the predetermined time. There are but two snags; first, if the contents of the safe or strongroom should be required in an emergency before the set time they cannot be obtained, and in certain circumstances, where for example government emergency plans were concerned, this could be a serious matter. But this should be a very rare occurrence; if there were any indication that they might be wanted, which normally there would be, the time lock could be set on short periods—say four hours. The second snag is that it is possible for a spy to discover the predetermined time for opening, and to arrange to be present at the *moment critique* with an armed force. However, in spite of these possible difficulties, the high quality safe or strongroom doors fitted with a time lock remains the highest form of physical security yet devised.

If the reader has learned nothing else from the foregoing treatise on barriers one thing should be firmly fixed in his mind: it is the importance of keeping the intruder and any other unauthorised person as far as possible from his target. If he cannot get near the safe or strongroom he

will be unable to use his key copy if he has been able to get one;

will be unable to overlook the combination;

may not be able to discover what is the nature and strength of the final obstacle, and therefore be unable to make plans for overcoming it.


PHYSICAL SECURITY—DOCUMENTS

The Radcliffe report says:

'*It is important to grasp . . . that, while in certain cases verbal in-*

*formation or manuscript notes may suffice, the chances are that anyone engaging in espionage will be under pressure from his masters to provide information in documentary, probably photographic, forms.'*

The handling of a document of a security nature is governed by the classification accorded to it. By handling is meant the strength of the place of storage, the place where it is worked upon, who may have access to it, and how it is transmitted. It is not the intention to go further into these aspects since the ritual will vary in particular circumstances because of the many variables. The classic example of a security variable, not however applicable to industrial espionage, is the military dilemma of the body of troops who were surrounded by the enemy and adjudged by their commander to be capable of holding out for only half an hour more. The radio message he wanted to transmit to HQ was 'Situation desperate; send re-inforcements'. This is undoubtedly information of considerable value to the enemy and according to military standing orders should be sent in cypher. The message might, however, take ten minutes to encode and another ten to decode. Clearly although secret the message could correctly be sent *en clair*. An example closer to the subject is the case of the storage of secret information in a strongly protected keep, guarded day and night by armed soldiers. Here it might well be acceptable to keep it in fire-resisting files. But secret information in an unprotected office might well have to be stored in a burglar-resisting coffer inside a fire-resisting file. So on this subject generalisations may be dangerous.

The purpose of this section is to examine what more can be done to protect classified documents on the assumption of an ill-intentioned employee who has, in spite of all our security efforts, come through the nets of personnel and physical barriers. The industrial spy is now, therefore, working in the keep, a trusted servant of the company, with legitimate access to its secrets. But the resources of protective security are not yet exhausted. Even though the spy has access to the information he has still the problem of taking it out of the office, or photographing it and removing the copy—on the assumption of the truth of the statement from the Radcliffe report with which this section began.

Regular searches or snap checks of persons and their bags and briefcases can be ruled out at once. They are intolerable in principle and would cause deep resentment in practice. Searching on well-founded suspicion is a different matter and may be justified. In any case searching is most unlikely to be effective against a determined person, especially in days when miniature photographing is practicable.

Some of the practical security measures which can make the task of the spy within more difficult (and this is the essence of all security) are given below:

*Copying.* The original number of copies made of a classified document should be controlled and each copy should be numbered and accounted for. Any further copying should require the written consent of a senior official. Authorised copying should be carried out in a special section, say, of the registry, and a record kept.

*Removal of Classified Documents.* A rule forbidding the removal of documents and files from the office can be made, although there will undoubtedly have to be exceptions. Such exceptions should be recorded in registry. Incidentally the point should be made that it is very difficult, if not impossible, to have a satisfactory security system without a definite registry system; sometimes it is economical to split registries into classified and unclassified sections.

Whenever possible it should be insisted that documents are put in files immediately they are received or created, each page being numbered and indexed. This deters unauthorised removal of pages and reduces to a minimum the number of loose and uncovered papers circulating in an office—these are always a security risk.

*Brief-Cases.* In extreme circumstances a rule may be made that brief cases are to be left in a secure cloakroom outside the office. This is certainly a deterrent to the unauthorised taking of files out of the office, although it does not prevent single documents being taken out in pockets; however, this latter might be difficult if the advice given above is taken and all documents remain at all times on files. This rule is unfortunately unenforceable in the case of ládies' handbags.

*Late Working.* This is not necessarily sinister, but it does provide opportunities for espionage. A book should be provided and the times and other facts recorded. Working late should require permission and the security officer should be informed. Returns to the office at unusual times should be viewed with particular suspicion. The author, as a young duty officer of the august War Office, well remembers being called upon to handle a situation of this kind of remarkable delicacy. It was shortly after the Fuchs[1] case. At about midnight the Duty Officer was informed by a guard that a man dressed in civilian clothes was attempting to enter the War Office, giving as his reason that he wanted to go to his desk to do some work,

1. Klaus Fuchs was sent to prison for fourteen years in 1950 for betraying nuclear secrets to the Russians.

having had an inspiration. He claimed he was a scientist with the rank of major in the department of the Scientific Adviser to the Army Council. He was brought under escort to the office and was able to establish his identity, although some lingering doubts as to his motives remained. The Duty Officer, a captain, was about to suggest that the scientific major went home when the latter, in further extenuation, offered as final proof of his *bona fides* to take the former to the Cabinet Offices in Downing Street, where he would open the combination lock of the safe containing Britain's nuclear warfare secrets! After hearing this the author decided to invite the major to stay the night in the War Office. For a moment it looked as if an arrest was going to be necessary—it is unusual but not unheard of nor illegal for a captain to arrest a major—but the major eventually agreed to stay of his own volition. He was bedded down in a War Office strongroom with the duty sergeant for company.

In the morning there was great excitement and the author had interviews with a whole series of eminent personages. Fortunately investigations showed that the major was completely innocent of any evil intentions and that his somewhat eccentric behaviour was due to tension, the result of the stresses and strains of his job.

Vital documents can of course be taken out of the office by means other than hand of spy. The spy may arrange for them to be taken out with the wastepaper. The best way to deal with this is that in a highly classified office all waste paper should be regarded as secret and shredded, preferably in a $\frac{1}{32}''$ cut before being taken out of the office. The shreds should later be burned under supervision.

Another way of reducing opportunity for espionage, especially illegal copying, is to share—it is not suggested that all offices can be shared. The *need to know principle* alone may prohibit this; if it does it may be possible to arrange visual communication between offices by windows or glass panels.

A method of demoralising the spy who would try to smuggle documents or cameras in and out is to make the approach to the classified office as long and bare as possible. An entrance hall which is in effect a corridor with a guard standing at the far end is a long carry for the smuggler who in his guilt feels conspicuous. This method was used with partial success at key points in Cyprus during the Emergency to deter Cypriot girls from carrying in powdered explosive in their powder compacts for sabotage purposes.

It is hoped that the foregoing examples, which are far from exhaustive, have demonstrated that sound security procedures exist to defeat the spy within should other procedures fail to keep him outside. The extent to which any security procedures are applied must, because of their cost and inconvenience, depend upon the threat.

## PHYSICAL SECURITY—CAR PARKS

The significance of motor-cars and other vehicles to security is that they offer excellent smuggling facilities. A thorough search of a vehicle takes hours rather than minutes and is therefore impractical unless there is a background of information. For this reason vehicles should be parked outside keep areas and the example must come from the top. Unfortunately it seldom does; there appears to be some status symbol in driving (or being driven) into security areas. Certainly admirals, generals and air marshals do not take kindly to being asked to walk from the compound gate, especially in inclement weather. They take even less kindly to having their vehicles searched, but this is what should be done if they are brought inside. It is of course not for one moment suggested that they are spies or that spies will often disguise themselves as generals—although successful impersonations of senior officers have been carried out on a number of occasions, but that is another matter. The fact is that vehicles offer an opportunity for a person other than the owner to smuggle; if spies know that senior officials' cars are admitted, these cars immediately become a target and, because searching is impractical, a danger to security. If necessary special vehicles can be kept inside the perimeter or travelators may be installed.

## INTRUDER DETECTION—AUTOMATIC ALARMS

The purpose of an automatic intruder alarm is to give early warning of illegal intrusion to the owner or to the forces of law and order. The alarm may be locally or remotely given. The former has the disadvantage that it may warn the intruder as well. But the alarm which is given remotely will often enable the arrest of the intruder to take place on the job, thereby making his subsequent conviction easier and removing, for a time at any rate, the threat to society that he poses. The intruder who has heard an alarm bell may run away and live to fight another day, or he may be spurred to finish the job quickly before the police or guards can arrive.

Thus the 'silent' alarm, as it is often called, is in most circumstances to be preferred, and it is to this that the following explanations refer. It comprises three parts: an initiating device, a terminal device and a link between the two.

*Initiating devices:* These fall into three main categories: those which depend upon the making or breaking of an electrical circuit; those which respond to noise or vibration; and those which result from the interruption of a light-beam. There are others, so far of lesser importance.

The main requirements of the initiating device are that it shall be utterly reliable—it may only have to work once in its lifetime, but it must work on that occasion. It must be fool-resisting, to reduce the risk of inadvertent operation. It must have a low false alarm rate, be economic, as tamper-proof as possible, and fail 'safe', that is, if it fails an alarm or fault condition must be indicated.

*Terminal devices:* These are the actual alarms. They indicate an alarm condition to those in a position to render or summon help. They may be located in a police station, but there is an increasing reluctance on the part of the police to accept terminal equipment, mainly on account of the mounting strain on police resources as the use of intruder alarms becomes more widespread. The modern practice is to terminate the alarm system in a commercial central station specially designed for the purpose. These are available in most of the big centres of the United Kingdom. They are, or should be, constructed in secure premises themselves and be manned for twenty-four hours a day by trained operators who, with the aid of special equipment, monitor the devices and inform the police station by direct line of attempted intrusion.

*Link:* This in the United Kingdom is usually by land-line. In special cases of high risk a private line may be hired from the Post Office as a direct and permanent link between the initiating and terminal devices. Special precautions are taken to ensure that the line is not easy to tamper with, but, should it be, an alert is given. For lesser risks and offering a very reasonable degree of security the '999' system is used. Coupled to the initiating device is an apparatus which when triggered off will dial 999 and pass a recorded message to the police information room to the effect that an intruder is on the premises. In the future, it may be possible to use radio links, but at present these do not offer a sufficiently high degree of reliability or security.

It is important to realise, as has been stressed elsewhere in this book, that alarms are not protective in the sense of offering a physical barrier to the progress of an intruder, and that they are not a substitute for such barriers. In theory the initiating device should be sited so that the time taken by an intruder after he has set off the alarm to reach his target should be not less and preferably more than the maximum amount of time required for the help summoned by the alarm to arrive. Thus, while the most important part of the physical defence is at the heart, the most important burglar alarm is that which operates earliest, and its siting is again a matter for considerable expertise and close co-ordination with the physical barriers.

Obviously the neutralising of an alarm is a primary task for an illegal intruder. For him to have a good chance of doing this he must either obtain the plans or carry out a detailed reconnaissance. The best alarm companies do not keep records of their installations, and a good system of access control will prevent reconnaissance. But even if the intruder is able to obtain one or both of these advantages, a sophisticated modern alarm system is extremely difficult to defeat—one mistake by the intruder and the alarm will operate.

It is, however, important that alarm systems themselves be given physical protection. They should certainly not be situated outside the outer barrier of physical defence. If they are not protected physically, apart from the possibility of tampering, there will be the risk of a high false alarm rate which considerably detracts from their value.

Wherever there is a high risk, intruder alarms should be employed in depth just as are physical barriers. Additional security is given if they are of different types.

Intruder alarms can be used to increase the efficiency and economy of a works guard force. Alone or in conjunction with closed-circuit television (see below) they enable remote places to be monitored from a central point, where guards can be held in readiness to reinforce any threatened point or sector.

INTRUDER DETECTION—CAMERAS AND CLOSED-CIRCUIT TELEVISION

*Cameras* may be concealed in the target area with the object of photographing an intruder; they may be actuated by an alarm device such as is described above. If their use is not suspected their film may be useful evidence of alleged intrusion. But they are usually difficult to conceal and once their presence is known the intruder can take steps to disguise himself or mask the view of the camera.

*Closed-circuit television.* Modern developments have made this a useful visual aid to security. Cameras at suitable points, if possible out of reach of an intruder, can be made to cover wide areas with reasonable economy; the latest design of camera can be swung to left and right or moved up and down through wide angles or closely focussed on any particular point of interest within its purview—these motions, known respectively as pan, tilt and zoom, being remotely controlled from the monitoring area. Cameras can be so sited that a complete view of an installation, its environment and individual rooms, is obtained on monitor screens. CCTV is at present an expensive form of security and can only be justified in the protection of a very high risk.

CCTV is a useful supplement to other forms of security, but not, of course, a substitute for any of them. Its main effect is to extend the range and vision of guards and it can reduce the number which are needed, but some guards are still needed—to monitor the screens, to act upon information received and, if necessary, to arrest intruders and stand in in the event of mechanical or electrical failures.

It is difficult to remain alert or even awake watching a TV screen where the picture does not change for hours on end. One way of ensuring alertness is to have intruder alarms closely co-ordinated with CCTV, so that in each sector covered by a camera movement or intrusion will set off an alarm in the monitoring rooms and indicate the relevant sector.

As has already been indicated, CCTV has application to access control, enabling remote supervision of gates and doors, including the examination of passes and identity cards.

INTRUDER DETECTION—SECURITY LIGHTING

Nearly all illegal intrusion takes place under the cover of darkness and then lighting is an important facet of defence. It is also a strong deterrent to the intruder and its power to deter varies directly with the skill in selection of the equipment, its siting and installation. These are complicated matters best left to an expert, who should insist among other things that the security lighting is—

of sufficient intensity to enable the defence to discriminate between friend and foe;

not patchy nor leaves shadows for intruders to hide in;

not dependent on any one source of power;

the kind of light which accentuates contrasts of colour rather than blends them as some very strong lights tend to do;

not so positioned that it dazzles the defence.

An effective and economical method of using security lighting is to link it to intruder detection devices, so that initiating the latter switches on the former and illuminates the intruder, for whom this can be a frightening experience. He may be temporarily dazzled and demoralised and will be vulnerable to a quick follow-up by guards and dogs.

INTRUDER DETECTION—TECHNICAL INTRUSION

The term technical intrusion connotes the use of technical equipment to eavesdrop or espy classified information.

Most, but not all, of the equipment available (see Chapter 7, p. 72) has to be taken into and concealed within the premises where the information is held or discussed. The exceptions are the use of telescopes and telescopic cameras and long-range hearing devices of the type described on p. 73 and 74 which can be sited in adjacent premises.

There is as yet no widespread use of technical intrusion equipment in the United Kingdom for industrial espionage, but according to the evidence it is becoming established practice in the United States. It is also frequently used by the state espionage and security services of the major powers. This country tends to follow the American pattern in many ways and so-called 'bugging' and other devices may therefore be encountered here in the future on a large scale also. The likelihood of this is a part of the threat assessment.

While there are technical methods of detecting the presence of eavesdropping equipment, it is doubtful whether the purchase and use of such equipment is as yet justified for industry in the United Kingdom. The best defence for the present is proper control of access to keeps so that the instruments cannot be placed. To defeat telescopic eavesdropping and spying it is sufficient to cover windows with lace curtains or to install frosted or opaque glass.

Other non-technical means of defeating eavesdropping include the last-minute changing of venues and times for important conferences or discussions, or the choosing of unusual places. An example of the latter was quoted in the *Evening Standard* of 9th April 1963. According to their correspondent, the 'Ind Coope-Tetley-Ansell merger was launched on an icy hilltop in Derbyshire'. In another connection it was a last-minute change of conference venue that saved Hitler's life on 20th July 1944. Instead of using the usual concrete bunker, the conference assembled in a wooden hut. If Stauffenberg's bomb had exploded as planned, its force, confined within thick concrete walls, would certainly have killed everyone there, including Hitler; the thin wooden walls of the hut offered little resistance to the blast and Hitler lived.

Ignoring the evil which resulted from the prolongation of Hitler's life, the security theoretician would like to think that some security genius had responsibility for this most effective surprise move, but it appears to have been fortuitous. The concrete bunker was being repaired at the time, and this, together with the fact that it was a hot summer day, appears to have determined the change. It is nevertheless a remarkable illustration of the value of surprise in security. Nothing is more devastating to carefully thought out and meticulously executed plans than surprise moves of this kind.

Neither changes of venue nor normal control of access will defeat the 'mini-bug' or the mini-camera carried in by a member of the staff or a visitor authorised to be present. There is, as has been pointed out, little threat of this at the moment; if and when there is, technical means of detection may have to be employed.

Lastly, mention should be made of telephone interception. This can be done externally, but would be difficult unless the espionage organization had penetrated the Post Office. Internally, it can be done on the switchboard by interconnection, or by inserting a miniature microphone in the handset.

Technical intrusion and interception, although not a serious threat, may become so in the future, not only because it may spread from the United States, but because rapid technological advance in the electronic and photographic spheres may render it even more formidable than it is now. George Orwell's Big Brother could be a fact before 1984.

INSTALLATION AND MAINTENANCE OF SECURITY EQUIPMENT

The installation and maintenance of security equipment presents special problems.

The first and perhaps most obvious one is the opportunities which are created for reconnaissance by persons not members of the owner's firm. It is for this reason that reputable firms sell not merely the equipment, but a complete service. In addition to selecting exactly the right equipment for the particular job, they will superintend its installation and, where appropriate, service it throughout the years of its life. The employees of such a security firm are as carefully selected as is humanly possible and great care is taken to avoid keeping telltale records which could be used to defeat the system.

Next is the importance of correctly fitting such items as locks, locking bars, grilles, window bars. The author has repeatedly seen on tours of inspection good locks that have been rendered quite useless by being badly fitted. Some common installation faults are—

locks fitted to badly made doors so that the bolt of the lock is not fully through into the striking-plate and the door can be prised open;

mortice locks fitted to doors that are too thin so that the doors become weakened and vulnerable;

locks placed too near unprotected letter-box apertures;

window bars and grilles not properly grouted into the masonry.

Leading security firms provide a service whereby specialists fit locks and other security devices.

Once installed, locks and safes need little maintenance although it is considered wise to have high risk equipment inspected by the makers' service organisation say once a year.

There is no branch of security that requires more precision work in the customer's premises than intruder alarms. Safes or locks arrive complete in working order, works tested and ready for use. If by chance they do not work it is immediately apparent and the fault can be rectified without undue prejudice to security; locks and safe doors can, it is true, jam, but this is exceedingly rare.

Each intruder alarm is a system on its own and has to be carefully tailored to the particular premises and situation. The systems comprise a number of delicate and sensitive mechanisms, each of which has to be incorporated into the 'purpose-built' system, and each one of which—

must work on 'the day';

must give as few false alarms as possible;

must be sophisticated enough to resist tampering;

must be simple enough for the owner to be able to control when the premises are occupied by his own employees and to 'set' at the end of the day;

must operate whether or not the main electricity supply is functioning.

The wiring up and balancing of even the simplest system calls for high installation expertise. Similarly with maintenance; because of the nature of the equipment it should be expertly serviced, and in fact most intruder alarm companies insist on a maintenance contract as a condition of sale.

One of the most important security tasks for both advisers and security officers is to ensure that installation and maintenance of equipment are properly carried out—by specialists.

# CHAPTER 15

# Management's Defence System against Industrial Espionage—Part II: Personnel

The most certain way of finding out what is going on within an organization is to carry out the espionage operation known technically as penetration. There are two ways of penetrating an organisation: one is to 'turn' somebody who already works for it, and the main preventive weapon in the hands of management against this hazard is psychological security.

The second method, which usually takes much longer, is to procure the employment in the target organisation of one's own agent. This may have to be very long term. Confidential or secret information is not usually given to junior employees and vacancies in the senior ranks are usually few and far between. A short cut, however, can be achieved through the secretarial channel. Top-class secretaries are, at the best of times, difficult to find. According to a recent survey by a secretarial agency, there are fifteen good jobs available for every one competent secretary. A good secretary therefore could easily achieve a high position almost immediately on employment, especially if she happened to be attractive as well. This is not necessarily to suggest any immorality on the part of management; even the most happily married man is not averse to seeing an attractive woman in the office and her charm can be a material business asset. Alternatively an approach, especially of the confidence trick type, may be made to an existing secretary with a view to alienating her loyalties as in the case related on p. 69.

The preventive measures relevant to both types of penetration fall into six clear parts:

indoctrination and personal security
psychological security
selection procedures
security of temporary and visiting employees
after-care
education and training

and it is a combination of all these which gives the maximum possible degree of personnel security.

Indoctrination is the process of initiating a person in the responsibilities of secret work. When a man is posted from unclassified to classified work, or from classified to more highly classified work, the responsibilities should be clearly explained to him; for example, the following may be stressed:

The nature and extent of likely espionage, especially techniques which may be used;

Those parts of his work which are particularly sensitive to espionage;

The names of colleagues, if any, with whom he may freely discuss his work—i.e. who have also been similarly indoctrinated;

The relevant details of the security system including the security rules (it is often better to read these out rather than hand out copies);

The consequences to the company and to him personally of a breach of security.

All this should be explained on the *need to know* basis.

In addition the person to be employed must be trained in the art of being personally secure and of setting a security example. In particular he must—

scrupulously observe security rules however high or humble his position;

at all times be courteous and helpful to security officers and men;

be discreet in his conversations with others who do not need to know about his work;

not expose himself to blackmail, especially by personal irregularities and excesses;

be careful of his own office security. He should not leave classified papers on his desk if he goes away; for a few minutes absence it may be sufficient to lock them in the drawer of his desk if it is strong and has a good lock. But for longer periods they must be locked up in their proper container. If he has a separate office it will be sufficient for short periods to lock the door provided it and the lock are of good quality and the papers are left face down if there is any danger of being overlooked. Security pairing is a useful drill; in this a manager and his secretary or two colleagues in the same work arrange to check each other's security; at close of business they try each other's safe and files to see that they have been properly locked, that papers have been put away and so on. It is sound practice never to close the door of a safe or the drawer of a file without locking it.

Indoctrination of a man or woman and instructing them in the art of being personally secure is a proper responsibility for the security adviser.

### PSYCHOLOGICAL SECURITY

For the purpose of this book psychological security may be defined as a state of morale which will enable and encourage the members of an organisation to remain loyal to it. It is well known that morale is the most important single factor in the ability to prosper of any organisation, be it an army, a football team, or a company.

Clearly a state of high morale does not prevent the infiltration type of penetration, but it may inhibit it. The spy may enjoy working in the firm concerned and his or her will to carry out espionage weakened; or he or she may be a conspicuous misfit in a tightly-knit, happy working community and draw too much attention to themselves, thus rousing the suspicions of alert managers or security personnel.

Psychological security as defined here is of course only one industrial dividend arising from high morale. There can be many others, such as improved productivity, fewer demands for pay rises, happier human relations and higher profits.

Because it is so closely connected with the overall success of the enterprise and because they are the only persons who have the means and authority to ensure it, the responsibility for the establishment and maintenance of psychological security is a primary one of the managing director and his line managers. The security adviser's job is to draw their attention to any shortcomings which may prejudice security.

The precepts of Chapter Eleven should form a sound basis for the attainment of high morale for most industrial purposes, including particularly resistance to espionage and subversion. This basis should be reinforced by security education (see p. 172). In a nutshell, what is needed is good leadership and an *esprit de corps* which will at once form an outer psychological barrier and provide the climate of understanding in which the inner and outer barriers are accepted as necessary without rancour.

### SELECTION OF EMPLOYEES

A man's past life usually, but not always, has some bearing on his future conduct. If he has been unreliable in previous employment or at school or university, this may be a pointer to future unreliability, although it is important not to mistake the normal follies of youth for chronic weakness. It is therefore perfectly reasonable for any employer to seek references from previous employers, and from other people who have known the candidate for employment, such as his headmaster or tutor.

However, a different situation arises in the matter of criminal records. A man who has committed a crime and who has been punished for it is reckoned to have paid his debt to society, and for this reason the police are understandably reluctant to give particulars of any criminal record there may be to prospective employers.

At the same time there is no doubt of the existence of recidivism in crime and many employers, especially those with which this chapter is concerned, might feel unable to take the risk of employing someone with a previous criminal record. Quite apart from a danger of recidivism, the employer may well have to declare, if he is aware of it, the fact that he is employing someone with a previous record to his insurance company and thereby incur an additional premium. Should he fail to do so and he suffered loss of cash, for example, whether due to the ex-criminal or not the insurance company might well be able to disclaim liability.

The position is aggravated where jobs which involve the national security are concerned. Here there is a government procedure known as positive vetting. This consists of a check against police and Security Service records, completion by the subject of a security questionnaire, references and a field investigation into character and circumstances. Government is, of course, mainly concerned to discover politically subversive backgrounds or future potential for subversion.

According to the Radcliffe report, positive vetting facilities are available to industry where government contractors are involved in classified work: 'The application of . . . PV (positive vetting) to contractors' employees is on the same basis as in the public service.' Obviously this assistance would not be given for purely commercial purposes and firms other than government contractors must therefore deal with this problem themselves.

The problem is far from unknown in the security industry, particularly in those companies concerned closely with the responsibility for the transport and storage of large sums of cash. Here it is usually the practice to make detailed background enquiries with the consent of the subject.

There are in the UK firms like Management Investigation Services (see p. 46) which make such investigations part of their business, but these do not operate on anything like the scale in the United States. Here, according to Vance Packard, one corporation, the Wackenhut, has grown 'in less than a decade from four private eyes into the fourth largest investigative and security organization in the nation, with a staff of 3,500, complete with a lie-detector division.' Not all their investigations are concerned with vetting for jobs of a security nature; much of their work is to investigate the general suitability of a person for a particular job. Full investigation could cost £100 or more.

In spite of the most careful checks, spies and traitors continue to operate even in the government service. It is not to be expected therefore that industry, except perhaps the security industry, lacking investigative resources, and probably for the time being reluctant on ethical and expense grounds to employ specialist agencies for the purpose, will be able to control the industrial spy by care in selection alone. Nevertheless, much can be done. For persons who are or who are likely to be employed in responsible positions of a security nature, verification of particulars given and the taking up of references is essential. The previous record of employment should be checked by writing to all the firms or employers mentioned and replies should be insisted upon. The existence of the firms should be checked in appropriate registers and directories. It may sometimes be worthwhile to call on a previous employer; a manager may be more forthcoming in conversation than he can be on paper. Of course, such detailed procedures are costly in time and effort and can only be justified in appropriate circumstances.

The applicant for the job should be required to explain and substantiate explanations of gaps in employment. Referees other than previous employers should again be capable of verification—like doctors, lawyers and other professional persons who are registered. The employer's reference is usually the best.

There is a vetting technique much used in Germany and increasingly in this country to ensure that personnel occupying positions of responsibility are free from serious character blemishes and that round pegs are fitted into round holes. This is graphology. The study of handwriting in this country tends to be regarded as something on a level with astrology, but there is reliable evidence to show that it is a valuable aid to personnel selection which should not be overlooked in a security context. (See Appendix J.)

It would be a great advantage if the police were freely permitted where jobs of a very high security nature were concerned to advise

G

employers of adverse previous records. The fact that they cannot does not prevent heavy and unfair criticism of security companies by magistrates and judges when it is revealed in the course of legal proceedings that they have inadvertently employed persons with criminal records.

Apart from a previous criminal record there are other defects of character which may make a person a security risk. These include insobriety, financial or emotional instability, vanity, abnormal sexual or marital relations. Very careful thought needs to be given before employing (or continuing to employ) such people in key security positions.

### TEMPORARY AND VISITING EMPLOYEES

Categories in this class are—
replacement staff hired during holiday periods or illness;

contractors' men who have regular access to the vicinity of the premises, e.g. drivers, fuel suppliers;

contractors' men who have temporary access for special purposes such as building alterations or extensions;

visiting maintenance personnel, e.g. telephone, electrical, and other service engineers.

All these men and women may 'need to go' into the factory or office premises and yet the owner neither has nor can have any control over or say in their selection!

At first sight this security problem may seem insoluble and there is no doubt that it does pose serious difficulties. It is not surprising that much subversive activity has been carried out through or in conjunction with temporary and visiting personnel. Nor is it surprising that subversive organisations often seek as a priority to obtain maximum influence in trade unions whose members fall into these categories, particularly the last. Some of the most significant union activities by British communists have been in the Post Office, electrical and engineering unions.

The main defence is physical and rests on the keep system and temporary extensions of it. Building extensions and alterations to or near classified premises should be physically isolated from them by temporary fences which can, if necessary, be guarded by temporary guards. Fuel tanker and transport parks should be outside information keeps. In high security areas maintenance engineers (including security maintenance engineers) should be escorted.

Temporary staff should not be used to replace any of the permanent staff of a security keep. It is far better in the security sense, although probably less convenient administratively, to replace them with personnel from a non-security area who are nevertheless tried and proved permanent employees, using temporary staff in the non-security area. An illustration of this point is given by the following extracts from Hansard of 11th August 1966:

'Mr. Marten: *As the implications of the previous Answers were that the Prime Minister should be kept well informed about security matters, can he tell us whether the temporary secretary, Miss Wells, employed at No. 10 Downing Street, was positively vetted beforehand? If so—*

Mr. Speaker: *Order. Security Questions are not allowed on the Order Paper, and I do not think that they should be allowed in supplementary questions.*

The Prime Minister: *On a point of order, Mr. Speaker. In view of the slur made by the hon. Member for Banbury (Mr. Marten), may I be allowed to reply?*

Mr. Speaker: *Since the question has been asked, yes.*

The Prime Minister: *The hon. Member for Banbury (Mr. Marten), who spends most of his time snooping on this kind of question, gave a statement to the Press. I wish now to give the facts. This lady was sent for a few days as a replacement for a sick secretary to my wife. She was employed on exactly the same terms as have always been the case at Downing Street, although we have in fact greatly tightened up the security provisions in the recruitment even of temporary staff as compared with the position under our predecessors.*

*It was when she was asked to type a stock letter on Vietnam and began to query the text that one of my secretaries threw doubt on her position when she was replaced and returned to the place from which she had come. There has been the fullest vetting of anyone who has anything to do with security work. This lady had no access to any security work, and I repeat that the rules are tighter than in the time of the Government of which the hon. Member was a member.'*

According to the *Daily Telegraph* of 12th August 1966, 'The secretary, Miss Sylvia Wells . . . is now married to Mr. Brian Wright, a former member of the Woking branch of the Communist party.'

AFTERCARE

Moral principles and practical difficulties are not the only limitations no the value of selection procedures for security classified work. A man or woman with a perfectly sound past record may suddenly defect. If Professor Radzinowicz is right about the dark figure of crime, that 'Crime brought fully into the open and punished represents no more than about fifteen per cent of the total', there is a good chance that there are many thousands of undetected criminals in circulation. No checks against police records, even if these could be obtained, would be likely to be fruitful in such cases.

It is quite clear therefore that this defence is far from being a complete one. To this must be added the obvious fact that in spite of great efforts and wise rule high morale cannot always be maintained; adverse national or international economic or political forces quite beyond the control of management may cause psychological insecurity through fear of unemployment or reduced emoluments.

Aftercare is the name given to those security measures which are designed to detect

(1) spies who have slipped through the selection procedure net;

(2) those hitherto loyal servants of the company who decide to betray it.

It should be said at once that any form of counter-penetration by management agents is not only wrong in principle, but likely to do more harm than good. Sooner or later it would become known and the damage to security and management's image would be immense and irreparable.

The job of aftercare, like psychological security, is essentially one for line management. By knowing the men and women who work for him, by being in touch with them, by participating in their recreation and extra-mural activities, the manager will soon learn who are the misfits. Now most spies, except those of the top rank, who so far are more likely to be employed on state than industrial espionage, are apt to be and look like misfits. It is very difficult for a man or woman to lead a double life for any long period. Some of the signs are:

(1) lack of real friends—because of lack of time to cultivate them and fear that intimate friends would discover their double life;

(2) exceptional ability at job—this is an essential quality for spies: without it they are unlikely to graduate to key positions;

(3) lack of hobbies—because of lack of time to develop them;

(4) quiet, reserved and generally introverted—this is really the security barrier which a spy must have.

But not all persons displaying these symptoms are spies!

If there are grounds for suspicion certain tests may be applied; for example, the employee may be moved without previous warning to other employment. If he (or she) is a spy, his activities will be dislocated and there may be no time or opportunity to make alternative arrangements; the shock or surprise may make him careless, he may protest too much or too little. A case in point is that of Judith Coplon, a brilliant young American political analyst who worked in the Department of Justice. She was also a communist sympathiser feeding a Russian espionage network. In 1949 she was convicted and sentenced to a long term of imprisonment. According to Ronald Seth[1]:

*'Towards the end of 1948 . . . the FBI learned that the contents of some of their papers were reaching Moscow. A thorough investigation was instituted, and one by one all possible channels of leakage were eliminated until suspicion came to rest on Judith Coplon. But it was still only suspicion. There was no proof. However, the Department of Justice could run no risk of her seeing and handling any further secret papers, and she was transferred to another division.*

*'When she learned of the transfer, according to her chief, "she was very much disturbed. She protested again and again in vehement terms against being moved. It was on account of these loud protests that the FBI were convinced that she was their quarry."'*

There are other tests which are however beyond the scope of this chapter.

A hitherto loyal employee who turns against his employers usually gives ample early warning of disaffection (before it actually occurs) to the intelligent manager. Only on very rare occasions does a happy and contented employee succumb to a direct espionage approach—and very few intelligence officers are foolish enough to try; they much prefer the soft target.

There is almost always a pre-disposing reason. A man may become disgruntled because someone has been promoted over his head without, he thinks, just cause. Very few people object to being over taken in the promotion sense so long as it is not only fair, not only seen to be fair, but also made intelligible. His disappointment will show in many ways; there may be a falling off in the standard of his work; he may start to drink heavily or become morose and ill-tempered.

One of the most common causes of disaffection in individuals (and for that matter in teams) is, of course, bad management. Very few people object to tough managers so long as they are fair and just; so long as they can be talked to; so long as they are not repressive of ideas. The most deadly type of manager is the bully, who, unsure of himself and greedy for further advancement, spends more of his time

1. *Anatomy of Spying* (Arthur Barker, 1961).

with those who are in a position to grant it than with those who are
his direct responsibility. Such managers generally centralise all power
in their own hands, those who resist being side-stepped or broken.
They surround themselves with courtiers and sycophants more conspicuous for their fawning flattery than their management ability. In
these circumstances, morale is quickly impoverished and communications break down so that ideas do not find expression, and disaffection is not detected. The results are usually unexpected defections to
rivals by long-term and previously happy and loyal employees and, at
worst, subversive activity.

The message of this section may be summed up by quoting again
from the Radcliffe report. After stressing the importance of the basic
measures of physical security—in the passage with which Chapter
fourteen began—the report says 'No system of personnel security
however much elaborated can be effective enough to modify their
primary value'.

And if this is true of government departments, with the whole
machinery, expertise and records of the Security Service and the
police at their disposal, it is more so of industry.

EDUCATION AND TRAINING

*Security education* is to *security training* as—to use a horticultural
simile—general soil preparation is to the detailed care of the plant.

The object of security education is to obtain security by consent
which is much more likely to be successful than if it is merely imposed
without explanation. The main task is to explain the need for security
to the staff and work force, and to enlist their co-operation. This is no
easy matter, for very few people have an absolutely clear conscience,
and the mere mention of the word 'security' is apt to cause insecurity.
Whatever may be said in explanation the feeling is apt to persist that
the measures are aimed at depriving the worker of what he may regard as his legitimate perquisites—a shave on the company's premises
in the company's time using the company's electricity, or a bit of
'do-it-yourself' with the company's tools and materials. The fact that
many if not most security officers and operatives are ex-policemen
reinforces this feeling, as does the term 'works police' or the name of
the security officers' association 'Industrial *Police*[1] and Security
Association'.

Paradoxically, the situation is further complicated by the need to

1. Author's italics

maintain security. It will almost certainly not be possible to give the full facts about secret processes and plans. It may indeed be necessary to mask altogether the fact that there are information secrets.

Fortunately, as has been pointed out, the security precautions are essentially similar for all types of risk, be they information, cash, pilferage. It may well, therefore, be best to lay emphasis on that which is most tangible, say precautions against loss of cash and theft of valuable materials. One of the very best ways of educating staff is through the use of films. The National Coal Board have set a particularly good example of educating miners in safety precautions and drills through the use of closed-circuit television in canteens and places of recreation. Some excellent security films are available. One enterprising company, Proctor & Gamble, themselves victims of industrial espionage, produced an article on it in their house magazine *Moonbeams* and it could well be repeated in other house magazines or newsletters. Other firms have produced small security booklets for issue to all concerned including, where appropriate, employees' wives and husbands.

But the best security education stems from the establishment of a good security discipline. It must be efficiently administered and cause not only the minimum interference with operations, but the minimum personal inconvenience. Gate control which causes long queues in the rain; fences which interrupt communications with lavatories, rest rooms, recreation centres; officious security officials; car parks that are good in the security sense but are inconsiderately far from the place of work—are a few examples of security which will cause resentment. Security will be seen to exist and be loathed.

It will be seen that security education and its image are closely connected. The image can be helped if in addition to making security reasonable it is made contextual with such accepted disciplines as fire and safety. It can also be used to help workers and staff safeguard their own property; there are few large concerns—factory or office—in this day and age that do not suffer larceny of staff property which, although lost items may be replaced by the firm or insured, nevertheless causes deterioration of morale.

*Security training* is the nourishment which is given to the security plant to keep it healthy and fruitful. It is a continuing process and is closely linked with the important security concept of maintenance of momentum. Security, being defensive in character, is possessed of a natural inertia, which feeds and grows on the fact that for so long no attack takes place. The highest form of security would probably exist in conditions where an attack took place on average once a week, but at irregular times.

It is usually convenient to carry out training in groups, although the groups should if possible meet for certain subjects such as those taught by films; higher management particularly must display interest in security training of the other groups.

### HIGHER MANAGEMENT

An occasional lecture on the threat, especially if it is changing, and on advances in security technology, is important. Any necessary detailed instruction in the security art should be given personally by the security adviser. It is a security truism that the higher the position of the manager, the less likely it is that he will obey the security rules; the more senior, the more prone he is to leave secret papers lying about, safe keys in drawers, and safes open. No doubt this is largely because senior executives work at very high pressure. The answer lies in making personal assistants and secretaries responsible for the security of the senior executives for whom they work—a kind of security cushioning.

### SECRETARIES AND PERSONAL STAFF

These categories can and should form a strong security barrier round the top management. It is very seldom possible or desirable for top management to function within a security keep. Managing directors and their board colleagues must of necessity be accessible to visitors and executives; elaborate control of access would cause resentment and those who were senior enough would probably ignore it, causing immense damage to security. Here, then, the defence must rest largely on the personal staff which includes personal assistants, secretaries, chauffeurs, butlers and so on, and they must be a training target for the security adviser. On joining, personal assistants and secretaries should be first indoctrinated and as soon as possible afterwards given a comprehensive security course of at least a week's duration. Chauffeurs and butlers and other domestic staff should be impressed with the need for silence in regard to the affairs of their employers.

### FAMILIES

Many senior executives 'unwind' the worries and problems to loving, sympathetic and intelligent wives after the day's work is done, usually to the great benefit of their business. Wives not aware of the need for secrecy are often good targets for the 'conning' type of espionage.

Probably all that is needed is to remind husbands of the importance of explaining security requirements to wives. In very high security matters, formal indoctrination of wives by the security adviser may be necessary. To forbid husbands to discuss office matters with wives is not only to run the risk of impairing their relationships, but is unrealistic.

A slightly different problem arises with wives engaged on classified work. Some husbands tend to resent their wives being engaged on such work, which carries with it the inevitable security status symbol; it may seem to put her in a more important position than his own. But these same husbands may often be willing to believe that their wives' jobs are unimportant except for the reward they bring and so it may be convenient to leave them in blissful ignorance. In other cases, indoctrination may be the best course—the wives will be the best judges. Women, incidentally, are very good at keeping secrets; they are far from being the security risks that some men believe.

The above are simply a few categories to illustrate the importance and some of the main considerations of training. Other categories may need to be considered; for example, supervisory staff, shop stewards.

Security training and education may sometimes be extended too far—in its embrace may be included those whose affections have already been alienated or deliberate spies. Provided the security instruction has been correctly carried out in a secure way, with especial regard to the 'need to know' principle, little harm will be done and there may be positive good. The finest deterrent to espionage is the knowledge that the security is strong and that failure is highly probable.

*Momentum* in security is maintained by activity of which training and education are the mainsprings. But security, like most arts and sciences, must submit itself to tests of its health and strength from time to time. Checks and inspections carried out reasonably regularly and sensibly will provide a valuable impetus to security. Carried out too often and officiously, or in a Prussian way, they can cause not only immeasurable harm to security, but thoroughly bad industrial relations.

The object of checks and inspections is to improve security efficiency. This is achieved by the discovery of such weaknesses as exist and their rectification. Checks[1] are usually of the 'snap' variety carried out without previous warning and usually of a particular aspect, e.g. physical. Inspections are more prolonged affairs, carried out after reasonable notice has been given, regularly but at irregular intervals. Their purpose is to examine the whole security system of, say, a department or of the firm itself.

Checks are the responsibility of line management, not of the security adviser or security officer. They should be carried out by the departmental head or a senior executive appointed by him; it is usual for the security adviser or officer to be present to assist. It is *not* the job of security to carry out 'secret' checks or administer reprimands for breaches of security. These, like any other breaches of discipline, are the duty of line management.

Formal inspections are usually the responsibility of the security adviser acting on behalf of the managing director. The security adviser should arrange with the departmental head a time of mutual convenience and ask for a senior executive or the departmental security officer to accompany him throughout the inspection. When it is completed, a written inspection report should be submitted to the managing director; it is customary and courteous to discuss the report, particularly any adverse findings, with the head of department before submission to the managing director. Not only does this enable him to prepare his answers and, if necessary, to take immediate corrective action, but it is a valuable check on the accuracy of the report itself.

It will be seen that there is plenty of work to occupy the time and energies of security personnel in the sphere of preventing security inertia or complacency. The key nature of the security adviser's job will also be apparent; in addition to having a high degree of professional knowledge and expertise, he must be the soul of tact. His is the task of maintaining enthusiasm for what may be regarded by many as an expensive and inconvenient overhead, apt to interfere with operational efficiency, and as an infringement of personal liberty.

---

1. These checks should not be confused with those carried out every day or every night by guards and watchmen, when these are employed. The object of these is to see that everything is basically in order—that safes have been locked, windows closed and so on. These are of course a valuable part of security, especially security against theft and fire. Their value in security of information is more limited, for guards and watchmen are not normally in a position to check on information procedures.

# CHAPTER 16

## *The National Security Problem*

This book is intended primarily for management, but the point has been made, and it cannot be too often repeated, that security is a whole science; that the technology cannot be successful if it is applied piecemeal. Some suggestions are therefore made in this concluding chapter as to how a national and comprehensive application of security technology could be made to solve the whole problem of a society which is transiting towards area 'war'. First is a summary of the threat.

### THE AREA WAR

The transition from linear to area war is epitomized by the current struggle in Vietnam, where American and Vietnamese forces are involved in pitched battle against the Vietcong as well as having to face massive subversion. It is the latter which causes the greater anxiety; without it the war would have been already concluded. Vietnam is probably in any case now irrelevant to the main struggle which, while so much democratic effort is being spent in Vietnam, is being fought out on our doorsteps.

This country and much of the western world is the arena in which the ideological battle is being decided. It is largely an industrial arena where lives and works an industrial society. Today we cannot live without the comforts and government cannot function without the facilities which industry provides. Our heating, lighting, piped water, refrigeration, telecommunications, roads, aeroplanes, railways, motor vehicles, ships, oil supplies, and the maintenance of all these, are vital to our whole society. Without exportable surpluses of our production we cannot buy from other countries the things we lack. Those who control the labour forces control industry and control us.

The submission of this book is that major threats to our democratic way of life, to our western ideology, arise from espionage and subversion, whose close relationship has been demonstrated. Espionage networks are used to obtain information for competitive, criminal, prison escape and subversive purposes, to proselytise, to disrupt, to punish, to disturb the precarious balance between mob rule and dictatorship which is democracy.

All the purposes for which espionage may be used against industry affect the economic and therefore the political strength of the state, and this is especially true of crime. The cost of crime is not confined to the losses. The overhead of crime also includes prisons, police, security equipment and guards, and the total annual cost is in the same area of value as our entire exports to South Africa.

Espionage and subversion in industry must for all these reasons be regarded as attacks against the state. But even if the forces of law and order were stronger than they are there would be little diminution of management's security problem. The vast acreage over which the manager holds sway is private property. He is responsible for what goes on in his domain; the police and other authorities normally can only enter at his request or with his permission. Yet his domain is the main target in the area war.

In this domain espionage and subversion must be detected and prevented. The spy and the shop floor bully must be evicted and dealt with according to law, which must be brought up to date. If the manager fails to secure his area of responsibility it will eventually be done for him. The government's prices and incomes policy has been necessitated by management's failure to contain the appetites of organised labour, and this failure is in no small measure due to activity such as that in the National Union of Seamen (Appendix F), the Electrical Trades Union (Appendix E), the motor industry (Appendix G), and elsewhere, which, it is asserted, is subversive. If this policy is not successful due to subversion, then further intervention will be necessary. If industrial courts are set up there will be a need for official enquiry and investigation within the manager's offices or on his factory floor, thus intruding on his operation. If, on the other hand, neither state nor management control subversion, subversive forces eventually will control them—and all of us.

SECURITY COMMITTEES

Co-ordination of effort is the essence of the technology of security. In a democratic society this inevitably means 'war' by committee, but there are plenty of successful precedents. For example, in Malaya during the area war there after the Second World War the major part of the defence effort of the country was run by committees. At the top, admittedly, there was one man of exceptional ability, Field Marshal Sir Gerald Templer, who, to use his own words, 'was not a committee', and had considerable personal power. But each state of Malaya was controlled for the purpose of defence against communist subversion by a committee known as the State War Executive Committee (SWEC) on which were represented all the parties concerned in or affected by the prosecution of the campaign. Under the SWECs were District War Executive Committees similarly constituted. These committees embraced the whole country and made touch with the lowest and highest levels. Through them, representatives of every major facet of national life—military, police, government and civilian—had a voice in the conduct of defence affairs and, knowing what was wanted and feeling part of the show, were able to contribute to the success of the campaign, which must rank as one of the most brilliant of its kind.

Once the strength of England lay in its village and community life, whose cohesion is lacking in today's society. In the anonymous urban and industrial life of today, security committees could have a welding effect. It is suggested therefore that a structure analogous to that used in Malaya might be established here. There will be those who consider such a proposal alarmist, but it can confidently be asserted that the threats posed by subversion and espionage to us here at home are greater than those which faced us in Malaya.

Such committees should be at national, regional and local level and should embrace representatives from all relevant walks of national life. At national level there would be representatives of government, the armed services, police, prison board, trade unions, employers, education authorities, the security industry, the press. At local level[1] the committees would in addition to their cohesive effect provide a forum where greater understanding of the role and difficulties of the forces of law and order would lead to greater co-operation; the policeman could come out of his ivory tower and again become a real member of the community; he might collect much useful information. The knowledge that these committees existed would itself discourage minor and potential criminals and strengthen the hands of parents and other leaders.

1. It is possible that existing watch and equivalent committees, many of whose functions are disappearing with police amalgamations and increasing Home Office assumption of their powers, could be adapted to these purposes, thus reverting to something more like their original role. But only a proportion of the committee should be elected; the remainder should be appointed so as to ensure the necessary coverage. (See Appendix H for further information on early security organisation.)

In case of need, and this may well be now, these committees could and should be set up in every community, village, town, ward, parish, each with a police officer to guide and assist them. They could—

collect information (but not in the espionage sense);

arrange for contact between the police and frightened or intimidated people;

encourage local education authorities to teach elementary security in schools;

encourage local residents to take security precautions in their homes.

It should be borne in mind that a primary task of subversive organisations will be to penetrate and subvert or gain control of police, security committees, the security industry, and any other organisations which inhibit the achievement of their aims.

The recent Home Office White Paper, *The War Against Crime* (Cmnd. 2296) in a paragraph 'The Co-operation of the Community' gives an example of how committee work in a related field can be useful. The following are extracts from paragraph sixteen:

'*Effective prevention of criminal behaviour requires a joint effort by all social agencies—statutory and voluntary—and indeed by the whole nation. Accordingly, in February 1959, on the day of publication of "Penal Practice in a Changing Society", the then Home Secretary convened a conference of church leaders and others prominent in public life . . . to consider how they could combat delinquency and improve by positive measures the moral health of the nation. Another conference, of a more widely representative kind, took place in November 1961 . . . Since then, two local conferences on the problem of juvenile delinquency have been held in Leeds and Preston. They stimulated active local interest in the problem.*'

These conferences are not, of course, quite the same thing as the permanent security committees envisaged above. Their success shows, nevertheless, that there is considerable scope for thought and action along these lines in the wider sphere.

In Bristol, where there has been for some time a highly progressive approach to the crime problem, a crime prevention panel believed to be the first of its kind in the country has been set up under the chairmanship of the Chief Constable. It embraces industry, commerce, the local authority and police. Sheffield's campaign against crime is taking a similar form. No doubt other enterprising cities will follow suit, but there will only be local results until the matter is put on a national footing.

## GRAND STRATEGY

The government has already set up a broadly based standing committee to consider the question of crime prevention on a national basis. This is progress, but if it is to be effective such a committee must be able to evolve a grand security strategy. This may be defined as the art of applying the whole of the national power in the most effective way to compel the criminal, the spy, the subverter, to abandon his evil way of life.

The committees at various levels would need to be linked by a national secretariat to provide the necessary communications, horizontal and vertical, and, above all, technical expertise. There can be no doubt that the Head of National Security should be a political appointment—a statesman of the highest calibre. Some would argue that the subject fell naturally into the Defence sphere. But it should be remembered that the Security Service, police and prisons, for example, already fall within the realm of home affairs; moreover, the problem is essentially of a civilian and social nature. In all the circumstances the Home Office seems the best administrative location for overall security.

But wherever the security power resides its custodian must be advised by a security chief of staff whose standing should be on a par with that of the Chief of the Defence Staff.

## BREAKING THE SUBVERSIVE STRANGLEHOLD—A FOURTH ARM

Although the total espionage usually necessary to the growth of subversion may be detected and prevented by security and intelligence measures, there may come a time when a subversive political party without technical abuse of the democratic process gains such a grip on key work forces (as it nearly did in the Electrical Trades Union and the National Union of Seamen – see Appendices E and F) that it cannot be dislodged. In spite of all the effort of government, managers, and security committees, crippling strikes in key industries or public utilities are threatened or actually take place. It would be a dangerous illusion to think that the armed services could take over in the circumstances envisaged. In the first place, their use for strike breaking would almost certainly be provocative to many sections of organised labour, who might otherwise behave entirely responsibly.

Secondly, the entire strength of the armed forces, some of which would in any case be abroad, would be quite insufficient in numbers or skills to replace the essential workers of vital industry. Thirdly, prolonged strike-breaking might place intolerable strains on the loyalty of men whose relations and friends might be among the strikers and who were recruited for quite different purposes.

It is not perhaps generally known that a major function of security in its counter-sabotage context (not explained in this book) is to ensure the provision of alternative sources of essential supplies in the event of the sabotage of one. Carried into the counter-passive sabotage sphere, this would imply the provision of a fourth arm of alternative labour; for example—

to man power stations;

to load and unload ships;

to run telecommunications;

to distribute food and fuel reserves.

Since many of these jobs require technical and local knowledge, the replacement labour force would have to be recruited and trained in advance. There is no reason why this should not be a form of national service, perhaps grafted on to civil defence or the Territorial Army, and run on para-military lines.

It is not to be expected that such a proposal would be received with joyful acclaim by all sections of the community; among the noisiest protesters would be those whose interest was ultimately subversive.

But its accomplishment would do a great deal to restore the present imbalance of power between organised labour on the one hand, and the rest of the nation on the other. It would fortify men of goodwill everywhere.

ECONOMIC WARFARE

Espionage and subversion are moral, if not always legal, crimes and both are concerned with gain and redistribution of wealth.

It has been argued *pace* Clausewitz that crime for gain is a continuation of industry by different means. The Government controls legitimate industry by both legal and fiscal measures. But while the Inland Revenue goes to considerable lengths to extract the maximum tax from law-abiding industry, no serious attempt is made to wage economic warfare against its illegal continuation. On the contrary, the main disincentive to crime for gain is deprivation of liberty. This is a curious paradox, for the primary aim of the criminal is profit, not liberty. Deprivation by sentence of the law of such liberty as he had is a doubtful disincentive. In the congenial circumstances with connubial privileges and early release on licence to live on the loot which a prisoner can increasingly expect today, it is becoming a case of 'Heads, I win; tails, I don't lose.'

Just as no industrialist would continue in an industry which was not profitable, so for the criminal crime would be exceedingly unattractive if there were little likelihood of profit, or if such profit as there was suffered sooner or later high taxation. There should be the right, subject to suitable appeal machinery, to tax apparent wealth, including the apparent wealth of wives of convicted criminals.

Economic warfare against the big criminal, if carried out relentlessly by a special intelligence organisation set up for this purpose, or grafted on, say, to the Security Service, would, in the opinion of the author, be the most important single step which could be taken to prevent the spread of crime and kindred evils, such as industrial espionage and subversion. At every stage of these operations, agents, spies, receivers, etc., have to be paid and a proportion of the ultimate spoils promised as well. It should not be difficult to make each stage more and more expensive and to deprive the criminal of many of the tools of his trade, human and material.

It may be observed that such means of waging war against crime are not open to criticism on humanitarian grounds, as are harsh sentences of imprisonment or capital punishment.

THE POLICE

Some main hopes for security against evils which this book portrays must rest on the police and those who are responsible for them. By the time this book is published many improvements may have taken place. It is devoutly to be hoped that these will include:

dispensing with the Police Federation in its present vociferous and insubordinate—almost intimidatory— form;

the establishment of an officer corps with as much recruitment from outside and at whatever levels as may be required by the public interest, with the goal of a culture;

the creation of a national criminal intelligence organisation to act in concert with the CID as does the Security Service with the Special Branch, and to provide intelligence coverage of those areas of major crime not covered by the Security Service. The new organisation should be of the Security Service type, that is, comprised of un-uniformed and un-uniform civilians with the same legal powers as civilians. There might be advantage in extending the function of the Security Service rather than starting a new organisation.

*        *        *        *

The concept of defence against subversion and espionage in our industrial society is therefore one of communal responsibility and organised total resistance. It would not be the first time in England. Our first great law-giver, Alfred the Great, laid it down that the free men of a neighbourhood were responsible for the good conduct of each other. There is an old quotation about Alfred which is an appropriate note on which to end this book: 'It must excite both our highest wonder and reverence to behold a man pursuing solitarily in the midst of ferocity, barbarism and ignorance . . . so many various and noble schemes for the civilisation and the true glory of his country.' The dark forces of subversion and total espionage are the modern equivalents of ferocity, barbarism and ignorance and, today, pose at least as great a challenge to us and our leaders.

Security is always preventive or symptomatic treatment. It does not itself answer the original problem. It should be regarded as a holding operation which gives time for help to arrive, time for correct political solutions to be found, time for the lies and hate on which subversion is based to be demolished by constant assault with the truth and love which are the foundation of all that is worthwhile in man.

# BIBLIOGRAPHY

## *of Works Consulted and Quoted*

The author has been able to discover no previous works of reference bearing directly on the subjects of this book, and he has already pointed out in the *Acknowledgments* that much of his information has come from press sources. The following works have been found most useful in its writing; they, or the relevant parts of them, should be read by any student who wishes to probe wider and deeper.

Bulloch, John.

His book *MI5* (Arthur Barker, 1963) relates the origin and history of the British counter-espionage service, nowadays usually referred to as the Security Service.

*Spy Ring* (Secker & Warburg, 1961) was written jointly with Henry Miller and is an account of the Portland naval secrets case.

De Gramont, Sanche.

*The Secret War* (Andre Deutsch, 1962) is a story of international espionage since 1945 and develops the theme of total espionage.

Fleming, Peter.

*The Sixth Column* (Rupert Hart-Davis, 1951). This book was described in its blurb as 'very funny' and 'an urbane, light-hearted and ingenious satire on the state of our country.' Some of it reads less funnily today. For example:

'Too much security is far worse than too little for a country which owes its position in the world to its spirit of enterprise and its readiness to take risks. If you run England as a Welfare State, *and* penalise initiative, *and* promote first frustration and then dishonesty by having too many unenforceable regulations and too many incompetent officials, then, says the author of Plan D, you set in motion processes which must inevitably impair the country's one really vital and irreplaceable asset, the character of her people.'

Irving, David

*The Virus House* (William Kimber, 1967) — This excellent account of the German wartime atomic research programme includes in

Chapter 7 details of the famous sabotage attacks on the Norwegian heavy water plant at Vemork near Rjukan.

Mattingly, Garrett.

*The Defeat of the Spanish Armada* (Jonathan Cape, 1959) includes information about Walsingham's espionage networks in Spain and in the Low Countries.

Miller, Henry—see Bulloch, John.

Packard, Vance.

*The Naked Society* (Longmans Green, 1964) examines the increasing invasion of individual privacy and is useful background reading. Espionage is an important violation of privacy.

Radzinowicz, Professor Leon.

*Ideology and Crime* (Heinemann, 1966)—A collection of lectures given to the Columbia University Law School—a study of crime in its social and historical context which illuminates the increase of espionage and subversion.

Rolph, C. H.

*All Those in Favour* (Andre Deutsch, 1962)—A condensed report, with an eye-witness commentary, on the High Court action against the Electrical Trades Union and a number of its Communist, or pro-Communist, leaders.

Sampson, Anthony.

*Anatomy of Britain* (Hodder and Stoughton, 1962)—A journalist's view of Britain's managers. It does not include the Police in the management panorama, which may be significant.

Sargant, William.

*Battle for the Mind* (Heinemann, 1957)—A study of the mechanics of brain-washing.

Schlesinger, Jr., Arthur M.

*A Thousand Days* (Andre Deutsch, 1965) includes an eye-witness account of President Kennedy's relationship with the Central Intelligence Agency.

Seth, Ronald.

*Anatomy of Spying* (Arthur Barker, 1961) is an explanation of the trade of espionage by a man who has carried it out.

*Unmasked* (Hawthorn, New York, 1965) is a comprehensive account of Russian espionage from the Revolution of 1917 to the Cold War of today.

Trevelyan, G. M.

*English Social History* (Longmans Green, first published in Great Britain in 1944) includes information on Defoe and Defoe's intelligence and public relations work.

# APPENDIX A

## *The Nature of Competitive Information*

(Excerpted with permission from *Chemical Engineering* 25th April 1966, © 1966, McGraw-Hill Inc.)
The intelligence department will be concerned with the following types of information about your competitors:

### CORPORATE AND FINANCIAL

(This is basic information upon which you build your file):
Corporate structure, interlocking directors
Management personnel changes, organizational changes
Mergers, acquisitions, joint ventures
New financing (domestic and foreign)
News of capital investments
Quarterly and annual financial reports

### PRODUCTION

Raw materials—nature, sources, costs
Present capacity, present output, planned capacity
Production costs
Processing techniques—use of new equipment and instrumentation
Product improvements
Byproduct and waste disposal
New plans—where, when, what and why

### MARKETING

Method of marketing
Warehousing—location, types of inventory
Price lists, discounts, contracts, reciprocal agreements
Customer services
Advertising plans

Market area tests
Customer brochures
Consumer surveys
Export sales, foreign distribution

### TECHNICAL

R & D staff—quantity, quality and location
Analysis of technical recruitment advertising
New products and processes—research findings, pilot-plant work
Government research contracts
Competitor's contracts with outside laboratories or technical consultants
Quality and properties of products as per analysis and tests

### LEGAL

Trademarks used and pending
Patents issued and pending
Patent or trademark infringement suits
Antitrust suits
FTC violations
Robinson-Patman Act violations
Income tax suits and rulings
ICC and tariff rulings
Senate investigations

# APPENDIX B

## *Hiring a Competitor's Employee*

(Excerpted with permission from *Chemical Engineering* 25th April 1966, © 1966, McGraw-Hill Inc.)

One way of gaining specific commercial intelligence is, of course, to hire an engineer or scientist working for your competitor. If you have your eye on such a man, you should consult with technical people in your own company and find out as much as you can about the special attributes and experience of the competitor's expert. The next step is to write an advertisement that reads exactly like that man's qualifications. This may result in an inquiry, which should be directed to a box number and not your company's name.

A second procedure is to have an employment agency write direct to the competitor's employee asking him if he knows anyone having such and such qualifications for a position paying a high salary. (Of course, the qualifications set forth should exactly describe the man to whom the letter is sent). This may prompt him to write the agency 'What about me?'

Before hiring such an applicant, your personnel department should ask to see the contract between him and his present employer. Is he restricted as to the industry or business he can offer his services to? Is there a 'holdover' clause that prohibits him from working for a competitor for one or more years?

If none of these clauses appear, then it will be proper to employ him, but most large corporations, desiring to avoid litigation, will require the new employee to sign an agreement including the clause:

'Employee agrees that, in performing his service for ———— (the new employer), he will not disclose or use any confidential information obtained by him from his former employer; and the company ———— (the new employer) will not require, as a condition of his employment, that the employee disclose any confidential information of his former employer.'

If an agreement of this type is made, then the new employer is usually well protected against suit by the former employer.

## APPENDIX C

# How to Hire and Use a 'Special' Investigator

(Excerpted with permission from *Chemical Engineering* 25th April 1966, © 1966, McGraw-Hill Inc.)

Suppose your salesmen report that your chief competitor has told its customers that 'within a few months we will be able to offer this product at a five per cent reduction in price'. A conference should be held with top management, sales management, research and development, and production to consider ways and means of meeting such a price reduction. If this conference reaches the conclusion that the competitor is going to employ a new raw material, or have subcomponents built abroad, it may be advisable to hire an investigator.

There are available a number of reputable firms and individual investigators who can be hired to obtain a specific piece of information. Of course, their fees are relatively high, and they should be used only in special cases where quick, precise information is essential. Also, their use may or may not be legal, depending on how they accomplish their task, and on other circumstances. Even in apparently legal situations, it is well to use the following protective procedures:

(1) Never make a direct contact—investigators should be contacted through a consultant or industrial laboratory.

(2) Your corporate name should never be revealed to the investigator.

(3) The investigator should be interviewed in your consultant's office or laboratory by one of your technical men who is thoroughly familiar with the problem. The investigator should be carefully instructed as to the precise information desired and the potential sources of this information.

(4) The timing and the price should be agreed upon in advance. It is understood that the company will have to pay the consultant or intermediary a commission of from five per cent to ten per cent for services.

(5) The investigator should render his report orally in the presence of

your agent and your representative. There should be no written memos regarding the matter.

(6) Payment is made to your agent (consultant or laboratory), who then pays the investigator. No link between your company and the investigator should be apparent.

Let us assume that the investigator finds that your competitor plans to purchase a partly manufactured component from a Japanese producer. (He can import such an item at reduced duty rates because it is not fully manufactured.) Your company should consider sending a technical representative to Japan and contacting, through a Japanese agent, firms who might be producing such a component. Experts from Japan are handled chiefly by so-called 'Trading Companies' and it is not difficult to ascertain which company will handle your competitor's exports.

Moreover, by checking with the MITI agency of the government, which regulates and approves such agreements, it may be easily ascertained whether your competitor has entered into a know-how agreement with a Japanese firm. By moving rapidly through a competing Japanese firm, your company may be able to import such components as soon as or before your competitor. Thus you may be able to offer your customers the same product, at the same price reduction, at the same time, as your competitor.

Special investigators may be used also for finding out whether your competitor is infringing one of your patents, buying his raw material from another source not known to you, or preparing to build a new plant that could affect your own plans.

## APPENDIX D

# *Cost of Competitive Information*

(Excerpted with permission from *Chemical Engineering* 25th April 1966, © 1966, McGraw-Hill Inc.)
In a small company, or in a semi-autonomous division of a larger company, the annual operating budget of a newly established CI department might look as follows:

| | |
|---|---|
| Salary of manager | $12,000 |
| Salary of secretary-librarian | 6,000 |
| Payroll-related expenses | 3,000 |
| Subscriptions to magazines, newspapers and reporting investigators | 1,500 |
| Fees of special investigators | 3,000 |
| Fees of foreign agent or part-time Washington representative | 5,000 |
| Office supplies, telephone, misc. | 1,000 |
| Annual budget | $31,500 |

Is it worth the cost? The question you must decide is not so much whether your company can afford such a department, but rather whether it can afford *not* to have one.

# The Case of the Electrical Trades Union

In the successful High Court action in 1961 against the ETU and a number of its communist or pro-communist leaders, in which John Byrne and Frank Chapple, both members of the Union, successfully claimed that elections for the union's chief officials had for some years been fraudulently conducted. Counsel for the plaintiffs in his opening words explained how the defendants were alleged to have achieved their main object—the rigging of elections,

(1) By arranging that there should never be more than one candidate offering himself for election in any given position;

(2) By arranging who that candidate was to be;

(3) By ensuring that the candidate was proposed by as many branches as possible;

(4) By sending 'national officers' (employees of the union) to branch meetings just before an election, ostensibly on some official business, but really to canvass for the communist candidate;

(5) By making trivial charges against prominent non-communists, so that they could be disqualified from union office for a period of years;

(6) By 'disqualifying' non-communist branches, using the impossibly complicated rules as a source of reported irregularities in election procedure, and condoning the same irregularities at communist ones;

(7) When all else had failed, by altering the returns of voting sent in by branches.

The two principal defendants, Frank Haxell, then Secretary, and Frank Foulkes, President of the Union, were also members of a number of special committees of the Communist Party of Great Britain whose function it was (though they denied this) to secure the election of Communist leaders in the Union and thus control its policy.

In his judgement in favour of the plaintiffs, the Judge had this to say about communism:

'*Communism is not illegal in this country. Nor are communist gatherings proscribed, provided they are not aimed against or calculated to subvert the State. In this action I have heard no evidence of gatherings or activities of that character . . .*'

But what other purposes have communists in seeking to gain and maintain control of vital trades unions? Communism is a political creed whose ultimate purpose is clearly the assumption of political power in the state. What better way is there of subverting the state than by holding it to ransom through the big vital unions? Like the National Union of Seamen. Like the Electrical Trades Union. The learned Judge should have borne in mind Lenin's dictum mentioned in Chapter 7 and repeated here to stress its importance:

'*It is necessary . . . to resort to all sorts of stratagems, manoeuvres and illegal methods, to evasions and subterfuges, in order to penetrate the trades unions and to remain in them carrying on communist activities inside them at all costs.*'

Perhaps a large notice carrying this message should be hung in such places as boardrooms, government offices, and trades union headquarters.

# The Seamen's Strike 1966

The seamen's strike provided a clear demonstration of how Britain could be ruined by the intrigues of a few and the greed of many and is a fitting summary of the main theme of this work.

The strike began with

*A Blunt Pay Demand.* A vital sector of the transport industry and therefore in a position of high bargaining power decided to make 'a blunt pay demand' not unlike that made by Mr. Reginald Webb of the Police Federation a few days after[1] the seamen's strike began on the 16th May, 1966.

Of the seamen's subsequent decision to threaten a strike the court of inquiry set up by the Government under Lord Pearson had this to say:

*'The Executive Council (of the National Union of Seamen) were . . . calling a strike on the assumption that they would get their own way— that the owners, after all the concessions which they had made and offered, would eventually under pressure from the strike threat offer more.'*

The country was at the relevant time in the middle of a grave financial crisis, of which the executive council of the NUS must have been aware. From their point of view therefore the timing of the strike threat could not have been more propitious; it could reasonably be anticipated that the government would be compelled to exert pressure on the ship owners to give way to the demands of the NUS.

Of the justification for striking the court of inquiry said:

*'In our view, the executive council (of the National Union of Seamen) were not justified in using the strike weapon without further attempts to resolve the position, because there was nothing to call for the use of this very drastic and dangerous remedy. There was no remaining issue of principle; there were only questions as to the terms of the offer. Their members were not suffering hardship. There had been a major and costly improvement in seamen's wages in March 1965, and enormous*

1. 24th May 1966.

*minor benefits gained and now, in 1966, there is another costly im-*
*provement offered.'*
*Political Exploitation.* A dangerous strike designated by an impartial
inquiry as 'unjustified' having been achieved by one means or another,
the next step in subversion is to increase and prolong the damage by
all practicable means. On 28th June the Prime Minister addressed the
House of Commons on the subject of the Communist Party's attempt
to do just that. The following extracts and story are from the report
of his speech in *The Times* of 29th June, 1966:
'*For some years the Communist Party had had as one of their objectives*
*to build up a position of strength not only in the seamen's union, but in*
*other unions concerned with docks and transport. . . This is (he said)*
*a takeover bid. . . The whole formidable power of the Communist*
*Party's industrial apparatus has been for some time directed towards this*
*end.'*
    The Prime Minister unfolded a story which showed that the in-
formation necessary to the communists' exploitation had been
acquired and that this had been used to great advantage. For example, the communists had been able to 'capture' two key strike
committees—those on London and Liverpool. Although there were
no members of the Communist Party on the executive council of the
NUS, a small group of
'*articulate, intelligent and well-briefed members could exercise in-*
*fluence far beyond their number.'*
    The Prime Minister referred to Mr. Joseph Kenny and Mr. James
Slater, neither of whom was a member of the Communist Party, both
of whom were members of the executive council of the NUS. He said
'*I must acknowledge their political and argumentative skill. I can*
*testify to their ability, to their mastery of the details of the seamen's*
*complaints, to their ability to absorb skilled briefing, and to their*
*dominance among their colleagues. . . .*
    '*They live in Liverpool and South Shields respectively, and over the*
*past few weeks when attending the executive council in London, they*
*have stayed at the same flat as Mr. Jack Coward. Of course, they are*
*free to stay where they like, but Mr. Ramelson has visited the flat when*
*they were there, and Mr. Norris has been in constant touch with them.*
*They have been in continual contact with Mr. Ramelson and Mr.*
*Norris.'*
    Coward, Ramelson and Norris are members of the Communist
Party. The Prime Minister who has met the executive council at 10
Downing Street, went on
'*I need no evidence, other than my eyes and ears, to recognise that*

*these two have dominated the executive council throughout the negotiations.'*

The Prime Minister did not mention that it is established communist practice to have an undercover structure—a party living underground—as well as one in the open. This has many advantages:

(1) In the event of proscription of the 'legitimate' open party the work can go on.

(2) It can be used to infiltrate organisations whose members are hostile to communism. For example—
trades unions like the Electrical Trades Union, where communists are not permitted to hold office; other trades unions where communist support is weak and whose ballot boxes cannot be manipulated (see p. 193);
other political parties with the object of gaining control or of weakening them so that their power can be usurped.

(3) There is a ready-made espionage, sabotage and secret propaganda machine which can also be used for intimidation, for psychological pressure, for secret courts, for the elimination of traitors, for such work as that described by the Prime Minister in the same speech, according to *The Times*:

*'All of us are used to hecklers, but the treatment anyone who in the past six weeks advocated a return to work on almost any terms would have received from strike committees—and some of them did from picket lines outside union headquarters, and the more vociferous members of the strike meetings—would have daunted many of us. I had it in Liverpool ten days ago, and like many I am an old hand. But it was not pleasant, and those who, through the history and organisation of this union, are less experienced than we, might find this treatment almost intolerable.*

*'He commended to MPs all the evidence produced in some newspaper reports—the telephone calls to branches, the organisation of brutal slogans, placards, interjections, the implications and suggestions, whether on the executive or at strike committees or at any other level— and this certainly took place—that anyone who advocated negotiations up to a few days ago was a traitor to the men who elected him and a marked man in the next election. These things were being said, and they knew that this is true.*

*'There was no more tightly-knit community than a ship. From a ship there was no escape. There was no happier hunting ground for the sea lawyers who could make the life of any man a misery who had been*

*marked out as a blackleg even for exercising his democratic duties as a member of an elected body, than a ship on the high seas.'*

Such an underground organisation when operating in industry for secret political purposes can fairly be described as a *total industrial espionage network for purposes of subversion*—in this case, *the usurping of power in the National Union of Seamen.*

This was not, of course, the only object. The next one, as the Prime Minister said, was to spread the strike:

*'Time and again in this dispute the Communist Party's objectives have rapidly become the policy of the executive (of the NUS) . . . This is particularly true in relation to the determination of the party to spread the strike.'*

with, as a further object

*'The destruction of the government's prices and incomes policy.'*

The seamen's strike ended on 1st July 1966 shortly after the Prime Minister's denouement. The inevitable long and short term economic, military and political consequences to the pound sterling, to the British standard of living, to defence in West Germany and east of Suez, to our alliances, which are the basis of our defence, our influence in world affairs, must be gratifying to those whose overall strategy has the weakening of the West as the main objective.

# APPENDIX G

## *The Scamp Report on the Motor Industry and Subversion in the Amalgamated Engineering Union*

As a result of prolonged unrest in the motor industry a Joint Labour Council was set up in November, 1965, under the independent chairmanship of A. J. Scamp, JP, a man renowned for his tact and impartiality. The council consisted of six employers' and six trade union representatives. It was agreed that Mr. Scamp would from time to time report to the Minister of Labour on the work of the council and his first published report is dated 10th November 1966.

The great problem of the motor industry is unofficial strikes. In 1965 there were just over one thousand of these and in the first half of 1966 they were running at the yearly rate of 1,200. In the first six months of 1965 more than six million man hours were lost. Although this was reduced to about three million in the first six months of 1966, the disruption may have been even greater because of the increased number of stoppages.

The leading motor car manufacturers together with relevant trades unions are parties to formal agreements for the avoidance of disputes. The agreed procedure provides for five stages of discussion and that no stoppage of work, partial or general, shall take place until the procedure is exhausted.

Of the six hundred stoppages which took place between 1st January and 30th June 1966, all but five were unofficial and, in many cases, the procedure had not been used at all or had been abandoned at an early stage. At Morris Motors Limited, Cowley, for instance, the council had found that, in 1965, 256 out of 297 stoppages of work had occurred before the senior shop steward had even had a chance to put the grievance into procedure. In the first half of 1966 again, 128 stoppages out of 142 took place before the senior shop steward had had time to act on them, in spite of special efforts made by the company to provide facilities for the bringing in of senior shop stewards as soon as a problem was known to exist. A closer examination of 445 stoppages of work which took place in five motor manufacturing firms in the first half of 1966 shows that over two-thirds of

H

them lasted for short periods ranging from up to four hours, and over eighty per cent. lasted for no more than one working day. If therefore, in so high a proportion of these stoppages, a formula for the resumption of work could be found within a few hours, one is bound to ask oneself if the problem could not equally well have been resolved without a stoppage of work and its consequential effects on production and the livelihood of other workers.

Mr. Scamp says of the unofficial stoppages—

*'That all is not well with the present arrangements is clear from the fact that, all too frequently, stoppages of work occur with no attempt to invoke the procedure or, at best, before the procedural arrangements have been used to the fullest extent. This situation is frequently defended with the argument that the procedure takes too long and that men get better results if they stop work in order to call attention to their grievances. Whilst I would be the last to advocate avoidable delay in resolving industrial relations problems, I believe that this argument should be treated with reserve.'*

and

*'It is difficult to identify precise and coherent reasons why this state of continuing indiscipline should prevail so strongly in the motor car industry in particular. Working conditions in the industry are not always beyond reproach, but in modern motor car plants they usually compare well with conditions in many other occupations and industries including other sections of the engineering industry. One recognises, of course, that some of the work is repetitive and may induce feelings of frustration or boredom. It is uncertain, however, how far such considerations are of material importance in determining the incidence of industrial disputes. There may be scope for research here, but it is interesting, and possibly significant, that no complaints or representations on this score have been made by the men's representatives at any of the inquiries conducted by the Council.'*

and

*'Failure by the industry to enforce whatever procedure agreement is in operation can only lead to anarchy, a state which seems already to be not very far away in some establishments. If the industry cannot itself evolve means of restraining minority groups of men from the selfish pursuit of immediate sectional advantage, without regard to agreements one is forced to the conclusion that the only solution may be for the power to impose sanctions against indiscipline to be vested in authorities outside or independent of the motor car industry.'*

There is no direct evidence available to the author that this unhappy state of affairs is due to subversive activity. The probability that it is is strong. It is useful to apply certain tests—

*Motive.* With all the information, access and skill available to him Mr. Scamp has been unable to find an explanation for the 'anarchy', which on the face of it seems motiveless.

Mr. Scamp did not apparently investigate the possibility of a political background. Yet the motor industry is one of the largest in the country and accounts for a substantial part of our exports. If any subversive political party wanted to create economic difficulties for Britain this, like the shipping or electrical industries, would be an excellent target.

*The Communist Position.* A prominent trades union in the motor industry is the Amalgamated Engineering Union. This is the largest union in the non-communist world which does not by its rules ban communist officer holders. It has a membership of 1,100,000, most of whom are highly skilled engineers performing important jobs in key industries, including particularly defence. According to *The Times* of 10th February, 1966, the 'communist dominated' AEU had been blamed by Vickers at Barrow-in-Furness for inspiring a strike threat to 'knock' Britain's Polaris submarine programme.

Quite apart from this evidence Polaris is an obvious target for communist subversive activity. And if this is not enough, *The Times* quotes Mr. F. Porter, the AEU district secretary, as having 'no comment' to make on the alleged communist-dominated structure of his committee, and as refusing to reveal communist membership.

On 1st July, 1966, *The Guardian* carried a report that Sir William Carron, president of the AEU, and one of the most highly respected trades unionists in the country, had accused communists of trying to take control of the union. The warning appeared in the July issue of the union's monthly journal alongside a report of a meeting held in Birmingham on 4th June at which extremists active in the engineering industry were present. The report says the meeting was dominated by communists. The *Daily Telegraph* of the same date said that the meeting was attended by about ninety supporters of a left-wing publication, *Engineering Voice*. One of the main speakers was Mr. Hugh Scanlon, a member of the executive council and prospective candidate for AEU presidency in 1967. Mr. Scanlon is also, with Sir William Carron, a member of the Motor Industry Joint Labour Council and therefore a colleague of Mr. Scamp's.

In an article in the *Sunday Times* on 3rd July Sir William Carron drew attention to the fact that he would have to retire in 1967 and this and other elections due involved the majority of the eight-member executive council and three newly created posts of full-time national organisers. 'Here', said Sir William, 'is a glittering prize for the subversive elements in our society and a unique coalition of Communist, Trotskyist and left-wing Labour rebels is already in action.'

He went on to say that the Birmingham meeting referred to above was for the purpose of discussing which of his successors should have the support of the 'Communist-Trotskyist-Leftist clique'. If the meeting had been confined to AEU members it would not have been so bad, but in fact it was attended by a number of members of other unions including Mr. Jack Coward of the National Union of Seamen, one of the communists named by the Prime Minister in Parliament in connection with the seamen's strike (see Appendix F).

Sir William also said—

*'Those who attended the Birmingham meeting were told by a Communist official of an outside union, Mr. William Warman of the National Union of Sheet Metal Workers and Coppersmiths, that "if we can change the position in the AEU we could change the position in the whole labour movement."*

*'What is meant by "labour" can be gauged from the fact that one candidate for my post who will certainly not be supported by the subversives is Mr. John Boyd, at present executive member for Scotland, who in a few weeks becomes chairman of the Labour Party. A strange situation where the chairman of the Labour Party can not only be rejected by his brother Labour members in his union but be actively plotted against by subversives.*

*'I use the word "subversive" advisedly because the policies of the Communists are well-known. Communists who are honest about their political affiliations can be countered. There have, however, sprung up in recent times other front organisations which seem to be anarchistic in their approach and which, it has now been proved, are definitely engaged in initiating or most certainly encouraging the spread of disruption. For most purposes, and certainly for the control of a key organisation such as my own union, there is a natural alliance between these subversive groups.*

*'To many trade unionists, this question of interference might seem to be a matter domestic to the AEU. I would hope that it is now recognised that this is not so. The union's influences on the nation's economy and defence make it a matter which has a far wider impact. Indeed, whatever the Government of the day, and its political complexion, the modern trade union has an influence and power far beyond its industrial base.*

'*I consider it my duty to make known, first to my own members, and then to the country as a whole, not only what is occurring but what may occur through the influences of those who capitalise upon apathy. There is still a need to alert the community to what is happening, despite the now-historic ETU case, Mr. Wilson's speech of last Tuesday, and my own decision to publish the circumstances of the Birmingham meeting.*

'*There is very proper resistance to any suspicion that we are becoming the type of society in which people are continually investigated by the police or other organs of the state. It has, nevertheless, to be recognised that all democracies are vulnerable to the potentiality of tightly-knit well-disciplined groups. We have surely had enough experience of this in Europe and in other parts of the world, especially in those post-war years. Recognising our national abhorrence of dictatorship, in my estimation it is the lesser of evils that we should know of the operations of those who would use democratic licence to destroy democracy and replace it with dictatorship.*

'*These facts are well known to many people, particularly trade union leaders. It is depressing that so few have been prepared to speak— publicly—about them. I believe that in the not too far distant future, circumstances will compel them to denounce the subversives and their tactics.*'

There is plenty of other evidence to suggest that communist subversion is strong in the motor industry. After Sir William Carron's article it is hardly necessary to say more, but two aspects of behaviour associated with the unofficial strikers of this industry are so typical of subversion, particularly communist subversion, that they are worthy of brief mention.

*The maintenance of subversive discipline.* The now celebrated 'noose' courts discovered to have been held at BMC Cowley in March 1966 resemble very strongly the courts of underground or espionage nets for subversive purposes. Unfortunately the evidence has been confused by subsequent 'whitewashing' and covering up operations, but it seems fairly clear, for example, that—

(1) there was no form of appeal;

(2) no legal representation was made available;

(3) judgement was by acclaim of a crowd, like lynch law or mob rule; and

(4) there was bullying, if not intimidation, as part of the 'trial'.

According to *The Sunday Express* of 20th March, 1966,

'*Four men are in hospital or too ill to go to work as the result of the notorious "noose" trial at the Cowley, Oxford, car factory. These are facts, whatever a high union official may say about grotesque distortion in newspaper accounts.'*

Such courts are vital to subversion, and will be found wherever it is.

*Agreed Procedures.* Nothing is more damaging to subversion than proper machinery for the ventilation of disputes and grievances. It is a primary objective of subversive organisations to discredit such machinery by all possible means and prevent its use if necessary by intimidation or bullying.

In all the circumstances Mr. Scamp's remark above: 'Of the six hundred stoppages which took place between 1st January and 30th June, 1966, all but five were unofficial and, in many cases, the procedure had not been used at all or had been abandoned at an early stage', is hardly surprising.

With all the foregoing evidence and much more available for the seeking from open sources, his other statement, 'It is difficult to identify precise and coherent reasons why this state of continuing indiscipline should prevail so strongly in the motor car industry in particular', seems naïve.


POSTSCRIPT

It was announced in April 1967 that BMC had made a 'disastrous loss of £7½ millions in the first half of 1966'. The company blamed, among other things, a series of strikes for its poor performance.

A continuation of losses on this scale might mean a foreign take-over to 'rescue' BMC, as in the case of Rootes. In this event almost the entire British motor-car industry would be in foreign hands.

It is impossible to escape the conclusion that the foreign motor magnates have nothing to lose by increased subversion in this industry.

# APPENDIX H

## *Early Security Organisation*

The importance of committee work in security has been stressed in the book, and the evolution of responsibility for it is therefore briefly described below.

While vegetable life ensured its survival by the random method of prolificacy, and other animal life risked the external hatching of its eggs, mammals nurtured their young in the mobile fortress of the womb, and enlisted the aid of the male as a guard and commissary. When other living beings left their children exposed to the dangers of cold and heat and the attention of wild beasts, the mammals kept their young with them while they were too weak to fight their enemies and taught them the arts of survival. The apprenticeship lengthening as life became more complex made the partnership of man and woman an enduring one, which gave rise to man's first committee and finest institution, marriage, whose purpose is now, as it was originally, security.

Man soon learned to give depth to the defence of his family, by hiding his wife and his children in a hollow tree or behind some heavy rocks, especially at night. Later caves were used with boulders for doors, and the site was carefully chosen so as to be difficult to find and to attack without making a noise. Like many animals, early man liked to jabber, and he soon found that he could use this noise to warn his family or his friends when danger threatened. A particular noise meant tigers, another elephants, and so on. The human voice was thus the first burglar alarm; security was probably the origin of language.

The rigours of early existence, and especially of the glacial period, which threatened to destroy the human race, taught man that he must provide against disaster. Soon he learned to store food in case of famine, animal skins and fuel for fire against extreme cold. Later there were communal stores for use in emergency. This was, of course, insurance—which is the concept of communal responsibility for individual loss.

As the family grew, so did a need for discipline. Disobedience could in certain circumstances lead to loss of life. Not only was this bad for the victims, but it weakened the family unit or the tribe. Mother was undoubtedly the first teacher; if her discipline failed she appealed to father, who was a suitable authority for two reasons. First, he was physically strong; secondly, being less involved (through being away from his family for much of the day) he was less partial.

It was this internal order of the family, later of the tribe, which was probably the first true police function in human society. The free man, the tithing man, the mutual pledging called frithborh by the Saxons and frankpledge by the Normans, are all developments of this responsibility of the father for the order of his family.

The *Encyclopaedia Britannica* (11th edition), quoting various authorities, says of frankpledge:

'*An early English institution, consisting of an association for mutual security whose members . . . were perpetually bail for each other. The custom whereby the inhabitants of a district were responsible for any crime or injury committed by one of their number is old and widespread; it prevailed in England before the Norman Conquest, and is an outcome of the earlier principle whereby this responsibility rested on kinship . . . About this time (1030) these societies, each having its headman, were called* frithborhs *or peace-borhs, and the Normans translated the Anglo Saxon word by frankpledge. But the history of the frankpledge proper begins not earlier than the time of the Norman Conquest. The laws, which although called the laws of Edward the Confessor were not drawn up until about 1130, contain a clause about frithborhs which decrees that in every place societies of ten men shall be formed for mutual security and reparation . . .*

'*The view of frankpledge, or the duty of ascertaining that the law with regard to frankpledges was complied with, was in hands of sheriffs, but held an itinerant court called the "sheriff's tourn" for this and other purposes . . .*

'*The machinery of the frankpledge was probably used by Henry II when he introduced the jury of presentment; and commenting on this connexion F. W. Maitland says, "the duty of producing one's neighbour to answer accusations (the duty of the frankpledges) could well be converted into the duty of telling tales against him". The system of frankpledge prevailed in some English boroughs. Sometimes a court for view of frankpledge, called in some places a mickleton, whereat the mayor or the bailiffs presided, was held for the whole borough; in other cases the borough was divided into wards, or into leets, each of which had its separate court.*'

The Encyclopaedia's point that frankpledge is the outcome of an earlier principle whereby security responsibility rested on kinship should be noted.

An older definition is given by Giles Jacob's *A New Law Dictionary* (London 1736):

'*Frankpledge signifies a Pledge or Surety for the Behaviour of Freemen; being the ancient Custom of this kingdom borrowed from the Lombards; that for the preservation of public Peace, every Free born Man at the Age of Fourteen (Religious Persons, Clerks, etc., excepted) should give security for his Truth towards the King and his Subjects, or be committed to prison; whereupon a certain Number of Neighbours usually became bound one for another, to see such Man of their Pledge forth-coming at all Times, or to answer the Transgression done by any gone away: And whenever any one offended it was forthwith enquired in what Pledge he was, and then those of that Pledge either produced the offender within thirty one days, or satisfied for his offence. This was called Frank-Pledge, and the custom was so kept, that Sheriffs at every County Court took oaths as young persons grew to the age of fourteen years, and see that they were settled in one Decennary or other; this branch of the Sheriff's authority was called Visus Franci-plegii, or View of Frank-Pledge. At this time, no man giveth other security for the keeping of the Peace than his Oath.*'

Gradually it became more convenient for these committees to delegate their security functions and it was out of this delegation that the constable, and later the police forces, arose. But the committees retained for many years supervisory rights, including the right to appoint constables. In their modern form, they are Watch Committees in the cities and boroughs of England and Wales, and in the counties, Standing Joint Committees. Their responsibilities and powers are being steadily eroded by central government.

Committee work in England has a long and honourable history, and it is fitting to end this Appendix with some words written by a distinguished historian and Master of Balliol, Mr. A. L. Smith:

'*Nowhere was the village community so real and enduring a thing as it was in England for at least 12 centuries of its history. In every parish men met almost daily in humble, but very real self-government, to be judged by their fellows, or fined by them, or punished as bad characters; to settle the ploughing times and harvest times, the fallowing and the grazing rules for the whole village. To these twelve centuries of discipline we owe the peculiar English capacity for self-government, the enormous English development of the voluntary principle in all manner of institutions.*'

# APPENDIX I

## *Defoe's Scheme for General Intelligence*

The following are extracts from a twenty-three page document written in 1704 by Defoe for Robert Harley, then Speaker of the House of Commons, now preserved in the manuscript room of the British Museum. It should be borne in mind that the principal purpose of this scheme was to help Harley achieve and maintain the supreme power. For those interested in history as well as intelligence it is worth reading in full:

(1) *'I ALLOW that in our constitution we admit of no supreme ministry*

*that the nation is particularly jealous of favourites*

*These are the two chief obstructions in the way of a refined and rising statesman and these are the two reasons why we have had no capital men in the Civil Administration, no Richelieus, Mazarins or Colberts in the State*

*But I must go back for a reason for these two principles and must say*

*(1) It would be best to have a supreme ministry*

*(2) The nation may easily be reconciled to it*

*Twill be needless to prove the advantage of a chief ministry; our confusions in Council, our errors in executing and unwariness in directing from the multitude and bad conduct of ministers make it too plain.'*

(2) *'Sir Francis Walsingham, though not a Prime Minister, yet if we read his story the ablest statesman and the longest employed, the most employed in difficult cases and the greatest Master of Intelligence in the age.'*

(3) *'How shall you make yourself Prime Minister of State, unenvied and unmolested, be neither addressed against by Parliament, intrigued against by Parties, or murmured at by the mob—?*

*With submission, tis very feasible with an accurate conduct.*

*They say those designs require most policy which have least of honesty; this design must be honest because it must be honest to serve our country.'*

(4)  '*The King of Sweden in his German wars always employed trusty persons in the towns and cities he reduced, to inform themselves of any known case where one was oppressed, or any family that had the general pity; and unlooked for, unasked, he would send for, right, and believe them.*'

(5)  '*Intelligence is the soul of all public business.*

*I have heard that our Secretary's office is allowed 12,000 per annum for this weighty article, and I am credibly informed the King of France has paid eleven millions in one year for the same article—and tis allowed he never spares his money on that head, and thereby outdoes all the world in the knowledge of his neighbours.*

*How much of the 12,000 allowed for intelligence is expended in our Secretary's office I will not guess at. But this I presume: that such a sum being so vastly disproportioned to the necessary expense, the work is not done, and consequently the money which is given for it is lost.*

*Our statesmen have been so far from acquainting themselves with other countries that they are strangers to their own, a certain token that they have sought their private advantage, not the public service, The Secretary's office should be an abridgment of all Europe.*

*Her Majesty's Secretary of State ought to have Tables of all the following particulars to refer to, stated so regularly that they might have recourse to any particular immediately they ought to have.*

(1)  *A perfect list of all the gentry and families of rank in England, their residences, characters, and interest in the respective counties.*

(2)  *Of all the Clergy of England, their beneficies, their character and morals and the like of the dissenters.*

(3)  *Of all the leading men in the cities and boroughs, with the parties they espouse.*

*They ought to have a Table of Parties, and proper calculations of their strength in every respective part, which is to be had by having the copies of the Polls sent up on all elections, and all the circumstances of such elections historically collected by faithful hands and transmitted to the office.*

*They should know the names of all the men of great personal estates, that they may know how and where to direct any occasional trust. They should have the special characters of all the Justices of the Peace, and men of note in every county, to have recourse to on all occasions.*

*Two trusty agents would easily direct all this so if their hands are not too much tied up as to money, and yet the persons entrusted no know who they serve nor for what need.*

*The Secretary of State should have a Table of all the Ministers of State, lists of the households, the Privy Councils and favourites of every court in Europe, and their characters.*

*With exact lists of their forces, names of the officers, state of their revenue, methods of government, etc., so just and authentic and regularly amended as alterations happen, that by this he may duly estimate their strength, judge of their interests and proceedings, and treat with them accordingly.*

*He should keep a correspondence of friendship in all courts with ministers of like quality, as far as may be honourably obtained, and without prejudice carried on.*

*Mr. Mitton kept a constant epistolary conversation with several foreign ministers of state, and men of learning, abstracted from affairs of state, but so woven with political observations that he found it as useful as any part of his foreign correspondence.*

*A hundred thousand pounds per annum spent now for three years in foreign intelligence might be the best money ever this nation laid out, and I am persuaded I could name two articles where, if some money had been well applied, neither the insurrection in Hungary nor the war in Poland should have been so fatal to the confederacy as now they are.*

(4) *If it may be of service I shall give a scheme for the speedy settling of those two uneasy articles and consequently bringing down such a force on the French as should in all probability turn the scale of the war on the Danube and the Po.*

*A settled intelligence in Scotland, a thing strangely neglected there, is without doubt the principal occasion of the present misunderstandings between the two kingdoms; in the last reign it caused the King to have many ill things put upon him, and worse are very likely to follow.*

*I beg leave to give a longer scheme of thoughts on that head than is proper here and a method how the Scots may be brought to reason.*

*There is a large article of spies abroad among the enemies, this I suppose to be settled, though by our defect of intelligence methinks it should not. But it reminds me of a book in eight volumes published in London about seven or eight years ago called Letters Writ By a Turkish Spy—the books I take as they are a mere romance, but the moral is good; a settled person of sense and penetration, of dexterity and courage, who reside constantly in Paris, though as tis a dangerous post he had a larger allowance than ordinary, might by one happy turn earn all the money and the charge be well bestowed.*

*There are three towns in France where I would have the like, and they might all correspond.*

*One at Toulon, one at Brest, one at Dunkirk. They therefore might trade together as merchants and the Tourts also with them.*

*As intelligence abroad is so considerable, it follows in proportion that the most useful thing at home is secrecy.*

*For as intelligence is the most useful to us, so keeping our enemies from intelligence among us is as valuable a head.*

*I have been in the Secretary's office of a post night when had I been a French spy I could have put in my pocket my Lord N——ms letters directed to Sir Geo. Book and to the Duke of Marlborough laid carelessly on a table for the doorkeepers to carry to the Post Office.*

*How many miscarriages have happened in England for want of silence and secrecy:*

*Cardinal Richelieu was the greatest master of this virtue that ever I read of in the world, and if history has not wronged him, has sacrificed many a faithful agent after he had done his duty that he might be sure he should not be betrayed.*

*He kept three offices for the dispatch of his affairs, and one was so private that none was admitted but in the dark, and up a pair of back remote stairs, which office being at the apartments of his niece made room for a censure passed upon her character, which the Cardinal chose to suffer that he might have the liberty to transact affairs there, of which more moment.*

*This is a principal reason why I object against bringing of things before the Council, for I will not affirm that the Minutes of our Privy Council have not been read in the Secretary's office at Versailles. Tis plain the French outdo us at these two things, secrecy and intelligence, and that we may match them in these points is the design of the proposal.'*

## APPENDIX J

## *Graphology as an Aid to Personnel Selection*

Graphology is being increasingly used, particularly in Europe, as an aid to management in its task of selecting the right people for the right jobs and for general assessment of character. So far as the author is aware, it has not yet been used in this country for security of personnel purposes, but some evidence available to him suggests that it should be given a trial. It is, of course, important that if it is so used graphology is regarded as an aid to other methods of assessing security and this point is clearly brought out in the following monograph, for which the author is indebted to Jane Paterson, the handwriting consultant.

The word graphology was originally conceived and used by a French abbot, Hippolyte Michon, who published his first book on the subject in 1875. It is now commonly accepted as denoting handwriting psychology, and the 1964 English Dictionary defines it as 'the study of hand-writing to deduce the characteristics of the writer'. Later the focus of graphological progress moved to Austria (particularly Vienna), to Germany and to Switzerland. Today in Germany courses in graphology are included in the syllabus of those pursuing academic studies in psychology, and in many cases, of those reading medicine; there is a chair of graphology at most of the large universities.

However, today, in 1967, the Graphological Foundation in Zurich is held to be the most advanced centre in the world for research, training and the practice of graphology.

In April, 1966, the first world congress of graphologists was held in Amsterdam. It was attended by delegates from seventeen countries and included eight representatives from Great Britain. The foundations were laid for a world graphological society.

In Great Britain police authorities and some businessmen are sceptical of the claims of graphologists. This is hardly surprising as there are no recognised professional qualifications or safeguards, and the public may therefore easily be misled or the 'profession' brought into disrepute by extravagant claims.

Graphology, like all projective techniques, has its weakness and its strength and should always be used in conjunction with other methods of assessment. It is a valuable additional aid to personnel selection and vocational guidance in that it can reveal some aspects of personality not readily discernible by other techniques. The danger of employing graphology lies in not appreciating its limitations. For example, no graphologist can assess the age, sex or IQ of the writer, and there are aptitudes which cannot be discerned.

A study of hand-writing can only reveal the characteristics which were present at the time of writing, and since personality is dynamic and not fixed, misleading results can be obtained from old hand-writing material, or specimens written under unusual stress. In some cyclic mental illnesses the patients have periods of complete normality and their writing at these times may show no sign whatsoever of abnormality. It is important, therefore, that the writing sent to the graphologist for analysis is current and that, if possible, there are several specimens written at reasonable intervals.

The strength of graphology is that it covers the whole personality—that the writing is fixed and measurable and can be studied at leisure without the influence of the personality concerned. Attributes such as leadership, acceptance of responsibility, energy and drive, enthusiasm, tenacity of purpose, organising ability, co-operation, and the ability to mix are indicated by hand-writing, as are physical and mental ill-health, weakness of character, over-indulgence in drink, drugs, etc., feelings of resentment, greed, avarice, repressions, tendencies towards sexual excess and perversion. Disabilities such as those listed above, undesirable in high positions in any calling but particularly security, might well not be evident at an interview. Referees might not know of them, or might not be impartial. But an employer who makes use of the services of a graphologist may well be forewarned of their existence. Graphology is particularly useful against the 'Flash Alf' type of person and those with superficial charm.

It must be emphasised, as Mrs. Paterson has done, that graphology would be useful in establishing security reliability only when used in conjunction with other recognised methods such as interview, background inquiries, etc. It would seem worth experimenting with it in the classification of prisoners—the results could hardly be worse than the system which appeared to prevail before the escape of the spy George Blake.

## APPENDIX K

# *Historic Examples of Espionage and Intelligence*

The following stories of intelligence, espionage and counter-espionage will, it is hoped, be useful as background reading or for teaching purposes. For those whose appetite is whetted, there is a bibliography elsewhere in the book.

JOSHUA

The history of espionage is, with a few exceptions, military and political. One of the earliest acts of espionage for military purposes is related in the Book of Numbers. In about 1380 BC twelve spies were sent by Moses to collect information about the strength of the Canaanites and the prospects of successful invasion of Canaan by the Children of Israel. Moses' briefing of them is noteworthy—

'*And Moses sent them to spy out the land of Canaan, and said unto them, Get you up this way southward, and go up into the mountain; and see the land, what it is, and the people that dwelleth therein, whether they be strong or weak, few or many; and what the land is they dwell in, whether in tents or in strongholds; and what the land is, whether it be fat or lean, whether there be wood therein or not. And be ye of good courage, and bring of the fruit of the land.*'

The chapter goes on to tell how they searched the land and returned and reported to Moses. One of the twelve was Joshua. It was he and Caleb who alone retained their courage and reported in favour of an armed advance, when the others returned disheartened and exaggerating the power of the opposition, saying,

'*The people be strong that dwell in the land, and the cities are walled and very great . . . We are not able to go up against the people, for they are stronger than we . . . The land through which we have gone to search, it is a land that eateth up the inhabitants thereof; and all the people that we saw on it are men of great stature. And there we saw the giants, the sons of Anak, which come of the giants; and we were in our own sight as grasshoppers and so we were in their sight.*'

214

Ronald Seth (see Bibliography) believes that the twelve spies split up into small parties, a sound policy technically, and that this fact may have accounted for the diverse views. As Seth also points out, the different stories illustrate one of the greatest difficulties of espionage: the making of accurate reports. Those who saw the famous Japanese film *Rashomon* will remember how four witnesses gave four materially different accounts of the same incident because all had different motives. The moral of the film was, of course, that personal motive is never entirely absent from human accounts, and this is undoubtedly true of espionage. When, as is almost always the case, the subject of espionage is of a technical nature, at least elementary training in that subject is mandatory. For example, a military spy in the field would usually need a detailed knowledge of enemy equipment, uniforms, unit identification marks, badges of rank and so on if he is to discover the enemy order of battle.

Joshua was one of the few spies who became a great general. One would expect the unobtrusive personality of the typical spy to be quite different from that required of a great leader of men, whose attributes usually include dominance and decisiveness. Lawrence of Arabia, whose main exploits, curiously enough, were in the same area as Joshua's, is another example of this unusual combination of great individualism, high intelligence and extraordinary, if unorthodox, powers of leadership, and ability to submerge them beneath a colourless exterior, which ensured equal success as a spy, saboteur and leader of men. Grivas (see page 220 of this Appendix) is not without a claim in this field.

### WALSINGHAM

A classic example of espionage for political purposes is Sir Francis Walsingham's surveillance of Mary, Queen of Scots. He was regarded by the adherents of Mary as the most insidious of her enemies in the English Privy Council. He arranged to intercept most of her letters, and after deciphering them sent them on to their destinations in order to obtain fresh information from the answers.

Walsingham's interception system remains a principal espionage and counter-espionage weapon today. John Bulloch in his book *MI5* relates the origin and history of the 'British Counter-Espionage Service' and in particular the life and work of its founder and director for thirty years, Sir Vernon Kell. He says, 'Kell's system of filing and cross-indexing, and his *reliance on the interception of the communications of spies*, is still the main weapon of MI5 today' (author's italics).

Even when she was brought to trial, Mary was not free of Walsingham, for he was appointed to the commission to try her—a somewhat unusual assignment for a chief of intelligence. During the trial, Mary charged him with having forged the correspondence produced against her, whereupon it is said Walsingham rose to his feet and solemnly called God to witness that he had not done anything unbecoming an honest man, and that he was wholly free from malice. There is little doubt that this was true; he was the devoted servant of Queen Elizabeth and the state and was recognised as a man of the highest character, and was deeply religious. His personal integrity and disinterested patriotism are facts which have not been challenged, and these virtues are upheld to this day in the administration of British intelligence and security. Because of Elizabeth's well-known parsimony, he was compelled to expend most of his private fortune on payment of his spies and agents.

Walsingham's intelligence and espionage achievements were not, however, confined to the political sphere. It is virtually certain that a large measure of the credit for England's victory over Spain, culminating in the defeat of the Spanish Armada, was due to the excellence of his military intelligence service. There were two major targets: the first was to find out the size and strength of the Armada which it was known Philip of Spain had decided to dispatch, and when it would sail. The second espionage target was the plan and dispositions of the Spanish army under the Duke of Parma waiting in the Netherlands to cross the Channel after the English fleet had been defeated by the Armada.

Admittedly, Spanish security was not all that it might have been. While the Armada waited in Lisbon harbour, its commander, the Duke of Medina Sidonia, who seems to have been something of a bureaucrat, caused an elaborate report to be drawn up showing the whole order of battle with the name of each ship, its tonnage, the number of its guns, its sailors and its soldiers. In the words of Garrett Mattingly in his book *The Defeat of the Spanish Armada*,

*'For good measure he (the Duke of Medina Sidonia) added the principal gentleman-adventurers on each ship, listed by name with the number of their combatant servants, also the gunners, the medical corps, the friars and regular priests (one hundred and eighty of these), the organization of the* tercios *with a list of their officers and the strength of every company, the siege-train, the field-guns, the small-arms of all kinds, the total supply of powder (all fine-corned arquebus powder, he noted proudly), the number of cannon balls of all weights (123,790), the lead for bullets, the match. The report also listed provisions, biscuit, bacon,*

*fish, cheese, rice, beans, wine, oil, vinegar, water, in so many thousands or tens of thousands of hundred-weights, or in so many pipes and tuns and casks.'*

To help Walsingham further, the Duke allowed or caused (it is not clear which) the report to be published. Official amendments were issued from time to time to bring it up to date. Again according to Mattingly, copies of the report were available for sale in Amsterdam before the Duke's flagship had passed the Lizard and, of course, a copy reached Walsingham.

Walsingham's elaborate espionage network included a link with the Marquis of Santa Cruz whom King Philip had appointed Grand Admiral of the Armada, but who died whilst the fleet was being assembled and was succeeded by Medina Sidonia. The espionage effort was not confined to getting the dispositions of the Spanish fleet; it was also able to report that Philip was in financial difficulty, due at least in part to the cost of the Armada, and that he was trying to raise cash from Genoese bankers. This information was passed to Walsingham, who let the Genoese authorities know that the Queen of England would deem it a most friendly gesture if the Genoese were unable to meet the King of Spain's wishes. England's importance as a trading nation and Genoese doubts of Spain's credit-worthiness were sufficient to ensure compliance with Elizabeth's request. This latter is an early example of an additional function of intelligence, which is to provide information by which economic warfare can be waged. In Britain today this appears to be a function of the Board of Trade; it may be an interesting exercise of the future to examine its handling of the intelligence problem posed by the decision to apply economic sanctions to Rhodesia.

In the Netherlands' intelligence operation against the Duke of Parma, the spy was a certain Jan Wychegerde, a Netherlands' merchant fluent in Spanish as well as Flemish who, as part of his trade, supplied items of the commissariat for the Duke of Parma's army. In so doing, he gained valuable information for Walsingham, not only about the intended junction between the Armada and Parma's army, but also tactical information of value to the English army then fighting with the Dutch in the Netherlands. According to Mattingly, 'He was one of the toughest and cleverest of Sir Francis Walsingham's spies'.

This exposition of Walsingham's intelligence and espionage brilliance would not be complete without the story of a Spanish counter measure. Most of the timber for the Elizabethan men-o'-war came from the Forest of Dean. It is related that the Spaniards, in preparation for the Armada, sent agents to try to bribe the foresters to sabotage the English defence by burning down the trees. It is not known whether or not they had any success. It was perhaps as well that the Court of Verderers of the Forest of Dean had appropriate deterrent powers which included the right to skin trespassers.

## FROM WATERLOO TO WORLD WAR II

The Battle of Waterloo was not only 'won in the playing fields of Eton'[1] but as a result of excellent *military espionage* organised by the Duke of Wellington's chief of intelligence, Colonel Henry Hardinge. His agents in France transmitted to him true accounts of Napoleon's plans, prior to Waterloo. Those who remember Wellington's celebrated dictum about the importance of 'the other side of the hill' (see p. xi) will not be surprised that his army should be excellently served in this respect.

There are no examples known to the author of any really successful leaders of men whose intelligence and espionage systems have not been of the highest quality. Where would Queen Elizabeth I have been without Walsingham's system, Bismarck without Stieber's, Napoleon without Schulmeister's, Stalin without Beria's, and so on? Beria's service in the espionage field is apt to be forgotten or ignored on account of his responsibility as head of the secret police for the reign of terror in Russia. They include the obtaining of early warning of German development of robot 'planes and the employment of Richard Sorge, said by some experts to have been the most successful spy of all time. Amongst Sorge's many brilliant coups were advance notice that Hitler intended to attack Russia (the Russians were also warned by Roosevelt and Churchill, who had received similar intelligence), of the Japanese decision not to attack Russia in 1941 but America and the British Empire instead, of the formation of the Berlin-Tokyo-Rome Axis, and the Japanese invasion of China.

## THREE HISTORIC EXAMPLES OF INDUSTRIAL ESPIONAGE

There is a story related by Ronald Seth in his book '*Anatomy of Spying*' which, if substantiated, would indicate that much of Britain's industrial power is due to an act of industrial espionage.

In the seventeenth century an important part of the growing iron and steel industry was located at Stourbridge in Worcestershire. One

1. A statement attributed by Montalembert to Wellington. This attribution has been refuted by the seventh Duke.

of the great ironmasters of the day was a Mr. Foley[1], whose family had been respected in that area for some time. Although the industry was prospering, according to the story Foley discovered that continental methods of producing steel from iron were superior to British ones. He knew that the processes were kept a close secret by the famous guilds and decided that the only way to learn them was by subterfuge. Being a violinist of some ability, he crossed to the continent and visited centres of the steel industry in Belgium, Germany, Czechoslovakia, Italy and Spain in the guise of a wandering minstrel. It appears that he was able to enter the foreign factories and carry out a sort of 'music-while-you-work' act. On the continent in those days minstrels were quite common, and 'Fiddler' Foley was accepted as such everywhere he went. He was able to make friends with the master craftsmen and with his technical knowledge quickly discovered their secrets. He returned to the United Kingdom and, back at Stourbridge, his works were soon producing a high-class steel equal, if not superior, to the continental steel, and it had the advantage of being considerably cheaper.

It is said that when they learned of Foley's espionage, the German and Belgian guilds attempted to assassinate him and to sabotage his works: both efforts failed.

In the first decade of the Twentieth Century an act of industrial espionage is said to have virtually ruined the economy of Brazil, which had been largely based on a great rubber monopoly. A British firm had illegally smuggled a rubber plant from Brazil, which was studied and cultivated in the hot house at Kew. From there it was taken to Malaya, whose climate was found to be ideal, and Malayan rubber rapidly replaced that of Brazil in world markets.

The famous Samuel Courtauld, known to family historians as S.C. III, suffered continual fears that his inventive genius would be the subject of espionage. It is related that a spy from Macclesfield had some success. It is believed that he managed to obtain information about a special spindle concerned with machinery for preparing silk for sale. In a letter written in about 1825 Samuel Courtauld says: 'I have nothing at the moment to tell you of machinery inprovements, but it is a sore thing . . . that a Macclesfield blackguard has had access to and free observation of them all.'

---

1. The Harley and Foley families intermarried about this time, and it is interesting to speculate that Defoe, Robert Harley's intelligence genius, and this Mr. Foley may have met, or influenced each other. There is unfortunately a dearth of information about Foley. The present Lord Foley, his lineal descendant, has no information to add, but is himself a musician of repute.

COUNTER-ESPIONAGE FAILURE IN CYPRUS

Of contemporary spies one of the most remarkable stories is that of Colonel (now General) Grivas, the Greek army officer who led the Cypriot underground in its struggle against the British authorities in the late 1950s. During this period, in spite of the most intensive manhunt, he evaded capture and commanded his force of spies, saboteurs and armed terrorists with considerable success, issuing the most detailed orders, almost daily, in writing. Grivas's story is especially remarkable not so much because of his achievements but because it demonstrates one of the greatest British counter-espionage failures of all time. There is little doubt that the capture of this one man would have brought the military struggle to an end and considerably eased the task of achieving a proper and final political settlement.

A manhunt amongst people largely friendly to the hunted is always a difficult matter, as the Germans learned from their efforts to capture Tito in Yugoslavia. But in the case of Grivas his pursuers had what should have been overwhelming advantages:

(1) Cyprus, which is smaller than Yorkshire, is an island with but sparse vegetation (as opposed to the jungles of Malaya).

(2) The British completely controlled the surrounding sea and air; it was virtually impossible for Grivas to leave, even if he had wanted to.

(3) The pursuers comprised nearly 40,000 soldiers, airmen and police —about twice the size of the Metropolitan Police Force. The population of Cyprus is about one-twentieth that of Greater London.

(4) About a fifth of the population was hostile to Grivas and (for a long time) sympathetic to the British.

The problem was therefore a simple counter-espionage one in particularly favourable circumstances and should have been solved in six months. In the result, Grivas evaded the hunt for the whole four years or so of the emergency, and was not located until he revealed himself when a political solution had been reached. It is surprising that no heads rolled for this disaster, which, apart from immense loss of prestige, must have cost the British taxpayer many millions of pounds.

We have travelled a long way from the genius of Walsingham, Defoe and Kell, whose own creation, MI5, by patient, accurate and skilled work from 1909 onwards, was able at the outbreak of war in 1914 to crush virtually the whole espionage network so painstakingly built up in Britain by the Germans. The bankruptcy of our counter-espionage effort in Cyprus, which was a police and not a security service responsibility, if it is representative of our present ability in this field, does not augur well for the outcome of our war against crime, which requires much the same attributes as were needed and not forthcoming there.

# APPENDIX L

## The Wade System of Gradation of Sources of Information

(Excerpted with permission from *Chemical Engineering*, 23rd May 1966, © 1966, McGraw-Hill Inc.)

Dr. Worth Wade, a Philadelphia management consultant, suggested in the American journal *Chemical Engineering* on 23rd May 1966, that information from or about competitors could be classified as follows:

1. Published material, and public documents such as court records.
2. Disclosures made by competitor's employees, and obtained without subterfuge.
3. Market surveys and consultant's reports.
4. Financial reports, and brokers' research surveys.
5. Trade fairs, exhibits, and competitor's brochures.
6. Analysis of competitor's products.
7. Reports of your salesmen and purchasing agents.
8. Legitimate employment interviews with people who worked for competitor.
9. Camouflaged questioning and 'drawing out' of competitor's employees at technical meetings.
10. Direct observation under secret conditions.
11. False job interviews with competitor's employee (i.e., where there is no real intent to hire).
12. False negotiations with competitor for license.
13. Hiring a professional investigator to obtain a specific piece of information.
14. Hiring an employee away from the competitor, to get specific know-how.
15. Trespassing on competitor's property.
16. Bribing competitor's supplier or employee.
17. 'Planting' your agent on competitor's payroll.

222

18. Eavesdropping on competitors (e.g., via wire-tapping).
19. Theft of drawings, samples, documents and similar property.
20. Blackmail and extortion.

The first seven methods are usually ethical and legal; the remaining thirteen are in a descending order of ethics or legality. The order may be affected by the means employed.

# Index

Aarvold, Judge, passed sentence in Proctor & Gamble case, 58

Acheson, Dean, xii

Alarm systems, as part of management's defence system, 156–8; maintenance of, 162

Aldomet, brand name of drug, the subject of industrial espionage in Merck case, 51

Amalgamated Engineering Union (AEU), use of strike weapon of, 37; subversive activity in, 126, 201–4

American Cyanamid Corporation — see Cyanamid

American Society for Industrial Security, 48

Arnold, Dr. Thomas, and the growth of public schools, 43, 44

ASLIB, independent but Government-sponsored information organisation, 128; and excess of security zeal, 132

*Attitudes to Efficiency*—Ministry of Labour publication advocating that management should take an interest in their employees, 114

Attorney-General, replied in the House to a question on amending the law relating to industrial espionage, 5; replied to a question on the Security aspect of the Kodak case, 55–6

Barriers, as part of management's defence system, 145–8

Bay of Pigs (CIA's unsuccessful attempt to overthrow Castro), failure in America's intelligence system, 18; 19

Beechams, may have been victims of industrial espionage, 56–7

Biggs, Ronald, his escape as an example of failure in defence, 146

Biorganic Laboratories, involved in Cyanamid case, 48

Blake, George, Russian spy, 24; 'ideological' spy, 66; his escape from prison as an example of poor security, 67; Mountbatten enquiry as a result of his escape, 91; 213

Board of Trade, export intelligence service, 40

Brand, John Louis, found guilty of receiving confidential documents, 57; sentenced, 58; 70

British Insurance Association, 141

British Security Industry Association, 136, 141

Brousse, Amy Elizabeth ('Cynthia'), spy who used sex as a weapon of espionage, 68

Bulloch, John, author of *MI5*, 24, 66, 67, 185, 215; *Spy Ring*, 185

Cameras and CCTV, as part of management's defence system, 158–9

Campbell, Alan, Q.C., his letter to *The Times* regarding the law on industrial espionage, 4

Cancelarich, John, and in the Cyanamid drug secrets case, 49

Car parks, physical security of, as part of management's defence system, 156

Carron, Sir William, accused communists of trying to gain control of the AEU by subversive activity, 201–3

Cartwright, W. F., advised British industry to copy the Japanese, 8–9

Castro, Fidel, and failure of US intelligence in Cuba, 18; and British intelligence, 19

Central Electricity Generating Board (CEGB), industrial espionage at their headquarters, 51–2

Central Intelligence Agency (CIA), its role in Cuba, 17–21; examples of its activity from 1950–60, 28–9

Centre-File Ltd., information service, 128

For Product Safety Concerns and Information please contact our EU
representative GPSR@taylorandfrancis.com
Taylor & Francis Verlag GmbH, Kaufingerstraße 24, 80331 München, Germany